SOCIAL WORK

History and Ideology

SOCIAL WORK
History and Ideology

Dr. Suman Ghosal

CENTRUM PRESS
NEW DELHI-110002 (INDIA)

CENTRUM PRESS
H.O.: 4360/4, Ansari Road, Daryaganj,
New Delhi-110002 (India)
Tel: 23278000, 23261597, 23255577, 23286875
B.O.: No. 1015, Ist Main Road, BSK IIIrd Stage,
IIIrd Phase, IIIrd Block, Bengaluru-560085 (INDIA)
Tel: 080-41723429
Email: centrumpress@gmail.com
Visit us at: www.centrumpress.com

Social Work: History and Ideology

First Edition, 2011

ISBN 978-93-81293-72-0

PRINTED IN INDIA

Printed at Tarun Offset Printers, Delhi-110053

Contents

Preface

Social work in its various forms addresses the multiple, complex transactions between people and their environments. Its mission is to enable all people to develop their full potential, enrich their lives, and prevent dysfunction. Professional social work is focused on problem solving and change. As such, social workers are change agents in society and in the lives of the individuals, families and communities they serve. Social work is an interrelated system of values, theory and practice.

Social work has its roots in the struggle of society to deal with poverty and the problems associated with it. Therefore, social work is intricately linked with the idea of charity work; but must be understood in broader terms. The concept of charity goes back to ancient times, and the practice of providing for the poor has roots in all major world religions.

In India Social Work never got established as an independent profession. The government social welfare departments, hospitals largely employed trained social workers against lower middle rung posts. When Indian labour laws made it compulsory to appoint welfare officers in the factories, Social Work degree became a passport to appointment against these posts. With time, welfare officers saw themselves becoming personnel officers and later human resource development (HRD) managers. People with Social Work background thus got higher status in society. When management education came to India (also from the USA), HRD became a preferred area of specialisation and management graduates soon replaced Social Work graduates from HRD jobs. A new attractive field opened for the Social Work graduates when some non-government organisations (NGOs) adopted corporate culture under the influence of its foreign donors. But these employment opportunities were limited in numbers because how many NGOs in India would find foreign funds? High profile jobs for Social Work graduates were therefore ruled out.

An ideology is a set of ideas that constitutes one's goals, expectations, and actions. An ideology can be thought of as a comprehensive vision, as a way of looking at things, as in common sense and several philosophical tendencies, or a set of ideas proposed by the dominant class of a society to all members of this society. The main purpose behind an ideology is to offer either change in society, or adherence to a set of ideals where conformity already exists, through a normative thought process. Ideologies are systems of abstract thought applied to public matters and thus make this concept central to politics. Implicitly every political tendency entails an ideology whether or not it is propounded as an explicit system of thought. It is how society sees things.

Social work and other professions struggle with the roles of knowledge and values in the study of society and human lives, and in professional practice. For those who separate theory and knowledge from values and ethics there is further discussion in the literature on which is the appropriate foundation for social work practice.

This book covers the aspects like historical ideologies, government policies thinking, community's changing needs and management needs, economic changes and movements that do influence social work and its history and ideology.

—*Editor*

1

Introduction

PRINCIPLES OF SOCIAL WORK

The social work profession is guided by a distinct set of abstract values and a Code of Ethics. These values are transformed into accepted practice principles for the purpose of informing our intervention with clients. What follows is a listing of nine Social Work Principles and brief description of each.

Acceptance-Acceptance is a fundamental social work principle that implies a sincere understanding of clients. Acceptance is conveyed in the professional relationship through the expression of genuine concern, receptive listening, intentional responses that acknowledge the other person's point of view, and the creation of a climate of mutual respect.

Affirming Individuality-To affirm a client's individuality is to recognize and appreciate the unique qualities of that client. It means to "begin where the client is." Clients expect personalized understanding and undivided attention from professionals. Individualization requires freedom from bias and prejudice, an avoidance of labelling and stereotyping, a recognition and appreciation of diversity, and knowledge of human behaviour. Purposeful Expression of Feelings-Clients need to have opportunities to express their feelings freely to the social worker. As social workers, we must go beyond "just the facts" to uncover the underlying feelings.

Non-judgmentalism-Communicating non-judgmentalism is essential to developing a relationship with any client. It does not imply that social workers do not make decisions; rather it implies a non blaming attitude and behaviour. Social workers judge others as neither good or bad nor as worthy or unworthy.

Objectivity-Closely related to non-judgmentalism, objectivity is the principle of examining situations without bias. To be objective in their observations and understanding, social workers must avoid injecting personal feelings and prejudices in relationships with clients.

Controlled Emotional Involvement-There are three components to a controlled emotional response to a client's situation: sensitivity to expressed or unexpressed feelings, and understanding based on knowledge of human behaviour, and a response guided by knowledge and purpose. The social worker should not respond in a way that conveys coldness or lack of interest while at the same time cannot over identify with the client.

Self-Determination-The principle of self-determination is based on the recognition of the right and need of clients to freedom in making their own choices and decisions. Social workers have a responsibility to create a working relationship in which choice can be exercised.

Access to Resources-Social workers are implored to assure that everyone has the necessary resources, services, and opportunities; to pay attention to expanding choices, and opportunities for the oppressed and disadvantages; and to advocate for policy and legislative changes that improve social conditions and promote social justice.

Confidentiality-Confidentiality or the right to privacy implies that clients must give expressed consent before information such as their identity, the content of discussions held with them, one's professional opinion about them, or their record is disclosed.

DEFINITION OF SOCIAL WORK

The social work profession promotes social change, problem solving in human relationships and the empowerment and liberation of people to enhance well-being. Utilising theories of human behaviour and social systems, social work intervenes at the points where people interact with their environments.

Principles of human rights and social justice are fundamental to social work.

Social work in its various forms addresses the multiple, complex transactions between people and their environments. Its mission is to enable all people to develop their full potential, enrich their lives, and prevent dysfunction. Professional social work is focused on problem solving and change. As such, social workers are change agents in society and in the lives of the individuals, families and communities they serve. Social work is an interrelated system of values, theory and practice.

Values

Social work grew out of humanitarian and democratic ideals, and its values are based on respect for the equality, worth, and dignity of all people. Since its beginnings over a century ago, social work practice has focused on meeting human needs and developing human potential. Human rights and social justice serve as the motivation and justification for social work action. In solidarity with those who are disadvantaged, the profession strives to alleviate poverty and to liberate vulnerable and oppressed people in order to promote social inclusion. Social work values are embodied in the profession's national and international codes of ethics.

Theory

Social work bases its methodology on a systematic body of evidence-based knowledge derived from research and practice evaluation, including local and indigenous knowledge specific to its context. It recognises the complexity of interactions between human beings and their environment, and the capacity of people both to be affected by and to alter the multiple influences upon them including bio-psychosocial factors. The social work profession draws on theories of human development and behaviour and social systems to analyse complex situations and to facilitate individual, organisational, social and cultural changes.

Practice

Social work addresses the barriers, inequities and injustices that exist in society. It responds to crises and emergencies as well as to everyday personal and social problems. Social work utilises a variety of skills, techniques, and activities consistent with its holistic focus on persons and their environments. Social work interventions range from primarily person-focused psychosocial processes to involvement in social policy, planning and development.

These include counselling, clinical social work, group work, social pedagogical work, and family treatment and therapy as well as efforts to help people obtain services and resources in the community.

Interventions also include agency administration, community organisation and engaging in social and political action to impact social policy and economic development. The holistic focus of social work is universal, but the priorities of social work practice will vary from country to country and from time to time depending on cultural, historical, and socio-economic conditions.

VALUES OF SOCIAL CARE

The following have been regularly cited in stakeholder publications as the key values to be pursued in the provision of services:

- independence
- citizenship
- empowerment
- social inclusion
- respect for diversity
- care and protection for vulnerable people/children and young people and the community.

In the remainder of this report, we consider in turn each of the key questions listed above. Where the evidence and issues for children and adults vary there are separate sections for each, but there are references to children's issues in the sections for adults and vice versa. For some issues we treat children first and for some we treat adults first. Although it makes for some inconsistency of style, we have chosen to try and start each section with the group for whom the issues are most important, rather than adhere to the same order for each question.

DEFINING CHARACTERISTICS OF SOCIAL MODELS

One of the key shifts in values which took place during the latter part of the 20th century was the notion that many of the disadvantages that service users face are the outcomes of social processes which serve to exclude them from the mainstream. The promotion of social inclusion for everyone is the starting point, which accepts that society as a whole has an obligation to eliminate (or at least to mitigate) the social disadvantages faced by users of social care services.

The key features below illustrate some of the principles on which modern social models are built:

- having a profound understanding of the complexity of human health and wellbeing
- addressing the inner and outer worlds of individuals, groups and communities
- embracing the experiences and supporting the social networks of vulnerable people
- understanding, collaborating with, and challenging institutions in civil society to promote the interests of individuals and communities
- emphasising shared knowledge and territory, across a range of disciplines making it [that is, the knowledge] accessible to service users and the general public
- promoting the need for empowerment and capacity building at individual and community level, thereby tolerating and celebrating difference
- placing equal value on the expertise of service users, carers and the general public
- challenging attitudes and practices that are oppressive, unjust and destructive
- critical understanding of the nature of power and hierarchy in creating inequalities and exclusion
- commitment to the development of theory and practice and the critical evaluation of process and outcome.

The model was originally defined by Oliver (2004). It challenged traditional approaches to physical disability which focused on individual limitations resulting from impairment, and came initially from disabled people themselves. Oliver (2004) states that, in the broadest sense, the social model of disability is about nothing more complicated than a clear focus on the economic, environmental and cultural barriers encountered by people who are viewed by others as having some form of impairment.

The social model is in principle equally relevant to all groups of service users. However, it has been developed differentially. Thus recent policy on people with learning disabilities, as embodied in *Valuing People,* has sought to extend the model for this group, while for older people the development of the model has not moved beyond opposition to age discrimination (Turner, 2003).

Beresford (2002, 2004) has written on the potential of such a model for mental health service users, taking as a starting point the social model of disability developed by the disabled people's movement.

The social model of disability has been critiqued both from outside and from within the disability movement. In respect of the former, Bury (2000) has argued that it is over-socialised and fails to take adequate account of impairment, although Oliver (2004) has rebutted this.

Thomas (2004), who supports the model, has suggested that it fails to take account of cultural and experiential differences among disabled people. Reeve (2004) feels that the psycho-emotional aspects of oppression operate at a public level affecting what people can do, but also at a personal level as to who they can be. This dimension, she argues, is not adequately highlighted in the social model of disability.

As far as children's services are concerned, the social model as articulated by adult service users has not generally penetrated, even for disabled children. Rather, official and academic literature on policy for children's services refers to an 'ecological model', most clearly in the context of an ecological model of human development.

This approach underpins the *Framework for the assessment of children in need and their families.* Its key characteristic is a central concern with the role of the wider family and of environmental factors in the community. Thus, the needs of the child must be assessed and tackled within his or her social environment. This model is at the heart of the development of the Assessment Framework under the Quality Protects programme.

The development of the Assessment Framework and its use as the basis for the assessment of all children in need, including those who may be at risk of significant harm, should, at best, succeed in integrating a previously twin-track approach to children in need and those potentially at risk of significant harm. It should also improve the consistency of social work interventions with children and their families and, in the view of policy makers, provide a clear evidence base for assessment:

Use of the framework should provide evidence to help, guide and inform judgements about children's welfare and safety from the point of first contact, through the process of initial and more detailed core assessments according to the nature and extent of the child's needs.

Houseman (2001) lists the key requirements of the Assessment Framework as follows:

Assessments must:

- be child-centred
- be rooted in child development
- be ecological in their approach
- ensure equality of opportunity
- involve working with children and their families
- build on strengths as well as identify difficulties
- be inter-agency in their approach to assessment and the provision of services
- constitute a continuing process, not a single event
- be carried out in parallel with other actions and providing services
- be grounded in evidence-based knowledge.

These principles are seen as underpinning all processes of work with children and families, including assessment, planning intervention and reviewing. The current Children Bill may also be seen to derive from the ecological model, whose values are evident in the five outcomes which flag up the centrality of the emotional, social and economic environment for children and young people (DfES, 2003):

- Be healthy
- Stay safe
- Enjoy and achieve
- Make a positive contribution
- Achieve economic well being.

Where children's services are concerned, current policy is, on the face of things, well developed to take forward the ecological model. Where this model is applied, it potentially reduces tensions between the educational model (with its emphasis on 'formal' intellectually measurable outcomes, such as GCSEs) and the medical model (with an emphasis on unilateral professionally informed assessment). The development of the Integrated Children's System, which will be implemented nationally in December 2005, commands a high level of agreement and support from stakeholders in all those agencies who are likely to work with children and their families (Ward and Rose, 2002).

This approach will be further reinforced by the forthcoming *National service framework for children* (DH, 2004) which encompasses six key areas: children needing acute/hospital care; maternity; mental health and psychological well being of children and young people; children in special circumstances; disabled children; healthy children and young people.

SOCIAL MODELS AND PROFESSIONAL DEFINITIONS

The Quality Assurance Agency (QAA) for Higher Education, in its benchmark statement for social work (QAA, 2000), requires that undergraduate students during their degree studies should:

... acquire, critically evaluate, apply and integrate knowledge [of] ... the social processes ... that lead to marginalisation, isolation and exclusion and their impact on the demand for social work services; explanations of the links between definitional processes contributing to social differences (for example, social class, gender and ethnic differences) to the problems of inequality and differential need faced by service users; the nature of social work services in a diverse society.

The Training Organisation for the Personal Social Services (TOPPS) England defines one of the key values in The National occupational standards for social work as the importance of social workers being capable of challenging discriminatory images and practices affecting users and carers (TOPPS, 2004). Such requirements suggest that the knowledge base and professional practice of social workers, while not completely embracing the social model, are underpinned by key elements of this model.

Bailey (2004) writes of "the almost unbelievable penetration of the language of the social model [of disability] into institutional and organisational literature", while Oliver (2004) notes that, by the 1990s, the model was being colonised by a range of organisations, interests and individuals and that the Disability Rights Commission is guided in everything it does by the social model of disability. A recent report for the SSI, *Independence matters*, states that it takes as its value base the social model of disability and found that "social services in the councils inspected were strongly committed to developing services that promoted the social model of disability" (Clark, 2003). The model has been similarly embraced in two recent reports on mental health.

Thus, at the level of values there seems to be a widespread acceptance of the social model. However, there is some doubt regarding the extent to which it has had a real impact on professional practice. Bailey (2004) comments that spread of the language of the social model of disability is often concurrent with "continuing oppressive practice".

Oliver (2004), reflecting on social work practice over the previous 20 years, concludes that the social model has "had no real impact on professional practice, and social work has failed to meet disabled people's self-articulated needs". Similar points were made by Clark in the SSI report (Clark, 2003) "only half the councils visited were able to demonstrate that the everyday practice of frontline staff reflected the strategic commitment to the social model". The Audit Commission/SSI (2004) report reached a similar conclusion:

While social care services are committed to developing services ... [which] enable people with disabilities to overcome barriers to full participation, it is also clear that the everyday practice of front line staff does not always reflect this.

However, neither report addresses the issue of how 'everyday practice' is to be changed to accommodate the social model. If the social model requires that "the way society is organised must be changed" then it is pertinent to ask whether simply changing working practices is sufficient. At the same time, a commitment to place the social model at the centre of practice would, at the very least, need the 'institutionalisation' of a respect for the expertise and experience of service users, in parallel with the development of capacity building, at both an individual and community level, to challenge disabling barriers.

2

History of Social Work

Social work has its roots in the struggle of society to deal with poverty and the resultant problems. Therefore, social work is intricately linked with the idea of charity work; but must be understood in broader terms. The concept of charity goes back to ancient times, and the practice of providing for the poor has roots in all major world religions.

Pre-Modern History

In the West, when Constantine I legalized the Christian Church, the newly legitimised church set up poorhouses, homes for the aged, hospitals, and orphanages. These were often funded, at least in part, from grants from the Empire. By 590 the church had a system for circulating the consumables to the poor: associated with each parish was a *diaconium* or office of the deacon.

As there was no effective bureaucracy below city government that was capable of charitable activities, the clergy served this role in the west up through the 18th century.

During the Middle Ages, the Christian church had vast influence on European society and charity was considered to be a responsibility and a sign of one's piety. This charity was in the form of direct relief (for example, giving money, food, or other material goods to alleviate a particular need), as opposed to trying to change the root causes of poverty.

The practice and profession of social work has a relatively modern (19th century) and scientific origin.

Modern History

Social work, as a profession, originated in the 19th century. The movement began primarily in the United States and England. After the end of feudalism, the poor were seen as a more direct threat to the social order, and so the state formed an organized system to care for them. In England, the Poor Law served this purpose. This system of laws sorted the poor into different categories, such as the able bodied poor, the impotent poor, and the idle poor. This system developed different responses to these different groups.

The 19th century ushered in the Industrial Revolution. There was a great leap in technological and scientific achievement, but there was also a great migration to urban areas throughout the Western world. This led to many social problems, which in turn led to an increase in social activism. Also with the dawn of the 19th century came a great "missionary" push from many Protestant denominations. Some of these mission efforts (urban missions), attempted to resolve the problems inherent in large cities like poverty, prostitution, disease, and other afflictions. In the United States workers known as "friendly visitors", stipended by church and other charitable bodies, worked through direct relief, prayer, and evangelism to alleviate these problems. In Europe, chaplains or almoners were appointed to administer the church's mission to the poor.

During this time, rescue societies were initiated to find more appropriate means of self-support for women involved in prostitution. Mental asylums grew to assist in taking care of the mentally ill. A new philosophy of "scientific charity" emerged, which stated charity should be "secular, rational and empirical as opposed to sectarian, sentimental, and dogmatic. " In the late 1880s, a new system to provide aid for social ills came in to being, which became known as the settlement movement. The settlement movement focused on the causes of poverty through the "three Rs"-Research, Reform, and Residence. They provided a variety of services including educational, legal, and health services. These programs also advocated changes in social policy. Workers in the settlement movement immersed themselves in the culture of those they were helping.

In America, the various approaches to social work led to a fundamental question – is social work a profession? This debate can be traced back to the early 20th century debate between Mary Richmond's Charity Organization Society (COS) and Jane Addams's Settlement House Movement. The essence of this debate was whether the problem should be approached from COS' traditional, scientific method focused on efficiency and prevention or the Settlement House Movement's immersion into the problem, blurring the lines of practitioner and client.

Even as many schools of social work opened and formalized processes for social work began to be developed, the question lingered. In 1915, at the National Conference of Charities and Corrections, Dr. Abraham Flexner spoke on the topic "Is Social Work a Profession?" He contended that it was not because it lacked specialized knowledge and specific application of theoretical and intellectual knowledge to solve human and social problems. This led to the professionalization of social work, concentrating on case work and the scientific method.

American History

Following European settlement of northern America, the only social welfare was in the area of public health. When epidemics occurred, quarantine facilities were built to prevent contamination. As populations grew, Almhouses were built to house vulnerable people with no other support, including people with a long term illness or older people without families. The first recorded Almshouse was built in 1713 near Philadelphia by William Penn, and was only open to Quakers. A second one was built nearby in 1728, this time with public money. In 1736 New York opened the Poor House of the City of New York (later renamed Bellevue Hospital) and in 1737 New Orleans opened the Saint John's Hospital to serve the poor of the city.

Over the next 80 years, the facilities began to change. The precursors to modern hospitals began to form on the grounds of Almshouses, while the Almshouses themselves focused more and more on vulnerable people.

Modern social work in America has its roots in the mass migrations of the 19th century. Many of the migrants landed in New York and moved to other eastern cities, where mass crowding lead to social problems and ill health. Dr. Elizabeth

Blackwell was the United States' first female doctor who set up the New York Infirmary for Indigent Women and Children in 1853. The dispensary was run to assist the poor communities of East Side, and it soon diversified beyond a basic pharmacy, providing social assessments and support to local families. In 1889 Jane Addams was a young medical student who set up Hull House in Chicago to work with poor and immigrant communities. The house was both a community service centre and a social research program. Precursors to modern social work arose in Blackwell's infirmary and in Hull House as health professionals began to work with social determinants of poor health.

The first professional social worker to be hired in the United States was Garnet Pelton, in 1905 at the Massachusetts General Hospital. Garnet retired after six months due to contracting tuberculosis in the course of her work. She was replaced by Ida Cannon who worked in the role for a further forty years. Dr. Richard Clarke Cabot was the a key advocate in the creation of the role, as he believed there to be a link between tuberculosis and social conditions.

Both Pelton and Cannon had trained as nurses before taking up the role. Cabot was in charge of the outpatient ward of the hospital, and together with the newly created social workers, they redefined the way in which health and wellbeing was managed. The economic, social, family and psychological conditions that underpinned many of the conditions that patients presented with were recognised for the first time. Social workers would work in a complementary relationship with doctors, the former concentrating on physiological health, and the latter on social health. In addition to this, he saw that social work could improve medicine by providing a critical perspective on it while working alongside it in an organisational setting. This approach soon spread through other American hospitals, and in 1911, there were 44 social work departments in 14 different cities. Two years later, the number of social work departments had grown to 200.

Professionalisation

After 1905, most social workers were trained as nurses. The American Association of Hospital Social Workers was set up in 1918 to increase the links between formal education and hospital practice.

In 1929 there were ten university courses in medical social work. Around this time, psychiatry and psychology began to compete with social work as the complementary discourse to medicine in hospitals. Social work practice adapted to this by aligning itself more closely with psychoanalytic ideas, and became less concerned with living conditions and social health. While this detracted from the social concerns, it added a more scientific basis to dealing with patients, and challenging behaviours were more likely to be seen as a mental disfunction than poor moral character. The increase of social spending after World War Two saw another rise in the number of social workers.

Australian History

Social work as a profession in Australia developed later than in England or America, with the first professional social workers being hired in the 1920s. Social work training began in Australia in 1940 at the University of Sydney. The profession took direction from the established schools in England until the 1960s, when a more American model took hold. Most high level training and theory was imported from abroad until the 1980s. Some Australian social work writers such as Jim Ife has criticised the impact that this has had on Australians being able to develop culturally appropriate theories and practices. Since the 1990s, Australian social work has increasingly affiliated itself with Pacific Islander and New Zealand approaches.

Social Work has been a mostly public sector or not-for-profit sector profession in Australia, with private practice being rare. The profession has experienced changes in two different direction in the last 30 years. One is a pull towards a more managerial, professionalised model, and the other is to a more community based, deprofessionalised approach. Further to this has been the trend by large organisations to replace the "jack of all trades" social work approach with less highly trained, more technical positions. Since the 1990s, other reactions to managerial control of social work have followed theories of feminism, ecological sustainability and critical theories.

English History

The growth of social work in England as a discipline had similar parallels to the American experience of mass migration and social upheaval. The Industrial Revolution was a major cause of these changes, as social and economic conditions changed, resulting in the massive growth of cities. The first social workers were called hospital almoners, and were based in medical institutions. The Royal Free Hospital hired Mary Stewart as the first almoner in 1895. Her role was to assess people requesting treatment at the hospital to ensure that they were considered "deserving enough" of the free treatment. The role soon developed to cover the provision of other social programs, and by 1905 other hospitals had created similar roles. By this time, the Hospital Almoners Council had been formed to oversee the new profession.

THE HISTORY OF SOCIAL WORK (1850-1925)

In the 1850s, Elizabeth Blackwell introduced "visitors" into the homes of New York's sick. Immigration accompanied by rapid urbanization and industrialization, increased city social problems. Poverty and its accompanying difficulties forced society to address needed services. As a result, new charities, both public and private, responded to the challenge. Many of the new relief efforts were inefficient and poorly organized. As charity resources expanded, experienced workers saw the need for improved organization and management and they began to apply order to the problems in their communities. The hardship and slow economy of the 1870s threw millions of men out of work and sparked riots and strikes. The strikes shut down most of the nation's railroad traffic and, as a result, commerce came to a halt. Elected officials, shocked and frightened by the poverty, destitution and general unrest, expanded local relief efforts hoping to moderate the depression's severity and to re-establish social order. During this time, a new movement of charitable organizations began to appear that we now associate more directly with the evolution of early social work.

The charity organizations were created to reorganize the public and private resources that had proliferated during the 1870s. In 1877, the first American charity organization society was established in Buffalo, New York. Over the next two decades the movement spread rapidly. At the turn of the century, virtually every major urban area in America hosted some form of charity organization society. Leaders believed poverty could be eradicated through planned intervention or treatment rather than by direct relief (i.e. monetary assistance) alone. Many were disturbed by what they saw as an inefficient and chaotic array of urban philanthropy. Therefore, a central record keeping system was created to track those who received assistance and prevented the indigent from receiving relief from more than one agency. Someone, though, had to perform the crucial tasks of investigation and treatment, and that someone was the "*friendly visitor*", and yielded the birth of what would be the social work profession was born. In the early 1890s, Mary Richmond, then director of the Baltimore Charity Organization, began developing training programs. In 1898, the New York Charity Organization started the first school for social workers. The original curriculum was designed as a six week set of summer classes and included formal lectures and field work.

The Birth of Social Work

The friendly visitors were women who were volunteers or missionaries and most from the upper class society. They strived to lessen the burden of the poor through direct service and prayer. The friendly visitors would first study and investigate relief applications, separate the recipients into deserving or undeserving classes and then treat them by making referrals and providing them with friendship. Friendly visiting put many members of the *upper classes* in close proximity with the *other classes*. This familiarity often forced them to confront situations where such broad factors as exploitive working conditions and industrial injury were more often to blame for poverty than character flaws or lack of morals among the poor. Some visitors began to see that poverty was a far more complex problem than they had been led to believe.

As the attitudes and policies of the charity organizations began to change, so, too, did the character of friendly visiting. As friendly visitors became more systematic and professional, a consensus spread that visitors needed training. In 1891, the charity organization movement in New York began publishing a journal to disseminate new ideas in the field. Training programs under the leadership of new professionals such as Mary Richmond sprang up around the country. In 1898 these activities culminated with the establishment of the New York Summer School For Applied Philanthropy. Soon the friendly visitors were replaced by, or became, "professional"' social workers. Early on the now educated/trained friendly visitors began to refer to themselves as "caseworkers". It wasn't until the 1890's that they began to use the term "*social workers*. The early professional social workers also broadened the application of their new skills to include other types of charity work through expanding "casework" practice into child welfare institutions and juvenile courts. By the beginning of the 20th century, the volunteer friendly visitor of the early charity organizations had evolved into what we now identify as social casework.

The Depression

The 1890s economic slump was even more severe than the one that had occurred in the 1870s. Banks closed, unemployment soared, and three million men were idle due to unemployment. Racism, so often a symptom of class tensions, rose to disturbing levels. Traditional agencies such as the Children's Aid Society and the Salvation Army were overwhelmed, incapable of meeting the demands placed on their services. Faced with the grim realities of the depression, many charity organization leaders began to change and suggested the need for new thinking about poverty. Even the charity organizations stance to not simply provide direct financial assistance had to change. As a result, by turn of the century, two-thirds of all charity organization societies were directly involved with relief efforts.

Settlements-a New Idea

In London, a new idea was formed that was focused on improving the circumstances and *causes* of poverty than the flaws of the poor. From this idea emerged the first settlement house, Toynbee Hall, which was established in 1884. It was located in the slums of London and was established to help bridge the gap between London's rich and poor. The Toynbee model provided a residence where university men settled. This provided an outpost of culture and education in the poverty driven neighbourhood. The premise was that university students could learn as much from the poor as the poor could learn from the university students. In the mid-1880's, a group of college-educated Americans visited Toynbee Hall. Upon their return to America, some of these students were so impressed by what they saw at Toynbee Hall that they created similar establishments in American cities. In 1886, Stanton Coit established a settlement house in New York (later to be known as University Settlement). In 1889, Vida Scudder opened another New York settlement staffed with recently graduated college women. In that same year, Jane Addams and Ellen Gates Starr opened Hull House in Chicago. These successes were quickly followed by others. Soon settlements were spread throughout urban America. By the mid 1890s there were fifty, and by 1900 there were more than a hundred recognized settlements. The efforts of the settlement worker were different from those of the friendly visitors who focused mostly on the so-called indigent population or those we refer to today as the chronically poor. The settlement movement, in contrast, devoted most of its energies in working with what we would today regard as the poorer segments of the working class, particularly immigrants. They sought to reform aspects of American society that they identified as problematic. Instead of focusing their efforts on changing the individual behaviours and values of the poor, settlement workers tried to change the neighbourhoods and expand opportunities for working class people who were poor, but not indigent. The entry of the settlements and their residents in low-income immigrant neighbourhoods brought new attitudes and perspectives to the charity field.

Settlement workers researched and surveyed the problems of the poor through studies that documented the systemic nature of the problem. They argued that the social problems were the result of structural circumstances based on the general situations in which the poor lived, rather than individual deficiencies. The studies had national impact that described the conditions and trials of a variety of groups including immigrants, working women, children, and the unemployed. Public education, juvenile courts, public playgrounds, citizenship, daycare, and cultural awareness programs are just a few examples of the reform activities adopted by settlement workers. Many found themselves pulled into union organizing and local politics as they searched for strategies to improve the lives of their neighbours. In 1906, several New York settlements sponsored the friendly visitor concept for three school districts to deal with those whom neither the attendance officer, school nurse, or classroom teacher were equipped. The teacher or principal refereed children whose educational experience was obstructed by deficient scholarship, demoralizing home conditions, misconduct, physical defect and similar handicaps. After an examination into the background and personality of each child, the visitor used whatever personal influence or social adjustments were necessary to insure efficient performance.

Hull House was one of the most famous settlement sites. Many who lived there were immigrants from countries such as Italy, Russia, Poland, Germany, Ireland, and Greece. For these working poor; Hull House provided a day care centre for children of working mothers, a community kitchen, and visiting nurses. Jane Addams and her staff gave classes in English literacy, art, and other subjects. Hull House also became a meeting place for clubs and labour unions. Most of the people who worked with Addams in Hull House were well educated, middle-class women. Hull House gave them an opportunity to use their education and it provided a training ground for careers in social work.

Led by young Hull House resident, Mary Kenny O'Sullivan, the settlement served as a hub for organizing shirtwaist workers and pushed for the passage of the Illinois Factory Act, a bill that provided protective policies for working women and children. As reform issues emerged from their work in the community, settlement workers would then take on broader issues. Their crusade expanded to include creating basic services such as kindergartens, playgrounds, nurseries, child labour and eventually, under the adept leadership of Florence Kelly, led to the establishment of The Women's Trade Union League and The Children's Bureau.

Many groups had hope that government could be an instrument for improvement. This school of thought eventually led to the formation of the Progressive Party during Teddy Roosevelt's 3rd party campaign for the Presidency in 1916. Many of them, such as Lillian Wald, Florence Kelly, Jane Adams, and Paul Kellogg, rose to national prominence.

Jane Addams became one of the most well known figures in the nation. Such leaders continued their commitment to social change and reform. Until 1920, American women could not vote. Addams joined in the movement for women's suffrage (women's right to vote). Jane Addams also became involved in wider efforts for social reform, including housing and sanitation issues, factory inspection, rights of immigrants, women and children, creating kindergarten, playgrounds, child labour laws, anti-drug enforcement, pacifism, and the 8-hour day.

In Chicago, Mary McDowall helped create the National Consumer's League and hundreds of settlement workers joined the crusade for improving conditions of women and children workers led by Frances Kelly. Mrs. Kelly also became a leader in the early women's labour movement. In New York, settlement leaders such as Lillian Wald and Robert Hunter put social workers into public schools and promoted the idea of school-provided lunches. In some cities, leaders sought better housing for the poor. They gave keynote addresses at national conferences, wrote articles in national magazines and were commonly quoted in the nation's leading newspapers. Some of the more influential leaders developed interests in issues that extended beyond the neighbourhood. An example of this type of national activity was the crusade to improve the circumstances of women and children which led to the creation of the Children's Bureau.

The Country's infant and maternal mortality rates were the highest of any industrial country, the growing number of orphans was overwhelming local resources, both the public and private foster homes and orphanage networks were overcome by the sheer number of new wards, and millions of children were working instead of attending school. The same leaders who fought so prodigiously for maternal and infant health programs and widows' pensions were also prominent in the crusade against child labour. That problem proved to be more recalcitrant than either widow's pensions or health programs. Both industry and many poor families opposed laws that limited or prohibited young children from working. Industry for the obvious reason, were recruiting children to work, as they could pay child workers at a cheap rate. Poor families often needed the paltry contributions of their working children just to survive.

Leaders soon became involved in many issues. They included advocacy of labour, civil rights, suffrage and peace.

Seeking change, Florence Kelly called for the creation of a national Children's Bureau in 1900. In 1906, they created the National Committee on Child Labour (NCLC) which sponsored investigations and lobbied for legislation protecting children. Child labour was not eliminated until new legislation was passed as part of the NEW DEAL. After bringing her concerns before President Theodore Roosevelt, Kelly along with Lillian Wald, Edward Devine, James West, and Homer Folks brought together more leaders from communities throughout America to address such issues. With the support of President Roosevelt, a White House Conference On Children was held in 1909. Reformers began the campaign for what was then known as a widow's pension. These leaders felt that most children should be cared for in their own home as opposed to the all too common practice of removing children from the homes of poor single parents. They felt that the government was paying more for a child's care in an asylum or orphanage than it would cost to pay the mother to take care of her children at home. The resulting publicity put child welfare on the national agenda and generated enough political pressure to force the creation of the Children's Bureau in 1912. Julia Lathrop from Chicago's Hull House was named to head the U.S. Children's Bureau in 1912.

Initially, the Children's Bureau's role was limited to conducting research and collecting data on children's issues. One of the first studies undertaken by the new organization was of maternal and infant mortality. Armed with statistics showing a shockingly high rate of maternal deaths, bureau workers began a campaign for programs to directly address the problem. The Sheppard-Towner bill was introduced in 1918 by Congresswoman Jeanette Rankin. Ms. Rankin was the first congresswoman in the U.S. Congress and a social worker. The proposed legislation provided funds to local health departments for maternal and infant health services and after considerable opposition from conservative legislators was finally signed by the president in 1921. This legislation was so successful that funding, initially due to expire in 1927 was extended for an additional two years. When the act finally expired in 1929, there were more than 3,000 local programs and maternal and infant mortality rates were significantly improved. In 1911, Missouri enacted the first widow's pension. By 1919, 39 states had similar programs

Charlotte & Mecklenburg Couty

On August 4, 1919, The Mecklenburg Board of County Commissioners and the Board of Education organized the County's Department of Public Welfare. The department was located in the Charlotte City Hall. The staff included the superintendent, Mr. Lucius H.Ranson and a secretary. The budget for the first fiscal year was $2,239.76. Public Welfare activities included enforcement of school attendance laws, child labour laws, and supervision of Juvenile Court. On October 29, 1919, The Commissioners appointed a 3-member Board of Public Welfare which held their inaugural Board of Public Welfare meeting on November 17, 1919.

Nationally, leaders also played an important part in combating racism and civil inequality. Plans were made for the creation of a permanent organization which then evolved into the National Association For The Advancement Of Coloured People (NAACP). The NAACP's first central committee included William Walling, Jane Adams, and W.E.B. Du Bois. Adams also founded the American Civil Liberties.

Casework

By the time America became involved in the First World War, casework had developed as a major force in the new field of social work. No longer regarded as a technique only suitable for private charities serving the poor, casework was identified as a broad skill applicable in a wide variety of arenas including mental hygiene, schools, hospitals, and juvenile courts.

Dr. Richard Cabot introduced a medical social services department at Massachusetts General Hospital in 1905. Seven years after founding the service, a specialty in medical social work was offered by the Boston School of Social Work. A number of hospitals, mainly in the Northeast, established medical social work departments. Mental institutes also began to see the benefit of social services. Adolf Meyer, a prominent leader in the mental hygiene movement, believed that psychiatry needed to focus more of its efforts outside the asylum. He identified the social worker as a primary agent in providing a better understanding of the patient's social environment. By 1920, Social workers addressed mental hygiene problems in mental hospitals, outpatient clinics and juvenile courts.

In 1917 the National Social Workers' Exchange was formed. The Exchange dealt with a number of issues including employment, working conditions, and salaries. The success of the exchange provided evidence that there was a need for a national organization. By 1920, school social service programs were functioning Iowa, Massachusetts, and New York. In 1921 a group from the Social Workers' Exchange met at the National Conference and voted to change their name to the American Association of Social Workers. They opened their membership to accept everyone, trained or volunteer, who identified themselves as social worker. By 1919 this program had grown and changed its name to the New York School of Social Work, later to become the Columbia University School of Social Work. The University of Chicago was offering extension courses on social work which grew into a full curriculum known as the Chicago School of Civics and Philanthropy. In 1920 it officially became the University of Chicago, School of Social Work. By 1920 there were 17 schools of social work that formed the Association of Training Schools of Professional Schools Of Social Work. The organization was the predecessor to what is now known as the Council On Social Work Education. The new field of social work was now ready to begin creating a true and widely recognized profession.

By the end of the 1920s, most of the states and larger cities used an executive based system of administration for supervising public charities. This shift reflected the growing role state and local governments were playing in the field of relief. Social casework's began to increase shortly before the 1920s.

(1925-1940)

World War I provided unique opportunities for social caseworkers to prove the utility of their skills on non-poverty populations. Mary Richmond's *Social Diagnosis* was the first definitive text on casework. Much more than just another book, *Social Diagnosis*, propelled casework from one of a number of approaches used by charity workers into a major form of practice. In 1925, no longer would the social worker be viewed solely as a charity worker delivering relief and moral uplift, but rather employ new skills in aiding poor, middle class or even affluent clients. By 1926, the Red Cross had organized social service departments in federal hospitals. This in turn led to the establishment of a nationwide system of social services attached to Veterans Administration clinics, outpatient departments and hospitals.

The Great Depression

The trauma created by the depression produced a new kind of government and a new way of thinking about poverty. The depression, with its high unemployment rates among willing workers, shattered the dominant view that poverty was the result of personal failure. Before the depression, most people thought of welfare as something poor people received from mostly private charities. After the depression, welfare became a widely recognized responsibility of the federal government, and poverty was better understood as a situation caused by forces beyond individual control. Before the depression, relief programs were relatively simple arrangements. After the depression, welfare programs became a complex array of services, benefits, and taxes that affect virtually everyone.

The Great Depression left important marks on the social work profession. Largely due to the leadership of individuals who began their careers in settlements and moved into public service in the twenties, social work took its place on the national stage. Protégés of such early settlement leaders as Florence Kelly, Jane Addams, and Lillian Wald were major architects of what is now recognized as watershed public welfare policies. Harry Hopkins, Frances Perkins, Molly Dewson and Aubrey Williams not only led social work's advance into public welfare, but became public figures that greatly enhanced the public's previously low opinion of welfare and the social work profession.

President Herbert Hoover, along with most American leaders, assumed that the depression would be of short duration. Hoover refused to do anything until unemployment rates were inordinately high. By the early 1930s the nation was in crisis. Unemployment in some cities was over 40 percent and bankruptcy was a common occurrence. Thousands of unemployed males, called hobos or simply "Bo's", roamed the country in a fruitless search for work. Farmers from all over the heartland were losing their land.

Farm prices were so low that farmers were selling their produce for less than it cost them to transport the goods to market. Meanwhile, New York's Governor Franklin D. Roosevelt (FDR) was not afraid to act. FDR had a number of very gifted social workers on his staff, largely refugees from the settlement movement. Some, such as Frances Perkins, his state secretary of labour, he had inherited from previous governor Al Smith. Others, such as Harry Hopkins, he had recruited from private charities. Governor Roosevelt, with the help and encouragement of his social workers, crafted both unemployment and public works programs that were quickly imitated in other states.

Social workers realized the seriousness of the depression before most other professionals. Their work put them in a unique vantage point where they had an all too clear a picture of the people's plight. Social workers were also among the Great Depression's earliest victims. Faced with the dual hardships of increased demand and decreased donations, a third of all private agencies were forced to close their doors.

The New Deal

The nation was in crisis when FDR became president in 1933. Millions were unemployed. Farms were abandoned, banks were failing, industrial output was a trickle, and most public and private relief programs were out of money. The president wasted little time. In his first 100 days in office, he and congress passed an unparalleled number of bills designed to do something about the depression.

Taken as a whole, these programs became collectively known as the New Deal. The Federal Emergency Relief Act (FERA) was designed to pump new money into state welfare programs; the Civilian Conservation Corps (CCC) put thousands of young men to work in national forests and parks; the Public Works Administration (PWA) started public works such as schools, courthouses and bridges, employing thousands of construction workers. The National Recovery Administration (NRA), dubbed the *BLUE EAGLE*, created a network of policies and programs to help small businesses, and the Agriculture Adjustment ACT (AAA) promoted policies to help farmers.

The Second New Deal

By 1935, the nation had regained some of its confidence and economic indicators were improved. However, for much of the nation the depression continued to be a grim reality. Payrolls were still less than half of 1925 levels. Millions of the unemployed continued their fruitless search for work. It became obvious that the depression was going to be more stubborn than many hoped. In this context, Roosevelt and his inside group of planners put together a set of programs designed to be more permanent than the prior emergency measures. Those programs, taken as a group, quickly became known as the Second New Deal. Arguably, the most prominent (and in some ways the most infamous) of the new programs was the Works Progress Administration (WPA), headed by the social worker Harry Hopkins. The WPA was a work-relief program designed to replace the FERA. It reflected the strong bias of both FDR and Hopkins that work programs were a much superior solution to the problems associated with poverty than did welfare. The WPA eventually employed more than 8 million Americans.

Throughout the early years of the depression many in FDR's administration had advocated for a youth program. First Lady Eleanor Roosevelt was especially concerned about the plight of what she termed "America's unwanted youth". The CCC responded to this group in a small way but there were still millions of teens out of school, out of work, and out of luck. FDR issued the executive order creating a *works* program for these youths in the summer of 1935. The National Youth Administration (NYA) was headed by a young woman, Aubrey Williams, who was a protégé of Harry Hopkins and had been a staunch advocate for programs for women and children.

The Birth of Social Security

The real keystone of the second New Deal was an ambitious set of social insurances and permanent relief programs. These programs were welded into the 1935 Social Security Act. Certainly, the most important single piece of domestic legislation in the 20th century, the Social Security Act was far more encompassing than the program which now bears its name. Created by the Committee On Economic Security, this legislation was largely the product of social workers Harry Hopkins and Frances Perkins who worked closely with FDR throughout the process. Eventually a number of policy experts and legislators were involved in creating a broad set of programs that put the national government permanently in the business of welfare. The major components of the Social Security Act were the Social Insurance and the Public Assistance Programs

Social Insurance

The Social Security Act provided federal support for two social insurance programs that had been already initiated in many states. Unemployment Insurance and Workers' Compensation were crucial components in this set of provisions. However, the most ambitious part of the social insurance provisions was the creation of a federally administered program that provided limited insurance to workers in their old age. Officially this program was the Old Age Survivors and Disability Insurance (OASDHI) but is now known generally as Social Security. Together this set of social insurances was conceived as a matrix of programs offering working people some guarantees against economic and social problems beyond their individual control. The Social Security Act created two major elements. One provided aid to people with disabilities and the other granted aid for widows and their children.

The New Deal marginalized African Americans, Women, Hispanics and Asian-Americans. While the two New Deals were able to temporize some of the Great Depression's worst effects and created a welfare infrastructure that would serve the nation for the rest of the century, they failed to solve the economic problems that created the crisis. In retrospect, we now recognize that the various emergency measures, deemed so dramatic and radical in their time, were too meager to pull the country out of the depression. It took the enormous deficits created by World War II finally put an end to the depression. The emergency relief programs and the later creation of the Social Security system had a profound impact on the social work profession. First, it pushed the profession into the arena of public welfare. The crisis pulled thousands of social workers out of private agencies and into administrative and supervisory roles in the new public programs.

Another important impact created by the proliferation of public programs, was the increased number of people practicing social work. Thousands were recruited into social work through the gates of public programs. Many of these new social workers came from backgrounds quite different from their more experienced cohorts from established private charity programs. Most came from working class rather than upper class families. As the 1930's came to a close, social work had been transformed and had taken its place as an essential component of society.

3

Role of the Professional Social Worker

The main tasks of professional social workers are case management (linking clients with agencies and programs that will meet their psychosocial needs), medical social work, counselling (psychotherapy), human services management, social welfare policy analysis, community organizing, advocacy, teaching (in schools of social work), and social science research. Professional social workers work in a variety of settings, including: non-profit or public social service agencies, grassroots advocacy organizations, hospitals, hospices, community health agencies, schools, faith-based organizations, and even the military. Other social workers work as psychotherapists, counsellors, or mental health practitioners, normally working in coordination with psychiatrists, psychologists, or other medical professionals. Additionally, some social workers have chosen to direct the focus their efforts on social policy or academic research towards the practice or ethics of social work. While the emphasis has varied among these task areas in different eras and countries, some areas have been the subject of controversy as to whether they are properly part of social work's mission.

United States

In the United States of America, leaders and scholars in the field of social work have debated the purpose and nature of the profession since its beginning in the late 19th century. Workers, beginning with the settlement house movement, have argued for a focus on social reform, political activism, and systemic causes of poverty. Social workers of the Settlement House Movement were primarily young women from middle-income families and chose to live in lower-income neighbourhoods to engage in community organizing. These workers sometimes received stipends from charitable organizations and sometimes worked for free. In contrast to the settlement house movement, the friendly visitors were women from middle-income families who visited (but did not reside among) families in lower-income neighbourhoods. Friendly visitors emphasized conventional morality (such as thrift and abstinence from alcohol) rather than social activism.

Others have advocated an emphasis on direct practice, aid to individual clients and families with targeted material assistance or interventions using the diagnostic and statistical manual of mental diseases DSM-IV. While social work has been defined as direct, individual practice in the last quarter of the 20th century, there is a growing resurgence of community practice in social work. Of broad and growing significance are the relationship counselling and Relationship Education movements which seek to assist in interpersonal social skill building which can be of great societal value in promoting marriage and family stability. Relationship education and counselling primarily aid the majority of individuals who are free of pathology or who have found that DSM-IV based services are ineffectual. This majority can benefit from education and exposure to relationship skills that have not otherwise been discussed and distributed by social services in this time of weakened family, church, and societal conventions. Another new development in social work is the focus on informatics. For many social workers, the use of any online technology is problematic due to persistent concerns about privacy. However, other social workers recognize that clients are going on line for many purposes. Some schools of social work, such as University of Southern California are offering courses to build informatics skills at the graduate level.

Community practice is the new term of art for what used to be known as "macro practice" social work. Community practice includes working for change at the systems level, including human services management (administration, planning, marketing, and program development); community organizing (community development, grassroots organizing, policy advocacy); social policy and politics; and international social development.

The National Association of Social Workers (NASW) is the largest and most recognized membership organization of professional social workers in the world. Representing 150,000 members from 56 chapters in the United States and abroad, the association promotes, develops and protects the practice of social work and social workers. NASW also seeks to enhance the well-being of individuals, families, and communities through its work and advocacy. Although membership is generally not required for licensure, NASW survey data give a rough idea of how social workers are employed in the US. According to NASW:

Nearly 40% of NASW members say that mental health is their primary practice area. The health sector employs 8% of NASW's members, and 8% practice in child welfare or family organizations. Six percent of NASW members say school social work is their primary practice area, and another 3% work primarily with adolescents. (NASW, 2005) These figures are significantly confounded by the fact that NASW members are primarily licensed practitioners working in the clinical arena, and the fact that many social workers in the field do not actually hold a degree in social work. NASW is usually concerned with issues like licensing, reimbursement, etc., that are not relevant to child welfare practice, for instance.

Within the mental health field, social workers may work in private practice, much like clinical psychologists or members of other counselling professions often do. Social workers are often in the position of recommending the use of psychopharmaceutical agents, though not prescribing them. The increasingly widespread usage of these agents in the U.S. has received little scrutiny by the NASW, despite that fact that these drugs are prescribed far more heavily in the U.S. than anywhere else in the world. Social workers in private practice may take direct payments from clients and may also receive third-party reimbursement from insurance companies or government programs such as Medicaid. Insurance reimbursement for mental health services involves the designation of the recipient of services as mentally ill, or more specifically a label is assigned from the DSM-IV, the diagnostic and statistical manual of mental illness. This assignment, when recorded to an individual's medical history can prove to be a significant impediment to future pursuits. It can raise the cost to the individual for health or nursing home insurance; it can be the basis of denial for life insurance; and it can limit an individual's professional choices, such as in health care, motor vehicle operation, or airplane piloting.

Private practice was not part of the social work profession when it began in the late 19th century. It has been controversial among social workers, some of whom feel that the more lucrative opportunities of private practice have led many social workers to abandon the field's historic mission of assisting disadvantaged populations. The private practice model can be at odds with the community development and political activism strains of social work. Social workers in mental health may also work for an agency, whether publicly funded, supported by private charity, or some combination of the two. These agencies provide a range of mental health services to disadvantaged populations in the US.

Some social workers are child welfare workers, a role that looms large in the public's perception of social work. This role contributes to a negative view of social work in the U.S., since child welfare authorities can remove abused or neglected children from the custody of their parents, a practice that is fraught with controversy and sometimes with scandalous incompetence. Many child welfare workers in the US do not in fact have social work degrees (though all caseworkers in most states have at least a Bachelor's degree in a related field).

Some states restrict the use of the title social worker to licensed practitioners, who must hold a degree in the field. Such restrictions are a high legislative priority of NASW.

United Kingdom

In the United Kingdom and elsewhere, a social worker is a trained professional with a recognised social work qualification, employed most commonly in the public sector by local authorities.

Spending on social services departments is a major component of British local government expenditure.

In Social care UK, the title "social worker" is protected by law (since 1 April 2005) and can be used only by people who have a recognised qualification and are registered with the General Social Care Council (in England), the Scottish Social Services Council, the Care Council for Wales (Welsh: *Cyngor Gofal Cymru*), or the Northern Ireland Social Care Council.

The strategic direction of statutory social work in Britain is broadly divided into children's and adults' services. Social work activity within England and Wales for children and young people is under the remit of the Department for Children, Schools and Families while the same for adults remains the responsibility for the Department of Health. Within local authorities, this division is usually reflected in the organisation of social services departments. The structure of service delivery in Scotland is different.

Within children services some social workers are child protection workers, a role that looms large in the public's perception of social work. This role contributes to a negative view of social work in the UK since child protection workers for local authorities can remove suspected abused or neglected children from the custody of their parents, a practice that is fraught with controversy and media criticism.

In mental health care, social workers can train to become an Approved Mental Health Professional, involved in the application of the Mental Health Act 1983 (as amended by the Mental Health Act 2007) in England and Wales. Though now open to other professions, this involves a contributing a social care perspective to Mental Health Act assessments and is predominantly a social worker role.

In 2007, the General Social Care Council launched a wide-ranging consultation, in concert with a number of other social care organisations, to agree a clear professional understanding of social work in the UK.

SOCIAL WORK PROFESSION

The social work profession was forged in the cauldron of change that was a hallmark of the 19th century. At the beginning of the century, Americans possessed a world view that saw God and religion as both the purpose and cause of most life events. Gradually this view changed, and by the end of the century most Americans had a more secular and humanistic view of the world. Religion was still important but the belief that society could be shaped and even improved through the new discoveries of science and technology was widely accepted. The emergence of social work is a piece of this larger story. The beginning of the century "visitors" practiced a rudimentary form of social work that endeavoured to lessen the burdens of the poor through direct relief and prayer. The urban missionary movement and other similar philanthropies relied heavily on the use of the visitor in their work. This early form of visiting was very sectarian, bearing more a resemblance to missionary work than social work. Conversion was a common goal and prayer a typical treatment approach.

A more advanced form of proto social work was practiced by volunteers working with the Sanitation Commission and the Freedman's Bureau. The Sanitation Commission was a Civil War volunteer organization that developed services associated today with Public Health and the Red Cross. After the war, the Freedman's Bureau worked with newly emancipated slaves. Agents of the bureau delivered a wide range of social services to ease the assimilation of newly emancipated slaves. Activities in both of these agencies were heavily laced with the evangelical missionary spirit that was such a hallmark of the period, particularly among Protestant Americans.

THE STATE BOARDS

In the 1860s a new movement appeared that we now associate more directly with the evolution of early social work. Tagged with a variety of names: State Board of Charities, Board of Public Charities, Board of Charities and Corrections; the state board movement sought to bring some order to the management of state institutions. Many states experienced an institutional building boom, in part the direct result of Dorthea Dix's reform campaign before the Civil War.

In the 1850s and 1860s many Eastern states joined this public construction boom. They erected reformatories, prisons, mental asylums, poor-houses and orphanages. It soon became apparent that these institutions not only did not solve the problems that created them, but presented new problems in institutional management. Beginning in Massachusetts in 1863, states began appointing boards to oversee and manage the operations of their institutional structures. The idea quickly captured the imagination of early charity workers. In 1865, a convention to establish a national association was called. More than three hundred delegates attended.

The leaders of the boards turned to the then popular philosophy of science to create a new type of charity management: "scientific charity". This approach melded some of the new ideas about science with the principles of efficiency, which were being so impressively applied to business activities. In the words of historian James Leiby Scientific charity was to be:..*secular, rational and empirical as opposed to sectarian, sentimental, and dogmatic.*

More interested in studying social problems and management difficulties than in developing new techniques and skills, the state board movement's direct influence was relatively brief. It was quickly eclipsed by similar advancements among private charities. However, the pioneers in the state board movement were the first charity leaders who tried to develop a more systematic and rational approach to their work and to push it away from its traditional association with religion. The state boards took the first steps in developing charity work into a distinct activity.

THE CHARITY ORGANIZATION SOCIETIES

While state charities and institutions expanded, local charities also experienced unprecedented growth. Immigration accompanied by rapid urbanization and industrialization, increased city social problems. Poverty and its accompanying difficulties forced older established charities to expand their relief services. New charities, both public and private, responded to the challenge.

As charity resources expanded, experienced workers saw the need for improved organization and management. These developments were similar to what was then developing among state boards which followed a design earlier developed in England. Upper-class American Protestants often looked to

England for models to use in approaching problems in the United States. A charity organization to manage and organize relief was established in England in 1869. Using the English model, American charity workers began to apply order to the problems in their communities.

The Hardship of 1873

The general philosophy behind charity organization societies (COS) was a continuation of the state boards movement to promote scientific charity. The organizational framework was again borrowed from the English charities. However, much of the stimulus for their rapid development was the economic depression of the 1870s. Lasting most of the decade, the 70s depression threw millions of men out of work and sparked riots and strikes. In the summer of 1873, strikes spread throughout the urban East and shut down most of the nation's railroad traffic. Commerce ground to a halt and the strikes precipitated armed intervention in many states. City officials, shocked and frightened by the poverty, destitution and general unrest, expanded local relief efforts hoping to moderate the depression's severity and to re-establish social order.

Many charity workers were appalled by what they perceived as a serious step backwards in the progressive evolution of their new field. They felt that many of the new relief efforts were inefficient and poorly organized. Furthermore, they were convinced that the profligacy of the new programs would lead to the moral demise of the poor by spreading dependency and pauperism. This general concept that relief was, in and of itself a sinister activity, was a holdover from earlier days. However, it was reinforced by the conversion of many charity workers to the popular new social philosophy of social Darwinism. Social Darwinism was based on the teachings of Englishman Herbert Spencer who preached that relief was destructive to society and the poor because it created dependency and sapped their motivation.

The first charity organization societies were created to reorganize the public and private charities that had proliferated during the depression of the 1970s. Many charity leaders were disturbed by what they saw as an inefficient and chaotic array of urban philanthropy. Their strategy was to use the same blend of science and business efficiencies that had previously been applied by the state boards. The charity organization societies planned to apply the principles of scientific charity while carefully avoiding the common pitfalls of dependency and pauperism.

THE BIRTH OF THE CHARITY ORGANIZATION SOCIETIES

The first American charity organization society was established in Buffalo, New York in 1877. Over the next two decades the movement spread rapidly. At the turn of the century, virtually every major urban area in America hosted some form of charity organization society. Their basic approach quickly expanded beyond management and organization to include some characteristics that became trademarks of the movement.

First, the charity organization movement broke from earlier traditions by avoiding the dispensation of direct relief. Many leaders were, in fact, critical of agencies that did offer direct relief. Josephine Shaw Lowell, founder of New York's charity organization, and a major leader in the movement was once asked by a contributor how much money would go directly to the poor and she proudly replied,

Not one cent!

Second, most of the movement's members sought to inject order into the chaotic and often redundant mix of services so prevalent among local charities, through the creation of exchanges. The exchanges, or registries, were actually central record keeping systems that kept track of almoners and prevented the indigent from receiving relief from more than one agency.

A third important cornerstone of the charity organization movement and an important innovation was the introduction of a treatment component. Charity leaders did not simply wish to make charity more efficient and scientific. They believed poverty could be eradicated through the introduction of additional scientific techniques. The new techniques included planned intervention or treatment. Almoners would be able to lift themselves out of poverty because they would be morally elevated through engagement in this process. Someone, though, had to perform the crucial tasks of investigation and treatment, and that someone was the friendly visitor.

THE CHARITY ORGANIZATION SOCIETY ENTERS THE NINETIES

Even during the days of its greatest expansion, the charity organization movement had many critics. Labour leaders deplored the miserly attitudes of the organization and the punitive values of its visitors. Jane Addams admitted that all too many visitors were cold and stingy.

Leaders of the notoriously corrupt political machines actually capitalized on the conservative attitudes of the charity organizations. One such political leader admitted that while the charities studied and investigated he would find the poor unfortunate a job and a place to sleep and win both his gratitude and his vote. Writing about the charity organizations in general, radical John Reed said:

...there is none of Christ the compassionate in the immense business of organized charity; its object is to get efficient results- and that means, in practice to just keep alive vast numbers of servile, broken-spirited people.

Initially, leaders of the movement reacted to criticism defensively and continued to treat the poor like wayward children who needed guidance and advice from a socially superior person.

The Depression

On the other hand, the charity organization movement was gifted with an impressive array of flexible and talented leaders. The severe depression of the 1890s caused some charity pioneers to change the more punitive policies. Starting in 1893 and lasting through most of the decade, the 90s depression was even more severe than the one that had occurred in the 1870s Banks foundered and unemployment soared. Three million men were idle. Strikes became more numerous and violent. The strikes at Homestead in 1892 and Pullman in 1894, and the Mining Wars of 1898 were symptoms of extensive social unrest. Socialism, communism, and even anarchism became popular not only with intellectuals, but also among working people.

Farmers, frustrated by the low prices of commodities and unfair charges by the railroads, linked with labour to form the populist movement. General Jacob Coxey, advocated for a public works program to hire the millions of unemployed, capturing the imagination of thousands of Americans with his poor people's march on Washington. Racism, so often a symptom of class tensions, rose to disturbing levels. Some African-American leaders such as Booker T. Washington counseled patience. Other leaders, such as W.E.B. Du Bois an Ida Wells, advocated a more militant approach in opposing racism. Race riots broke out in several southern cities. Between 1892 and 1898 more than a thousand African Americans were lynched. These events accelerated the exodus of southern African Americans to the urban Northeast.

The cities suffered the worst. In New York City three-fourths of all its inhabitants lived in tenements. In Mulberry Bend, the heart of the Italian district, one-third of all babies born in 1888 died before their first birthdays. Traditional agencies such as the Children's Aid Society and the Salvation Army were overwhelmed, incapable of meeting the demands placed on their services.

The culture of the cities was also changing dramatically and that complicated relief efforts. The majority of inhabitants in America's largest cities were now immigrants and their children.

CHARITY ORGANIZATIONS REACT

Faced with the grim realities of the depression, many charity organization leaders began to change. Charity societies began publishing studies of the depression's effects. The studies of the 1990s evolved from the earlier friendly visitor investigations. They grew out of their intimacy with the situation's grim realities. The studies consistently suggested the need for new thinking about poverty. The old shibboleths commonly accepted as the major causes of poverty, low character, indolence, and intemperance, were replaced with more systemic theories. For example, one such study conducted in the city of New York found that only ten percent of the city's poverty was caused by shiftlessness and intemperance. The most substantial causes were found to be unemployment, sickness and industrial accidents. In 1896, Josephine Shaw Lowell, stalwart leader of the COS movement and previously a staunch proponent of traditional charity organization policies said,

It seems often as if the charities are the insults which the rich add to the injuries they heap upon the poor.

Edward Devine, general secretary of the New York COS stated:

We may quite safely throw overboard, once and for all, the idea that the dependent poor are our moral inferiors, that there is any necessary connection between wealth and virtue, or between poverty and guilt.

Even the charity organizations' most important attribute, its disdain for direct relief, changed under criticism and pressure produced by the depression. By turn of the century, two-thirds of all charity organization societies were directly involved with relief efforts.

Early Casework?

As the attitudes and policies of the charity organizations began to change, so, too, did the character of friendly visiting. Significance was placed on the visitors' investigations with a greater emphasis on objectivity. As visitors became more systematic and professional, a consensus spread that visitors needed training. The charity organization movement in New York began publishing a journal to disseminate new ideas in the field (1891). Training programs under the leadership of new professionals such as Mary Richmond sprang up around the country. In 1898 these activities culminated with the establishment of the New York Summer School For Applied Philanthropy. Volunteer visitors were replaced by "professional" social workers, some of whom now referred to themselves as "caseworkers."

Early social work began with visitors who primarily relied on prayers and a Christian view of the world to help the poor. By the 1870s, volunteer friendly visitors applied their new scientific tools of investigation and moral uplift. In the 1890s, this approach evolved into more sophisticated and realistic tactics. The increased demand for more refined techniques required training and suggested the beginnings of a profession.

The volunteer visitors of the 1880s became, in the 1890s, *social workers*. They attended training programs to upgrade their skills and returned to their agencies to take leadership positions for a salary. They no longer saw themselves as providers of friendship or moral uplift, but instead extended to their clients a professional relationship that aspired to be both scientific and objective.

The early professional social workers also broadened the application of their new skills to include other types of charity work through expanding "casework" practice into child welfare institutions and juvenile courts. By the beginning of the 20th century, the volunteer friendly visitor of the early charity organizations had evolved into what we now identify as social casework.

THE ROLES OF THE SOCIAL WORKER

In doing their day-to-day work, a social worker is expected to be knowledgeable and skilful in a variety of roles. The role that is selected and used should ideally be the role that is most effective with a particular client, in the particular circumstances. Social worker may be involved in a few or all of these roles depending on the nature of their job, and the approach to practice that they use.

SOCIAL WORK AND HUMAN RIGHTS

At the 1996 International Federation of Social Workers General Meeting in Hong Kong, an International Policy on Human Rights was approved. This is a milestone for social workers worldwide fighting human rights violations.

"The value base of social work with its emphasis on the unique worth of each individual has much in common with human rights theory. Social workers frequently operate in situations of conflict, and are required by their national codes of Ethics and in the international Ethical Principles and Standards to demonstrate respect for all regardless of their previous conduct. Their experience of the impact of social conditions on the capacity of individuals and communities to resolve difficulties means that they recognise that the full realisation of civil and political rights is inseparable from the enjoyment of economic, social and cultural rights. Policies of economic and social development have, therefore, a crucial part to play in securing the extension of human rights."

WHAT IS THE SOCIAL WORK PROFESSION

According to the Canadian Association of Social Workers (CASW) social work is: "a profession concerned with helping individuals, families, groups and communities to enhance their individual and collective well-being. It aims at helping them develop their skills and the ability to use their own resources and those of the community to resolve problems. Social work is concerned with individual and personal problems but also with broader social issues such as poverty, unemployment and domestic violence.

In a socio-political-economic context which increasingly generates insecurity and social tensions, social workers play an important and essential role."

SKILLS OF A SOCIAL WORKER

Social workers are involved in a variety of settings, and with a variety of people.

- understand the range of issues which make up the social welfare field
- direct intervention with individuals, families, groups or community services
- supervision, management and administrative skills
- legislative and policy analysis and development
- advocacy on behalf of individuals, families or the larger community

Values of a Social Worker

Social workers commit to a particular set of values including respect for worth and dignity of every person, the client's right to self-determination, confidentiality, advocacy and social action that promotes social justice. The CASW code of ethics summarizes these values as follows:

- Humanitarianism
- Egalitarian ideals
- Self-determination

- Mutual respect and dignity of every person
- Privacy
- Human rights
- Fair and non-judgmental
- Co-operation
- Knowledge and Theory of a Social Worker.

Social work knowledge and theory may include:

- human growth and behaviour
- family dynamics
- communication theory
- community development theory
- organizational theory
- theories of the state
- theories of oppression and empowerment
- social treatment interventions
- social action methods
- social research methods, and
- policy analysis.

There are 23 universities across Canada that provide professional education for social workers. Nearly 4,000 students enrol annually in social work education, and 370 faculty are employed to teach them.

Why a Social Work Profession?

Some key issues facing social work during the century continue to this day. Social work is a relatively recent profession. It grew up with industrial society and the development of a factory system, a vast division of labour, private markets, the use of money, and an unequal distribution of material gains. As industrialism expanded, many people were concerned about the existence of poverty in the middle of great affluence.

The Expansion of Social Work in the 20th Century

Data on the number of members in the Canadian Association of Social Workers founded in the 1920s. By 1939, it had 600 members. By 1966, there were 3,000 members, by 1986, 9,000 members. These are just members of the Association, not everyone who is a member of the field of social work.

The Education of Social Workers

The first Canadian trained social workers graduated from the University of Toronto, Department of Social Services in 1914. Until the early 1970s social work schools in Canada were accredited by the American Council of social Work Education.

Now, professional education of social workers takes place at 23 universities across Canada, and numerous community colleges. Nearly 4,000 students enrol annually in social work degree education, and 370 faculty are employed to teach them.

Most schools, faculties or the Canadian Association of Schools of Social Work accredits departments of social work. Degrees are granted at the bachelor, master and doctoral levels of study. The Bachelor of Social Work is the minimum educational requirement for entry into the profession. Post-graduate certificate programs are also offered in specialized aspects of social work practice.

SOCIAL WORKER DUTIES AND RESPONSIBILITIES

Purpose of Classification

Counsels and provides guidance to individuals and/or families with various social, medical, and/or psychiatric problems.

Distinguishing Characteristics: This is a specialized classification and not part of a series.

Examples of Duties:

- Interviews client to determine nature and degree of problem, disability or illness and interprets data for other social or health treatment agencies.
- Assists family members in understanding the clients' needs and aids client and family in working out realistic functional goals for client.
- Assists client and parents with problems concerning relationships or other aspects of social functioning effected by disability.

- Helps client and family members through individual or group conferences to understand, accept, and follow medical recommendations.
- Develops and writes informational material for educational purposes; conducts workshops and educational sessions.
- Provides psychiatric social work assistance to mentally or emotionally disturbed patients, collaborating with psychiatric team in diagnosis and treatment plan.
- Plans discharge of clients.
- Assists in training university students on field placement as a phase of their professional social work curriculum and conducts in-service training for mental health personnel.
- Coordinates referral and evaluation of client to interdisciplinary diagnostic teams; serves as case manager for referred client.
- Conducts psychosocial screening activities determining required specialized psychiatric assistance.

Knowledge, Skills and Abilities:

- Knowledge of the principles, practices, techniques and professional standards in the field of social work.
- Knowledge of community organizations and social service programs.
- Skill in communicating effectively with a variety of people of various socio-economic and educational backgrounds.

Minimum Qualifications: Master's degree in Social Work, Counselling, Psychology, Education or related field; OR, Bachelor's degree in a behavioural science or related field AND two years' experience working in a social service field or related capacity; OR, Any equivalent combination of experience and/or education from which comparable knowledge, skills and abilities have been achieved.

4

Concepts of Social Service

SOCIAL WELFARE SERVICES

The growth of social services is necessarily a slow process. Its principal limitations relate to the financial resources available and resources which can be spared for social services, lack of trained personnel and of organisations devoted to social welfare and lack of reliable data pertaining to social problems. These factors tend to limit the immediate objects of social welfare services to groups which are in a vulnerable position or need special assistance. The aims of social welfare are, however, wider in scope. Social Welfare is concerned with the well-being of the entire community, not only of particular sections of the population which may be handicapped in one way or another. Problems which have already come to the fore must no doubt claim attention; equally, it is necessary to take steps to prevent the occurrence of new problems.

In the field of social welfare, personnel provided by the Government or by public authorities generally represent only a nucleus for drawing into the service of the community the voluntary labours of large numbers of private individuals. In the past voluntary agencies depended entirely on donations from private persons. In the larger interest of the community these voluntary agencies have to be encouraged and assisted in extending the scope of their activities. The Central and State Governments and local authorities should therefore readily supplement private efforts in this direction. Eventually, the burden of maintaining social services has to fall in the main on local authorities. In the initial stages, however, special agencies are needed to provide the necessary impulse for the organisation of social welfare services and to bring about a measure of coordination between the efforts of public authorities and of voluntary organisations.

A comprehensive social welfare programme would include, for instance, social legislation, welfare of women and children, family welfare, youth welfare, physical and mental fitness, crime and correctional administration and welfare of the physically and mentally handicapped. It would also include in the special circumstances and background of India, a programme for fulfilling the objective of Prohibition. In this chapter developments in the field of social welfare services, including Prohibition, which have taken place during the period of the first five year plan and those projected for the second plan are briefly outlined.

SCHEMES OF THE CENTRAL SOCIAL WELFARE BOARD

As part of the first five year plan the Central Government set up a Central Social Welfare Board with the object especially of assisting voluntary agencies in organising welfare programmes for women and children and the handicapped groups. The Board has, in turn, in collaboration with State Governments, organised State Social Welfare Boards throughout the country. The building up of this organisational net work makes it possible to embark upon larger programmes of social welfare in the second five year plan. Already, during the past three years the foundations for these programmes have been laid. The Central Social Welfare Board has assisted 2128 institutions-of which 660 are women welfare institutions, 591 child welfare institutions, 151 institutions serving handicapped persons and delinquents and 726 institutions engaged in general welfare work. The grants given by the Board are intended to assist existing voluntary organisations in consolidating their activities. In the case of newly established voluntary organisations grants are given for enabling them to start their work on sound lines. The general object is to assist the establishment of voluntary institutions in all parts of the country. The Central Social Welfare Board has also taken up welfare extension projects, one in each district in the country, each project serving a group of about 25 villages. During the second five year plan the Board has a programme of setting up three more welfare extension projects in each district. By the beginning of 1956 the Board had established 291 welfare extension projects. During the second five year plan a programme for increasing the number of projects to 1320, so as to provide four projects to each district, is to be completed. When this programme is completed a total of 50,000 villages will have been provided with specially organised welfare services for women and children. It is proposed to establish about one-third of the new projects in each of the first three years of the plan period. In each district the projects are placed under an implementing committee, a majority of whose members are local women welfare workers. To meet the requirements of welfare extension projects, the Central. Social Welfare Board has organised extensive training programmes for women village level workers and for midwives. The Board has also made a beginning in Delhi, Poona, Hyderabad and Vijayawada in tackling the difficult task of providing work for women in their homes. For this purpose three match factories have been established and setting up of additional factories with the assistance of the Ministry of Commerce and Industry is under consideration.

Two Advisory Committees set up by the Board have also made proposals for social and moral hygiene and provision of after-care services. These envisage the establishment of a large number of homes and shelters. The general scheme is to have five types of homes in each State. Of these, one would be for rescued women for whom a fairly long period of social and environmental adjustment may be necessary. Two homes are proposed for the 'after-care' of persons discharged from correctional institutions, one for men and the second for women. At the remaining two institutions short-term rehabilitation services will be provided for, persons discharged from non-correctional institutions. There will also be one shelter in each district for the reception, medical examination and screening of these persons before they are passed on to the State Homes.

A sum of Rs. 14 crores is provided for the Central Social Welfare Board's Schemes, while for after-care and social and moral hygiene programmes Rs. 3 crores are provided in the plans of States and Rs. 3 crores in the schemes of the Ministry of Home Affairs.

WELFARE OF THE PHYSICALLY AND MENTALLY HANDICAPPED PERSONS

In September, 1955 the Ministry of Education constituted a National Advisory Council for the Education of the Handicapped. The functions of this Council are to advise the Central Government on problems concerning the education, training, and employment and the provision of social and cultural amenities for the physically and mentally handicapped, to formulate new schemes and to provide liaison with voluntary organisations working in this field. It is proposed to undertake a survey of the problem of the physically and mentally handicapped. There are at present about 60 schools for the blind, 44 for the deafmutes, 9 for the cripped and diseased and 5 for the mentally handicapped. The majority of these are private institutions which are aided by Government. In the second plan provision has been made for providing additional facilities such as model schools for blind children and deaf children, a women's section in the training school for the adult blind provision for scholarships etc. In the plans of a number of States also provision has been made for the welfare and education of physically and mentally handicapped persons. For the rehabilitation of persons suffering from incurable diseases provision has been made in the programme of the Ministry of Health.

Youth Welfare

A number of youth organisations and youth welfare programmes received active support during the first five year plan. In the plan a provision of Rs. 1 crore has been made for organising a comprehensive programme of youth camps and labour service for students. The object of this programme was to encourage youth participation in constructive national activities. Three-fourths of the amount was allocated for labour and social service camps and one fourth for work projects such as construction of swimming pools open air theatres etc. to be undertaken by students in and around their educational institutions.

By the end of 1955 about 900 camps had been organised and in these about 100,000 young persons participated. These camps took part in the construction of canals and roads, repair of buildings and tanks, slum clearance, sanitation drives, etc. The Bharat Sevak Samaj which has a special ancillary organisation for youth, the Bharat Yuwak Samaj also organised nearly 500 youth and students camps in which about 40,000 youths took part. The strength of the Bharat Scouts and Guides movement rose during the plan by about 50 per cent. The movement now includes 438.405 scouts and 68,118 guides. The work of the National Cadet Corps and the Auxiliary Cadet Corps also developed during the plan period on a large scale. The National Cadet Corps has now a total strength of 118,000, of whom 46,000 are in the senior division, 64,000 in the junior division, 8000 in the girls' division and 3,000 are teachers and leaders drawn from educational institutions. The Auxiliary Cadet Corps, which now counts 750,000 boys and girls on its rolls, has a programme of expansion to twice its present strength by the end of the second plan. In its plan, the Ministry of Education has provided for the establishment of National College of Physical Education for the development of sports and for support to various youth welfare activities such as youth leadership, training camps, youth hostels, etc. Provision has also been made for labour and social service camps and work projects and for assisting the work of the Bharat Scouts and Guides.

Other Welfare Programmes

For the second five year plan the Ministry of Home Affairs have formulated proposals, relating to juvenile delinquency, social and moral hygiene, vagrancy or beggary and probation. The man object of these proposals is to build up the essential institutions needed for developing social welfare work in relation to these problems. A provision of Rs. 2 crores has been made in the plan of the Ministry for the purpose of assisting States in which the necessary institutions are not already organised either by the State Governments themselves or by voluntary organisations.

Juvenile delinquency has been growing in large cities, the most common offence being theft. Legislation for dealing with juvenile delinquents exists in 15 States and has been recommended in others, but often it is not adequately enforced. Juvenile courts exist only in a few States; elsewhere trials of juveniles-are conducted by the ordinary courts. The number of institutions for juveniles are relatively small, being limited to 67 remand homes, 49 certified schools, 7 reformatory schools, 5 juvenile jails and 8 borstal institutions. The Central Government has suggested to States that there should be a remand home in each important town in which juveniles in custody may be lodged during the period of investigation of trial. It has also suggested that each State should have a certified school and a hostel for boys, where juveniles released on probation can be lodged if they cannot be attached to suitable families during this period. Finally, each State should have a borstal school for young delinquents between the ages of 15 and 21 years. Child guidance clinics and school social workers could assist in early treatment of behaviour problems and in reducing the incidence of juvenile delinquency.

The Central Government has also suggested that in States where a probation system does not already exist a beginning should now be made. It is further proposed that in the more important jails welfare officers should be appointed for the purpose of contacting prisoners during their stay in jails and for keeping in touch with them and their families after release.

The beggar problem has attracted attention for a long period but its extensive character and ramifications have hitherto impeded effective action. Study of the problem is being undertaken through two research schemes instituted by the Research Programmes Committee of the Planning Commission. It is important that steps to formulate a programme for eliminating the beggar problem altogether should now be taken. To provide for the worst cases, the Central Government has proposed that in each State there should be a home for 100 old, infirm, diseased or disabled beggars.

RESOURCES FOR SOCIAL WELFARE

The brief review which has been given above of programmes in the field of social welfare which have to be undertaken in the second five year plan will show that as a result of developments of the past three or four years social welfare programmes are now bring implemented as an integral part of planned development. The plan provides nearly Rs. 29 crores for schemes of social welfare. Rs. 19 crores at the Centre and nearly Rs. 10 crores in the States. A provision of about Rs. 11 crores is made for youth welfare and social welfare programmes in the plan of the Ministry of Education. Allied to these are the provision in the plan of Rs. IS crores for local development works and of Rs. 5 crores for social schemes connected with public cooperation. In this connection, full account should also be taken of the provision of about Rs. 91 crores for the welfare of backward classes and of the outlay provided in the plan on rural development programmes, including national extension and community projects and village and small industries. Where economic and social factors have such an intimate bearing on one another, it is difficult to draw too sharp a distinction between programmes for promoting social welfare and programmes for promoting economic development. They both subserve an identical purpose.

In the Five Year Plan the suggestion was made that funds available with endowments and trusts may be an important method of supplementing resources which States and private agencies can raise for social welfare. Enquiries on this subject were recommended with a view to evolving a basis for legislation concerning the use for approved purposes of funds held by endowments and trusts. In the past substantial sums for promoting social welfare activities were, made available through trusts and endowments. It has been observed that after a period many trusts became inactive, the r income is not spent for the purposes originally intended and unproductive investments occur. In mobilising private effort in support of social welfare programmes, a view should be taken of the contribution which trusts could make, especially towards the resources of voluntary organisations. These possibilities are being investigated.

Finally, it may be urged that in all fields of social welfare each local community has to assume the main responsibility for providing relief and assistance to the needy and the handicapped. The role of the State and the agencies setup by it cannot but be of a limited character. However, the experience of the first plan shows that resources provided by public authorities in money and personnel can go a long way in stimulating community effort and invoking much devoted voluntary service. This is the assumption on which the larger programmes proposed for the second five year plan have been formulated.

SOCIAL WELFARE AND THE PANCHAYATI RAJ

Democracy thrives in India today largely because it has always existed in some form at the micro level even during the long feudal era. The village council, Panchayat, consisting of village elders played a key role in this long survival of grassroot democracy. The Panchayati Raj (rule) now enjoys constitutional status with built-in mechanism for regular elections and minimum representation of women and members of the scheduled castes and scheduled tribes. There are over three million elected local representatives, making this the widest democratic base in the world. The Panchayati Raj helps in purposeful understanding of the masses and articulation of their responses. The Panchayati Raj is perhaps the best means of spreading democracy at the grassroot. Mahatma Gandhi called the Panchayats 'village republics'; these village republics contribute to making India a shining example of democracy in the world.

UPLIFTMENT OF THE RURAL POOR

Though the country has made tremendous strides in many fields, 27 percent of the rural poor live in poverty, often without basic facilities. With this in mind, the government has been increasing the allocation for rural development, which stood at approx.$3.1 billion. The percentage of rural poor, which was 56.44 in 1973-74,has been coming down over the years, but the actual number of the rural poor is still large —about 193 million.

The emphasis in some of the recent poverty alleviation programmes for the rural poor is on self-help, gainful employment, food security and strengthening of rural infrastructure.

Environment, Ecology and Forestry

In today's world, development has to harmonies with

environment. To ensure that, the government encourages use of pollution abatement techniques, especially in the critically polluted areas. Environmental considerations weigh heavily in clearing certain projects. For this purpose, laws have been framed, fiscal incentives given, agreements signed, educational programmes introduced and information disseminated through publicity.

India has taken major steps to control vehicular pollution in cities. In Delhi, all public transport vehicles are required by law to use CNG. Under the Kyoto Protocol, the government is committed to strengthening efforts to tackle global warming. At the World Summit on Sustainable Development held in Johannesburg in September 2002, India articulated its and other developing countries concerns with regard to the principles of international cooperation for protection of environment through sustainable development. Specific targets to provide access to safe drinking water and sanitation, clean energy, reversal of the present trend of loss in bio-diversity etc. have been outlined.

Breakthrough in Education

Being a signatory to the Delhi Declaration and a Framework for Action, which calls for Education for All (children), India has pledged to spend 6% of the GNP on education. Parliament has approved a legislation that makes free and compulsory education for all children in the 6-14 years age group.

Literacy rates have improved considerably over the years; from about 18 percent in 1951 the literacy rate today is over 75 percent for males and 55 percent for females. Despite this discrepancy, the female literacy rate has shown a higher growth in the last decade —about 15 percent against 12 percent for males.

It is estimated that about 80 percent of the children in the 6-14 years age group, who number close to 200 million, attend schools and their drop out rates have also been falling.

A Total Literacy Campaign is operational in many areas of the country. About five million volunteers are engaged in teaching the alphabets to about 50 million people in the 9-45 age group. It is estimated that 15 million of them have become functionally literate. The Elementary Education System in India is the second largest in the World with 149.4 millions children of 6-14 years enrolled and 2.9 million teachers.

Role of Women

Throughout Indian history, from the time of Sita, consort of Lord Rama, there have been women who occupied a special place in society. Laxmibai, Razia Sultan and Meerabai are names that now belong to history. From contemporary times, women who have left their imprint include Mrs. Vijayalaxmi Pandit, the first woman president of the United Nations, Mrs.Indira Gandhi, India's first woman Prime Minister and Mother Teresa, an Indian missionary who won the Nobel Peace Prize for spreading the message of love and care of the neglected.

India has set high standards for female representation in the policy and decision-making process. One third of the seats in local bodies — village panchayats, municipalities, city corporations and district bodies — are reserved for women. Many innovative programmes have been launched for generating employment, improving income and creating awareness among women. The ultimate goal is to make women economically independent and self-reliant. The year 2001 was observed as Women's Empowerment Year to create large-scale awareness about women's rights and issues.

In the world of sports and glamour Indian women have begun to leave a mark. K.Malleswari and Kunjarani Devi are the two top-most weightlifters in the world. In 1994 two Indians, Sushmita Sen and Aishwarya Rai, bagged the Miss Universe and Miss World titles respectively, a unique double for any country. The 1997,1999 and 2000 Miss World crown was bagged by Indians, Diana Hayden, Yukta Mookhey and Priyanka Chopra. Miss Universe crown in 2000 was won by Lara Dutta.

Indian women have left a mark among achievers in the social field also. Rashida Bee and Champa Devi Shukla of Bhopal won the 2004 Goldman Prize for Environment, the first Indians to be so honored. The award, considered to be the equivalent of the Nobel Prize for Environment, was in recognition of the work for survivors of the Bhopal gas tragedy of 1984. The two gutsy middle-aged women overcame sickness and defied social norms to fight for the rights of their fellow victims of the tragedy which had taken a toll of 20,000 lives. Ela Bhat, a Magsaysay Award winner, took the struggle for justice and recognition of self-employed women to national and international areas. She started south Asia's first labour and trade union for women workers in the informal sector.

Kiran Bedi, also a Magsaysay Award winner, is India's first Indian Police Service (IPS) woman officer. A former tennis champion, she has worked tirelessly for reforming prisoners and drug addicts, besides improving prison environment.

Welfare

As a welfare State, India is committed to the welfare and development of its people, particularly the vulnerable sections like the scheduled castes (SCs), scheduled tribes (STs), other backward classes (OBCs), minorities and the handicapped. There are specific articles in the Constitution, which outline this commitment. The strategy adopted for this aims at minimizing inequalities in income, status and opportunities. Taken together, the majority of the population of the country consists of SCs, STs, OBCs and minorities.

SCS, STS, BACKWARD CLASSES AND OTHERS

Almost a quarter of India 's population consists of the scheduled castes (SCs) and Scheduled Tribes (STs) who had remained neglected for centuries. The approach for their development has been enunciated by the Constitution. The government has taken several steps for their welfare. The representation of the SCs and STs in Parliament and all State Assemblies is assured. Provisions have been made in the constitution for reservation in appointments or posts for SCs, STs and OBCs. The government has implemented schemes for their educational development and rendering financial assistance to support economic activities.

In addition to Constitutional provisions for their welfare, there is a National Commission for SCs and STs, which while investigating and monitoring a matter relating to the safeguards for the SCs and STs enjoy the powers of a civil court. The Central as well as State governments consult this commission on all policy matters relating to the SCs and STs. Laws have been suitably amended to penalize anyone who tries to prevent the rights available to a person upon the abolition of 'untouchability ' in the country. Almost every state in the country has specified courts that try cases of atrocities against SCs and STs.

Minorities

At the national level, five communities have been notified as minorities —Muslims, Sikhs, Christians, Buddhists and Zoroastrians, who together constitute less than 18 percent of the country 's population. The Constitution guarantees them their right to conserve their religion, language and culture. Next to Indonesia, India has the world 's second largest Muslim population. The minorities have received a new deal with the establishment of the National Minorities Development Corporation, which has initiated schemes for micro financing of women belonging to the minority communities in various skills and trade, and also introduced schemes to offer concessional loans for education and pursuing professional courses. It also needs to be stressed that there is no bar against practicing any religion in India.

Children and Drug Abuse

India has adopted a National Policy on Children and was the first country to adopt a legislation in line with a UN Declaration on the Right of the Child. The Integrated Child Development Services aims at the holistic development of children in the 0-6 years age group —as also pregnant and lactating mothers from disadvantaged sections. There are over 450 day care centres, old-age homes and mobile medicare units. Over 60 units also function for the welfare of the street children.

A Central Adoption Resource Agency has been set up to act as the clearinghouse of information on children available for adoption. The government recognizes 56 Indian agencies for giving children to foreigners for adoption and another 280 foreign agencies have been enlisted for sponsoring applications of foreigners who seek guardianship of Indian children.

Population

India has 2.4% of the world 's land, but supports 16% of the global population. According to the latest census report (2001), India has a population of 1,027 million, about 150 million more than in the previous census (1991). The average exponential growth declined to 1.93 percent in 2001 compared to 2.14 percent in 1991. The infant mortality rate (IMR) came down to 70 (in 2000) from 146 in 1951. Life expectancy, which was 36.7 in 1951, increased to 64.6 in 2000 and in the same period the crude death rate came down to 8.7 per 1000 from 36.7. However, the task of removing poverty remains enormous.

Family

The aim of India 's National Family Welfare Programme is to stabilize the population at a level 'consistent with the requirement of the national economy'. The National Population Policy 2000, which has well-defined objectives, has set socio-demographic goals to achieve population stabilization by 2010.

The Family Welfare Programme in India is recognized as a priority area. It seeks, among other things, to popularize contraception, reduce the infant and maternal morbidity and mortality to bring down the level of fertility and to provide need-based, high quality, reproductive and child health care.

Planned Parenthood

The National Family Welfare Programme was launched to promote responsible and planned parenthood through voluntary family planning methods. Couples have the choice of adopting temporary or preventive measures. Facilities for medical termination of pregnancies in certain circumstances are also available. During 2002-03, the total number of family planning acceptors in the country as a whole was 7.8 percent higher than in 2001-02. The use of contraceptives has increased and in 2002-03 emergency contraceptive pills were introduced for the first time in the family welfare programme.

Child and Mother Care

In view of the close relationship between high birth rate and high infant mortality, various child and mother health care programmes are being implemented. A Child Survival and Safe Motherhood Programme is in operation to take up universal immunization and safe motherhood initiatives. NGOs are being given increasing support in an effort to involve the community for promoting spacing methods to stabilize population.

AIDS

With about four million victims, India has been hit severely by AIDS. A National Programme for the Prevention and Control of AIDS has been launched to bring down the current high rate of AIDS infection to zero by 2007. The threat of HIV transmission is being tackled through safe blood transfusion services, control of sexually transmitted diseases and information, education and counselling.

Medical Education

Medical research and education have received significant attention in the years following independence. While there were only 28 medical colleges in 1950, there are at present 106 medical colleges, 29 dental colleges and 11 other institutions providing medical education. Nearly 14,000 students graduate every year from medical colleges. Over 8,200 nurses qualify for service annually from 367 nursing institutions. Medical institutions in India also train a large number of students from other developing countries. India has world class hospitals manned by some of the world 's best physicians and surgeon. These hospitals have state of the art facilities but the treatment they offer is inexpensive, attracting many foreign patients.

Rural Health Services

The Government is paying increasing attention to integrated health, maternity and childcare in rural areas. A National Health Policy has been approved. It seeks to raise health care expenditure to 6 percent of the GDP by 2010. An increasing number of community health workers and doctors are being sent to rural health centres. Primary health care is being provided to the rural population through a network of over 150,000 primary health centres and sub-centres by 586,000 trained midwives and 410,000 health guides.

Housing and Urban Development

Various policies and initiatives of the Government have put the country on the threshold of a major qualitative and quantitative change in the housing and urban development sector. A Housing and Habitat Policy has been formulated and 'Housing for All ' is a priority for the government.

Social Welfare

The Indian government has established an extensive social welfare system. Among the many programs designed for betterment and enhancement of quality of life for SC, ST, BC, Minorities women and communities at large, we have -

- Minimum needs (food, cloth, housing, accessing education, health and drinking water) and social security programmes
- There are also services for the blind, deaf, mentally retarded, and orthopedically handicapped. Programs for displaced persons; rural community development
- Programs for women include welfare grants, women's adult education, working women's hostels, family planning & maternity care
- Special measures are aimed at rehabilitating juvenile delinquents, sexworkers, and convicts
- Other social welfare programs cover-emergency relief programs for natural disasters like-drought, flood, earthquake etc. and eradicating untouchability etc.,
- Apart from the above mentioned initiatives, the Government and NGOs are striving hard and working towards social sector like :
    - o Organizing awareness campaigns at various level on Social Evils (Women discrimination, child marriages, all are equal, Anti-dowry, Anti Alcoholism, No Tobacco, Child Trafficking, female infanticide and witchcraft/sorcery)
    - o Rehabilitation centres for Social Vulnerable groups (Migration, Persons with disability, Senior Citizens and Orphans/Street Children)
    - o Providing Social Security Schemes (Right to Food, Housing, Pension-family-maternal benifits and employment)

In this spirit, striving towards the similar objectives, the India Development Gateway aims to provide information, content, products & services for bringing awareness and to sensitize the rural communities on the subject.

SOCIAL REFORMERS

Decades come and go but what remain are the impression and great acts of the social reformers. India is privileged to have number of great souls like Dayanand Saraswati and Raja Ram Mohan Roy. They managed to bring revolutions by making radical changes in the society. Some of the reformers took up the challenges of breaking the jinx of prevailing caste-system while some fought for the introduction of girls'-education and widow remarriage. The contributions, made by these, simple yet eminent souls towards humanity are really extraordinary. Their activities and thoughts guided the nation to a new beginning.

Acharya Vinoba Bhave

Acharya Vinoba Bhave was a freedom fighter and a spiritual teacher. He is best known as the founder of the 'Bhoodan Movement' (Gift of the Land). The reformer had an intense concern for the deprived masses. Vinoba Bhave had once said, "All revolutions are spiritual at the source.

Baba Amte

From a child born with a silver spoon in his mouth, Baba Amte later transformed his life into a social activist. He devoted his entire life to serve the downtrodden people of the society. He left his lucrative profession to join India's struggle for independence.

Ishwar Chandra Vidyasagar

Ishwar Chandra Vidyasagar is considered as one of the pillars of Bengal renaissance. In other words, he managed to continue the reforms movement that was started by Raja Rammohan Roy. Vidyasagar was a well-known writer, intellectual and above all a staunch follower of humanity. He brought a revolution in the education system of Bengal.

Jyotiba Phule

Jyotiba Phule was one of the prominent social reformers of the nineteenth century India. He led the movement against the prevailing caste-restrictions in India. He revolted against the domination of the Brahmins and for the rights of peasants and other low-caste fellow.

Mother Teresa

Mother Teresa was a true follower of humanity. Many people considered Mother as the "reincarnated form of Lord Jesus". Mother Teresa devoted her entire life in serving the needy and abandoned people of the society. Although her mission started in India, she succeeded in bringing the people of all societies under one roof, i.e. humanity.

Raja Ram Mohan Roy

Raja Ram Mohan Roy is considered as the pioneer of modern Indian Renaissance for the remarkable reforms he brought in the 18th century India. Among his efforts, the abolition of the sati-pratha-a practice in which the widow was compelled to sacrifice herself on the funeral pyre of her husband-was the prominent.

Sri Ramakrishna Paramhansa

Sri Ramakrishna Paramhansa was a popular saint of India. He had a strong faith in the existence of god. He regarded every woman of the society, including his wife, Sarada, as holy mother. Swami Vivekananda was one of the prominent disciples of Ramakrishna, who later formed the Ramakrishna Mission.

Shahu Chhatrapati

King Shahu Chhatrapati was considered as a true democrat and social reformer. He was an invaluable gem in the history of Kolhapur. Shahu was associated with many progressive activities in the society including education for women. He was greatly influenced by the contributions of social reformer Jyotiba Phule.

Swami Dayanand Saraswati

Dayanand Saraswati was a reformer and believed in pragmatism. He preached against many rituals of the Hindu religion such as idol-worship, caste by birth, animal sacrifices and restrictions of women from reading Vedas. He was not only a great scholar and philosopher but also a social reformer and a political thinker.

Swami Vivekananda

Swami Vivekananda is known for his inspiring speech at

the Parliament of the World's Religions at Chicago on 11 September, 1893, where he introduced Hindu philosophy to the west. But this was not the only contribution of the saint. He revealed the true foundations of India's unity as a nation. He taught how a nation with such a vast diversity can be bound together by a feeling of humanity and brotherhood.

Mahatma Gandhi

Mahatma Gandhi: (2 October 1869 – 30 January 1948) was the pre-eminent political and spiritual leader of India during the Indian independence movement. He was the pioneer of satyagraha—resistance to tyranny through mass civil disobedience, firmly founded upon ahimsa or total nonviolence—which led India to independence and inspired movements for civil rights and freedom across the world. Gandhi led nationwide campaigns to ease poverty, expand women's rights, build religious and ethnic amity, end untouchability, and increase economic self-reliance. Above all, he aimed to achieve Swaraj or the independence of India from foreign domination.

Virchand Gandhi

Virchand Gandhi: Virachand Raghav Gandhi was from Mahuva. He is 19th Century Indian patriot who was friend of Mahatma Gandhi and contemporary to Swami Vivekanand. He and swami vivekananda drew equal attention at the first World Parliament of Religions in Chicago in 1893. He won a silver medal in same. His statue still stands at the Jain temple in Chicago. He was key member of Indian National Congress. And as a reformer established a] Gandhi Philosophical Society, b] Society for the Education of Women in India (SEWI). Under the banner of SEWI, several Indian women came to U.S.A. for higher studies. c] School of Oriental Philosophy, d] Jain Literature Society in London.. And he delivered 535 lectures in USA and Europe. He also died at young age of 37 alike Swami Vivekanand. Today Govt. of India has recognised his service by issuing Postal Stamp in his memory

Swami Vivekanand

Swami Vivekanand: (January 12, 1863–July 4, 1902) He was the founder of Ramakrishna Mission. Vivekananda is considered to be a major force in the revival of Hinduism in modern India. He is considered a key figure in the introduction of Vedanta and Yoga in Europe and America. He introduced Hinduism at the Parliament of the World's Religions at Chicago in 1893.

Swami Dayanand Saraswati

Swami Dayanand Saraswati: (February 12, 1824 – October 31, 1883) was an important Hindu religious scholar and the founder of the Arya Samaj, "Society of Nobles", a Hindu reform movement, founded in 1875. He was the first man who gave the call for Swarajay in 1876 which was later furthered by Lokmanya Tilak.

Raja Ram Mohan Roy

Raja Ram Mohan Roy: (August 14, 1774 – September 27, 1833) was a founder of the Brahma Sabha in 1828 which engendered the Brahmo Samaj, an influential Indian socio-religious reform movement. He is best known for his efforts to abolish the practice of sati, the Hindu funeral practice in which the widow was compelled to sacrifice herself on her husband's funeral pyre. It was he who first introduced the word "Hinduism" into the English language in 1816. For his diverse contributions to society, Raja Ram Mohan Roy is regarded as one of the most important figures in the Indian Renaissance. Ram Mohun Roy's impact on modern Indian history was a revival of the pure and ethical principles of the Vedanta school of philosophy as found in the Upanishads.

Jamnalal Bajaj

Jamnalal Bajaj: (4 November 1884 – 11 February 1942) was an industrialist, a philanthropist, and Indian independence fighter. Gandhi is known to have adopted him as his son. He is known for this efforts of promoting Khadi and village Industries in India. With the intent of eradicating untouchability, he fought the non admission of Harijans into Hindu temples. He began a campaign by eating a meal with Harijans and opening public wells to them. He opened several wells in his fields and gardens. Jamanalal dedicated much of his wealth to the poor. He felt this inherited wealth was a sacred trust to be used for the benefit of the people. In honour of his social initiatives a well known national and international award called Jamnalal Bajaj Award has been instituted by the Bajaj Foundation.

Vinoba Bhave

Vinoba Bhave: (September 11, 1895-November 15 1982) was an Indian advocate of Nonviolence and human rights. He is considered as the spiritual successor of Mahatma Gandhi. Vinoba Bhave was a scholar, thinker, writer who produced numerous books, translator who made Sanskrit texts accessible to common man, orator, linguist who had excellent command of several languages (Marathi, Hindi, Urdu, English, Sanskrit), and a social reformer. He wrote brief introductions to, and criticisms of, several religious and philosophical works like the Bhagavad Gita, works of Adi Shankaracharya, the Bible and Quran. His criticism of Dnyaneshwar's poetry as also the output by other Marathi saints is quite brilliant and a testimony to the breadth of his intellect. A university named after him Vinoba Bhave University is still there in the state of Jharkhand spreading knowledge even after his death.

Baba Amte

Baba Amte: (December 26, 1914 – February 9, 2008) was an Indian social worker and social activist known particularly for his work for the rehabilitation and empowerment of poor people suffering from leprosy. He spent some time at Sevagram ashram of Mahatma Gandhi, and became a follower of Gandhism for the rest of his life. He believed in Gandhi's concept of a self-sufficient village industry that empowers seemingly helpless people, and successfully brought his ideas into practice at Anandwan. He practiced various aspects of Gandhism, including yarn spinning using a charkha and wearing khadi. Amte founded three ashrams for treatment and rehabilitation of leprosy patients, disabled people, and people from marginalized sections of the society in Maharashtra, India.

Shriram Sharma Acharya

Shriram Sharma Acharya: (September 20, 1911 – June 2, 1990) was an Indian seer, sage, Indian social worker, a philanthropist, a visionary of the New Golden Era and the Founder of the All World Gayatri Pariwar. He devoted his life to the welfare of people and the refinement of the moral and cultural environment. He pioneered the revival of spirituality, creative integration of the modern and ancient sciences and religion relevant in the challenging circumstances of the present times. To help people, his aim was to diagnose the root cause of the ailing state of the world today and enable the upliftment of society. Acharyaji recognized the crisis of faith, people's ignorance of the powers of the inner self, and the lack of righteous attitude and conduct. During 1984-1986, he carried out the unique spiritual experiment of sukshmikaraña, meaning sublimation of vital force and physical, mental and spiritual energies.

Ishwar Chandra Vidyasagar

Ishwar Chandra Vidyasagar: (1820-1891) Vidyasagar was a philosopher, academic, educator, writer, translator, printer, publisher, entrepreneur, reformer, and philanthropist. His efforts to simplify and modernize Bangla prose were significant. He was a Bengali polymath and a key figure of the Bengal Renaissance. Vidyasagar championed the uplift of the status of women in India, particularly in his native Bengal. Unlike some other reformers who sought to set up alternative societies or systems, he sought, however, to transform orthodox Hindu society from within. Vidyasagar introduced the practice of widow remarriages to mainstream Hindu society. In earlier times, remarriages of widows would occur sporadically only among progressive members of the Brahmo Samaj.

Dhondo Keshav Karve

Dhondo Keshav Karve: (April 18, 1858-November 9, 1962) was a preeminent social reformer of his time in India in the field of women's welfare. Karve was one of the pioneers of promoting women's education and the right for widows to remarry in India. The Government of India recognized his reform work by awarding him its highest civilian award, Bharat Ratna, in 1958 (Incidentally his centennial year). The appellation Maharshi, which the Indian public often assigned to Karve, means "a great sage". Those who knew Karve affectionately called him as Anna Karve. (In Marathi-speaking community, to which Karve belonged, the appellation Anna is often used to address either one's father or an elder brother.)

Balshastri Jambhekar

Balshastri Jambhekar: (January 6, 1812– May 18, 1846) is known as Father of Marathi journalism for his efforts in starting journalism in Marathi language with the first newspaper in the language named 'Darpan' in the early days of British Rule in India. He founded Darpan as the first Marathi newspaper. He was editor of this newspaper during the British rule in India. This turned out to be the beginning of Marathi journalism. He had mastery in many languages including Marathi, Sanskrit, English and Hindi. Apart from that he also had a good grasp of Greek, Latin, French, Gujarati and Bengali.

Dr. Bhimrao Ramji Ambedkar

B. R. Ambedkar: (14 April 1891 — 6 December 1956) was an Indian jurist, political leader, Buddhist activist, philosopher, thinker, anthropologist, historian, orator, prolific writer, economist, scholar, editor, revolutionary and the revivalist of Buddhism in India. He was also the chief architect of the Indian Constitution. Ambedkar spent his whole life fighting against social discrimination, the system of Chaturvarna — the Hindu categorization of human society into four varnas — and the Hindu caste system. He is also credited with having sparked the bloodless revolution with his most remarkable and innovative Buddhist movement. Ambedkar has been honoured with the Bharat Ratna, India's highest civilian award.

Annie Besant

Annie Besant: (October 1, 1847 – September 20, 1933) was a prominent Theosophist, women's rights activist, writer and orator and supporter of Irish and Indian self rule. In 1908 Annie Besant became President of the Theosophical Society and began to steer the society away from Buddhism and towards Hinduism.

She also became involved in politics in India, joining the Indian National Congress. When war broke out in Europe in 1914 she helped launch the Home Rule League to campaign for democracy in India and dominion status within the Empire which culminated in her election as president of the India National Congress in late 1917. After the war she continued to campaign for Indian independence until her death in 1933.

Vitthal Ramji Shinde

Vitthal Ramji Shinde: (April 23, 1873 – January 2, 1944) He was a prominent campaigner on behalf of the Dalit movement in Maharashtra and established the Depressed Classes Mission to provide education to the Dalits in Maharashtra.

Gopal Hari Deshmukh

Gopal Hari Deshmukh: (1823-1892) was a social reformer in Maharashtra. Deshmukh started writing articles aimed at social reform in Maharashtra in the weekly Prabhakarunder the pen name Lokhitwadi. In the first two years, he penned 108 articles on social reform. That group of articles has come to be known in Marathi literature as Lokhitwadinchi Shatapatre.

Pandurang Shastri Athavale

Pandurang Shastri Athavale: (October 19, 1920–October 25, 2003) was an Indian philosopher, spiritual leader, social reformer and Hinduism reformist, who founded the Swadhyay Movement and the Swadhyay Parivar organization (Swadhyay Family) in 1954, a self-knowledge movement based on the Bhagavad Gita, which has spread across nearly 100,000 villages in India, with over 5 million members. He was also noted for his discourses or "pravachans" on Srimad Bhagawad Gita and Upanishads.

Kandukuri Veeresalingam

Kandukuri Veeresalingam: (16 April 1848-27 May 1919) was a social reformer who first brought about a renaissance in Telugu people and Telugu literature. He was influenced by the ideals of Brahmo Samaj particularly those of Keshub Chunder Sen. He got involved in the cause of social reforms. In 1876 he started a Telugu journal and wrote the first prose for women. He encouraged education for women, and started a school in Dowlaiswaram in 1874. He started a social organisation called Hitakarini (Benefactor).

Swami Ramdev

Swami Ramdev: Ramkishan Yadav popularly known as Swami Ramdev, is an Indian Hindu swami. He is known for his efforts in popularizing yoga as it is enunciated in Patanjali's

Yoga Sutras. He is also one of the founders of the Divya Yog Mandir Trust headquartered in Haridwar, that aims to popularize Yoga and offer Ayurvedic treatments. The New York Times calls him an "Indian who built Yoga Empire", "a product and symbol of the New India, a yogic fusion of Richard Simmons, Dr. Oz and Oprah Winfrey, irrepressible and bursting with Vedic wisdom".

Jawaharlal Nehru

Jawaharlal Nehru (14 November 1889–27 May 1964) was an Indian statesman who was the first (and to date the longest-serving) prime minister of India, from 1947 until 1964. One of the leading figures in the Indian independence movement, Nehru was elected by the Congress Party to assume office as independent India's first Prime Minister, and re-elected when the Congress Party won India's first general election in 1952. As one of the founders of the Non-aligned Movement, he was also an important figure in the international politics of the post-war era. He is frequently referred to as Pandit Nehru ("pandit" being a Sanskrit and Hindi honorific meaning "scholar" or "teacher") and, specifically in India, as Panditji (with "-ji" being a honorific suffix).

SOCIAL REFORM OR REVOLUTION

Reform or Revolution is the title of a pamphlet written by Rosa Luxemburg in 1900. It was published to confront the revisionist ideology beginning to emerge in Europe shortly after the internal conflicts amongst Marxists at the Second International.

Reform or Revolution has experienced an upswing in popularity lately due to conflicts amongst contemporary Marxists regarding this very same issue. While a detailed critique of the thinking of Eduard Bernstein it includes a short and devastating critique of marginalism and identifies credit and the stock market as things that will drive capitalism into crisis. When Polish-born socialist Rosa Luxemburg moved to Germany in 1898, it was the centre of socialist thought and home to the largest socialist party in the world—the Social Democratic Party (SPD). But within the SPD, a debate was raging.

On the one side were the revolutionaries—Marxists who believed that socialism can only be achieved through the self-emancipation of the working class. On the other side were the reformists, or revisionists, who argued that capitalism had reached a stage in which it was no longer necessary to call for revolution, but that enough reforms could be put into place—more democratic rights, more social welfare programs—that socialism would evolve over time. The revisionists, led by leading German socialist Eduard Bernstein, were gaining ground. This wasn't a new debate for the socialist movement. Some early socialist figures like Ferdinand Lasalle argued that socialism would be achieved through parliamentary means.

In 1878, Germany's chancellor Otto von Bismarck imposed anti-socialist laws. As a result, thousands were arrested and hundreds exiled, political newspapers were closed, and all political activity except elections was made illegal. During this period, the SPD declared itself to be revolutionary and repudiated the parliamentary road to socialism. The SPD's platform gave expression to the concerns of the urban working class in Germany, and its share of the vote grew from 312,000 in 1881 to more than 1.4 million in 1890. In 1890, the anti-socialist laws were lifted, and a wave of strikes and trade union militancy followed.

Fearing that the strikes would "scare off" conservative members or that repression might return, SPD leaders renounced the more revolutionary aspects of their program. So at the 1891 Erfurt Congress, the party program enshrined Marxism—and the overthrow of capitalism—as the "official" thinking of the SPD, but argued for practical tasks appropriate for a time when revolution wasn't on the immediate agenda. The party's campaign of opposition to the government won them a growing number of votes in elections. But a schism was developing within the party about how far to carry out this opposition.

Between 1896-98, Bernstein wrote a series of articles on the "Problems of Socialism" and later a book. Luxemburg's response was published in full in the 1908 pamphlet Reform or Revolution. If anyone suspected her of counterposing the two, Luxemburg sets the record straight in the first paragraph: "Can we oppose the social revolution, the transformation of the existing order, its final goal, to social reforms? Certainly not. "The practical daily struggle for reforms, for the amelioration of the condition of the workers within the framework of the existing social order, and for democratic institutions, offers to the Social Democracy the only means of engaging in the proletarian class struggle and working in the direction of the final goal—the conquest of political power and the suppression of wage labour. For Socialist Democracy, there is an indissoluble tie between social reforms and revolution. The struggle for reforms is its means; the social revolution, its goal."

Actually, it was Bernstein who counterposed the two, arguing, "The final aim of socialism, whatever it may be, means nothing to me; it is the movement itself which is everything." Seeing around him a period of capitalist prosperity in which workers were winning greater reforms, Bernstein argued that capitalism had created new mechanisms—such as trade unions, and electoral and legal reforms—that would make an evolution of society toward socialism possible. Luxemburg challenged Bernstein's arguments. She pointed out that Bernstein was little more than a utopian if he believed that socialism could be reformed into existence. Like the French utopian socialist Charles Fourier's "scheme of changing, by means of a system of phalansteries, the water of all the seas into tasty lemonade," Bernstein proposed changing "the sea of capitalist bitterness into a sea of socialist sweetness, by progressively pouring into it bottles of social reformist lemonade," Luxemburg wrote.

Luxemburg's explanation of the role of trade unions, elections and struggles in winning reforms—and sowing the seeds of revolutionary change—remain relevant 100 years later. The importance of unions, she argued, is that they are the body by which workers come together and understand that they are part of a class. Through struggles for reforms, they realize their class power. Not only do workers realize their ability to win reforms, but they also learn the limitations of reforms—and the need for the actual conquest of power. Luxemburg likened union struggles to the "labour of Sisyphus"—the mythical figure who was condemned to push a stone up a hill over and over again. The same applies to reforms won through the ballot box.

By proposing that trade unions or electoral reforms are enough to achieve a kind of socialism, Bernstein and the revisionists missed the importance of struggle in achieving reforms. They saw unions as the means of suppressing the contradictions in capitalism between the workers and bosses. Socialists, on the other hand, see unions as one means by which these contradictions can be pushed into the open and organized around. The truth is that struggles for reform, by their very nature, can launch an offensive against the attacks of the profit system, but not the profit system itself.

In the end, Luxemburg concluded, Bernstein wasn't simply arguing for a "more realistic" way to socialism, but had thrown out the prospect of socialism. "That is why people who pronounce themselves in favour of the method of legislative reform in place and in contradistinction to the conquest of political power and social revolution, do not really choose a more tranquil, calmer and slower road to the same goal, but a different goal," Luxemburg wrote.

"Our program becomes not the realization of socialism, but the reform of capitalism; not the suppression of the wage labour system but the diminution of exploitation, that is, the suppression of the abuses of capitalism instead of suppression of capitalism itself."

Rather than diminish the importance of the struggle for reforms, Luxemburg argued that these struggles are central. "In a word," she wrote, "democracy is indispensable not because it renders superfluous the conquest of political power by the proletariat but because it renders this conquest of power both necessary and possible." Today, in struggles that socialists are involved in, we meet people grappling with what kind of change is necessary. There are two potential stumbling blocks for socialists—one is to ignore the opportunities that exist; the other is to recognize them, but never try to take advantage of them.

The first danger discounts the value of reforms completely, abstaining from struggles to win limited changes that benefit working people. By setting themselves apart from issues that people are fighting for, socialists can relegate themselves to the sidelines of movements, remaining pure in their convictions, yet with little influence over anyone. On the other hand, if socialists throw themselves into fights for reforms without thinking about what the next step in the struggle is—about the next argument that could persuade others from simply viewing the future as a succession of reforms—they run the risk of never convincing anyone of the need to get rid of capitalism. They risk coming to believe, like Bernstein, that the "movement is the only thing."

A key part of this—and a question that Luxemburg didn't arrive at until much later—is the role of a revolutionary socialist organization in convincing others that they should join the fight for a socialist world.

ETHICS IN SOCIAL WORK, STATEMENT OF PRINCIPLES

Definition of Social Work

The social work profession promotes social change, problem solving in human relationships and the empowerment and liberation of people to enhance well-being. Utilising theories of human behaviour and social systems, social work intervenes at the points where people interact with their environments. Principles of human rights and social justice are fundamental to social work.

International Conventions

International human rights declarations and conventions form common standards of achievement, and recognise rights that are accepted by the global community. Documents particularly relevant to social work practice and action are:

- Universal Declaration of Human Rights
- The International Covenant on Civil and Political Rights
- The International Covenant on Economic Social and Cultural Rights
- The Convention on the Elimination of all Forms of Racial Discrimination
- The Convention on the Elimination of All Forms of Discrimination against Women
- The Convention on the Rights of the Child
- Indigenous and Tribal Peoples Convention (ILO convention 169).

PRINCIPLES OF HUMAN RIGHTS AND HUMAN DIGNITY

Social work is based on respect for the inherent worth and dignity of all people, and the rights that follow from this. Social workers should uphold and defend each person's physical, psychological, emotional and spiritual integrity and well-being. This means:

1. Respecting the right to self-determination-Social workers should respect and promote people's right to make their own choices and decisions, irrespective of their values and life choices, provided this does not threaten the rights and legitimate interests of others.
2. Promoting the right to participation-Social workers should promote the full involvement and participation of people using their services in ways that enable them to be empowered in all aspects of decisions and actions affecting their lives.
3. Treating each person as a whole-Social workers should be concerned with the whole person, within the family, community, societal and natural environments, and should seek to recognise all aspects of a person's life.
4. Identifying and developing strengths – Social workers should focus on the strengths of all individuals, groups and communities and thus promote their empowerment.

Social Justice

Social workers have a responsibility to promote social justice, in relation to society generally, and in relation to the people with whom they work. This means:

1. Challenging negative discrimination-Social workers have a responsibility to challenge negative discrimination on the basis of characteristics such as ability, age, culture, gender or sex, marital status, socio-economic status, political opinions, skin colour, racial or other physical characteristics, sexual orientation, or spiritual beliefs.
2. Recognising diversity – Social workers should recognise and respect the ethnic and cultural diversity of the societies in which they practise, taking account of individual, family, group and community differences.

3. Distributing resources equitably – Social workers should ensure that resources at their disposal are distributed fairly, according to need.
4. Challenging unjust policies and practices – Social workers have a duty to bring to the attention of their employers, policy makers, politicians and the general public situations where resources are inadequate or where distribution of resources, policies and practices are oppressive, unfair or harmful.
5. Working in solidarity-Social workers have an obligation to challenge social conditions that contribute to social exclusion, stigmatisation or subjugation, and to work towards an inclusive society.

Professional Conduct

It is the responsibility of the national organisations in membership of IFSW and IASSW to develop and regularly update their own codes of ethics or ethical guidelines, to be consistent with the IFSW/IASSW statement. It is also the responsibility of national organisations to inform social workers and schools of social work about these codes or guidelines. Social workers should act in accordance with the ethical code or guidelines current in their country.

These will generally include more detailed guidance in ethical practice specific to the national context. The following general guidelines on professional conduct apply:

1. Social workers are expected to develop and maintain the required skills and competence to do their job.
2. Social workers should not allow their skills to be used for inhumane purposes, such as torture or terrorism.
3. Social workers should act with integrity. This includes not abusing the relationship of trust with the people using their services, recognising the boundaries between personal and professional life, and not abusing their position for personal benefit or gain.
4. Social workers should act in relation to the people using their services with compassion, empathy and care.

5. Social workers should not subordinate the needs or interests of people who use their services to their own needs or interests.
6. Social workers have a duty to take necessary steps to care for themselves professionally and personally in the workplace and in society, in order to ensure that they are able to provide appropriate services.
7. Social workers should maintain confidentiality regarding information about people who use their services. Exceptions to this may only be justified on the basis of a greater ethical requirement (such as the preservation of life).
8. Social workers need to acknowledge that they are accountable for their actions to the users of their services, the people they work with, their colleagues, their employers, the professional association and to the law, and that these accountabilities may conflict.
9. Social workers should be willing to collaborate with the schools of social work in order to support social work students to get practical training of good quality and up to date practical knowledge
10. Social workers should foster and engage in ethical debate with their colleagues and employers and take responsibility for making ethically informed decisions.
11. Social workers should be prepared to state the reasons for their decisions based on ethical considerations, and be accountable for their choices and actions.
12. Social workers should work to create conditions in employing agencies and in their countries where the principles of this statement and those of their own national code (if applicable) are discussed, evaluated and upheld.

5

Social Work Philosophy

INDIAN PHILOSOPHY

India has a rich and diverse philosophical tradition dating back to ancient times. According to Radhakrishnan, the earlier Upanisads constitute "...the earliest philosophical compositions of the world." Traditionally, schools (Skt: *Darshanas*) of Indian philosophy are identified as orthodox (Skt: *astika*) or non-orthodox (Skt: *nastika*) depending on whether they regard the Veda as an infallible source of knowledge. There are six schools of orthodox Hindu philosophy and three heterodox schools. The orthodox are Nyaya, Vaisesika, Samkhya, Yoga, Purva mimamsa and Vedanta. The Heterodox are Jain, Buddhist and materialist (Carvaka).

Despite their diversity of opinion all schools are united in their belief in a universal law and order (Dharma and Rta) according to which human life must be lived for the well-being of the individual and society. Similarly, nearly all the schools are concerned with religious and metaphysical questions and express views on the precise nature of liberation depending on the philosophical presuppositions of each school. The main schools of Indian philosophy were formalized chiefly between 1000 BC to the early centuries AD. Subsequent centuries produced commentaries and reformulations continuing up to as late as the 20th century by Aurobindo and Prabhupada among others.

One of the characteristics of Indian philosophy is its plurality and inclusiveness. Philosophers from different schools can still have a rich and meaningful conversation agreeing on many points while differing on subtle points of difference. Competition and integration between the various schools was intense during their formative years, especially between 800 BC to 200 AD. Some like the Jain, Buddhist, Shaiva and Advaita schools survived, while others like Samkhya and Ajivika did not, either being assimilated or going extinct. The Sanskrit term for "philosopher" is *darúanika*, one who is familiar with the systems of philosophy, or *darœanas*.

Common Themes

The Indian thinkers of antiquity (very much like those of the post-Socratic Greek philosophical schools) viewed philosophy as a practical necessity that needed to be cultivated in order to understand how life can best be led. It became a custom for Indian writers to explain at the beginning of philosophical works how it serves human ends (purucartha). Brahmin thinkers centered philosophy on an assumption that there is a unitary underlying order (rta) in the universe which is all pervasive and omniscient. The efforts by various schools were concentrated on explaining this order and the metaphysical entity at its source (Brahman). The concept of natural law (Dharma) provided a basis for understanding questions of how life on earth should be lived. The sages urged humans to discern this order and to live their lives in accordance with it.

In modern times, the most important school of Hindu philosophy is *vedanta*, which is further divided into three ways of understanding the same truth as *dvaita*, *visisthadvaita* and *advaita*. While these concepts might seem different and sometimes contradictory, they represent the three stages of the development of the human consciousness.

Schools of Hindu Philosophy

Many Hindu intellectual traditions were classified during the medieval period of Brahmanic-Sanskritic scholasticism into a standard list of six orthodox (astika) schools (darshanas), the "Six Philosophies" (*cad-darœana*), all of which cite Vedic authority as their source:

- Nyaya, the school of logic

- Vaisheshika, the atomist school
- Samkhya, the enumeration school
- Yoga, the school of Patanjali (which provisionally asserts the metaphysics of Samkhya)
- Purva Mimamsa (or simply Mimamsa), the tradition of Vedic exegesis, with emphasis on Vedic ritual, and
- Vedanta (also called Uttara Mimamsa), the Upanishadic tradition, with emphasis on Vedic philosophy.

These are often coupled into three groups for both historical and conceptual reasons: Nyaya-Vaishesika, Samkhya-Yoga, and Mimamsa-Vedanta. The Vedanta school is further divided into six sub-schools: Advaita (monism/nondualism), also includes the concept of Ajativada, Visishtadvaita (monism of the qualified whole), Dvaita (dualism), Dvaitadvaita (dualism-nondualism), Suddhadvaita, and Achintya Bheda Abheda schools.

The six systems mentioned here are not the only orthodox systems, they are the chief ones, and there are other orthodox schools such as the "Grammarian" school. These six systems, accept the authority of Vedas and are regarded as "orthodox" (astika) schools of Hindu philosophy; besides these, schools that do not accept the authority of the Vedas are categorized by Brahmins as unorthodox (nastika) systems. Chief among the latter category are Buddhism, Jainism and Carvakas. Carvaka is a materialistic and atheistic school of thought and, is noteworthy as evidence of a materialistic movement within Hinduism.

Jain Philosophy

Jainism came into formal being after Mahavira synthesized philosophies and promulgations of the ancient Sramana philosophy, during the period around 550 BC, in the region that is present day Bihar in northern India. This period marked an ideological renaissance, in which the patriarchal Vedic dominance was challenged by various groups. Buddhism also arose during this period.

Jain philosophy is traditionally believed to have been revived by Mahavira, whom the Jains see as the 24th and final Jain Tirthankar (enlightened seers), a line that stretches to time immemorial. The 23rd seer, Parsva is traditionally dated to around 900 BC.

Jainism is not considered as a part of the Vedic Religion (Hinduism), even as there is constitutional ambiguity over its status. Jain tirthankars find exclusive mention in the Vedas and the Hindu epics. During the Vedantic age, India had two broad philosophical streams of thought: The Shramana philosophical schools, represented by Buddhism, Jainism, and the long defunct Samkhya and Ajivika on one hand, and the Brahmana/Vedantic/Puranic schools represented by Vedanta, Vaishnava and other movements on the other. Both streams are known to have mutually influenced each other.

The Hindu scholar, Lokmanya Tilak credited Jainism with influencing Hinduism in the area of the cessation of animal sacrifice in Vedic rituals. Bal Gangadhar Tilak has described Jainism as the originator of Ahimsa and wrote in a letter printed in Bombay Samachar, Mumbai: 10 Dec, 1904: "In ancient times, innumerable animals were butchered in sacrifices. Evidence in support of this is found in various poetic compositions such as the Meghaduta. But the credit for the disappearance of this terrible massacre from the Brahminical religion goes to Jainism."

Swami Vivekananda also credited Jainsim as one of the influencing forces behind the Indian culture.

A *Jain* is a follower of *Jinas*, spiritual 'victors' (*Jina* is Sanskrit for 'victor'), human beings who have rediscovered the *dharma,* become fully liberated and taught the spiritual path for the benefit of beings. Jains follow the teachings of 24 special Jinas who are known as *Tirthankars* ('ford-builders'). The 24th and most recent *Tirthankar*, Lord Mahavira, lived in c.6th century BC, which was a period of cultural revolution all over the world. Socrates was born in Greece, Zoroaster in Persia, Lao Tse and Confucious in China and Mahavira and Buddha in India. The 23rd Thirthankar of Jains, Lord Parsvanatha is recognised now as a historical person, lived during 872 to 772 BC... Jaina tradition is unanimous in making Rishabha, as the First Tirthankar. One of the main characteristics of Jain belief is the emphasis on the immediate consequences of one's physical and mental behaviour. Because Jains believe that everything is in some sense alive with many living beings possessing a soul, great care and awareness is required in going about one's business in the world. Jainism is a religious tradition in which all life is considered to be worthy of respect and Jain teaching emphasises this equality of all life advocating the non-harming of even the smallest creatures.

Non-violence (Ahimsa) is the basis of right View, the condition of right Knowledge and the kernel of right Conduct in Jainism.

Jainism encourages spiritual independence (in the sense of relying on and cultivating one's own personal wisdom) and self-control which is considered vital for one's spiritual development. The goal, as with other Indian religions, is *moksha* which in Jainism is realization of the soul's true nature, a condition of omniscience (Kevala Jnana). Anekantavada is one of the principles of Jainism positing that reality is perceived differently from different points of view, and that no single point of view is completely true. Jain doctrine states that only Kevalis, those who have infinite knowledge, can know the true answer, and that all others would only know a part of the answer. Anekantavada is related to the Western philosophical doctrine of Subjectivism.

Buddhist Philosophy

Buddhist philosophy is a system of beliefs based on the teachings of Siddhartha Gautama, an Indian prince later known as the Buddha (Pali for "awakened one"). From its inception, Buddhism has had a strong philosophical component. Buddhism is founded on the rejection of certain orthodox Hindu philosophical concepts. The Buddha criticized all concepts of metaphysical being and non-being as misleading views caused by reification, and this critique is inextricable from the founding of Buddhism.

Buddhism shares many philosophical views with other Indian systems, such as belief in karma, a cause-and-effect relationship between all that has been done and all that will be done. Events that occur are held to be the direct result of previous events. However, a major difference is the Buddhist rejection of a permanent, self-existent soul (atman). This view is a central one in Hindu thought but is rejected by all Buddhists.

Modern Philosophy

Modern Indian philosophy was developed during British occupation(1750–1947). The philosophers in this era gave contemporary meaning to traditional philosophy. Swami Vivekananda, Rabindranath Tagore, Sri Aurobindo, Mahapandit Rahul Sankrityayan, Swami Sahajanand Saraswati, Ananda Coomaraswamy, Ramana Maharshi and Sarvepalli Radhakrishnan interpreted traditional Indian philosophy in terms of contemporary significance. Osho and J. Krishnamurti developed their own schools of thought.

Today, there are several spiritual personalities: philosophers, teachers (gurus) or thinkers, such as Maharishi Mahesh Yogi, Sri Sri Ravishankar, Amma, Anadamayi and movements such as the Brahmakumaris and ISKON.

Political Philosophy

The Arthashastra, attributed to the Mauryan minister Chanakya, is one of the early Indian texts devoted to political philosophy. It is dated to 4th century BCE and discusses ideas of statecraft and economic policy.

The political philosophy most closely associated with India is the one of ahimsa (non-violence) and Satyagraha, popularized by Mahatma Gandhi during the Indian struggle for independence. It was influenced by the Indian Dharmic philosophy (particularly the Bhagvata Gita as well as, secular writings of authors such as Leo Tolstoy, Henry David Thoreau and John Ruskin. In turn it influenced the later movements for independence and civil rights, especially those led by Nelson Mandela and Martin Luther King, Jr.

CHARACTERISTICS AND VALUES OF INDIAN CULTURE

At the first press conference after his election, Indian President Abdul Kalam emphasized the need for the Indian younger generation to learn scientific knowledge and also correct values from their older generations, and added that India should get rid of poverty and become a developed country in twenty years. Why did President Kalam mention Indian values anew in his first press conference? This question deserves studying. But what's more important is to clarify what Indian values are. Before we start, we should have some knowledge about Indian culture and its characteristics. The reason is Indian values have taken shape in the fertile soil of Indian culture, which has cultivated the specific values of Indian people and made them differentiate from those of Chinese culture and Western culture. These are issues affording food for thought and research.

Characteristics of Indian Culture

Being an Oriental ancient civilization, India has a history of 5000 years. And its culture, extensive, profound and mysterious, has made immeasurable contributions to the world progress and civilization. Its distinct characteristics and personalities have made scholars and experts of academia today excited and confused, arousing their interest in probing the mysteries inside. But no consensus has been reached among them up to now. Some experts divide the characteristics of Indian culture into eight aspects, while others argue that there are no more than three.

Religiosity

India is a religious country, and almost all the people sincerely believe in religion. Religion touches every corner of the Indian society and the soul of all the ordinary people, thus maintaining tight and close links with Indian society, politics, economy, military, art and literature. Indian people witness the great and irresistible pacts imposed by religion on themselves in every aspect of life. In short, 'Life' will have no meaning without religion. In the first few years since independence, the Indian Government headed by Nehru took the policy of secularism as the fundamental one of developing economy, getting rid of poverty and stabilizing the society in order to mitigate the conflicts among different religious sects. The Indian National Congress, however, didn't comply with this policy consistently due to the deep and vast influence of religion on the Indian society. It was unable to fully pursue secularism and sometimes even made use of religion to meet some interests of the government due to the interweaving religious and caste contradictions. It's the incomplete secularism policy of the Congress that led to the soaring power and influence of Hinduism throughout the 1980s. The Bharatiya Janata Party (BJP) used this as an excuse to attack the Congress's secularist program and dismissed it as "camouflaged secularism" because it couldn't represent the interests of Hindus. The Muslims, for their part, also didn't consider this policy in their interests. This is one of the main factors that led to the humiliating defeat of the Congress Party (despite a history of more than 100 years) in the 1990 election.

If we try to analyze and do some studies on the language, literature, art, music, dance and sculpture of India, it will not be hard to find that they are all centered on religion, both in form and content. Even the legislation of the country, the shaping of individual morals and traditional customs and habits of ethnic groups are developed under the influence of religion. Religion has been fully integrated into Indian culture. In short, there will be no Indian culture without religion. For example, in literature there are many works regarded by the academia as the purely religious literature such as the well-known Pancatantra, which was edited and disseminated by religious figures especially for their descendants and is full of passionate feelings that preached the religious spirit.

Even in the liberation movement of the Indian people against the British colonial rule and for national freedom and independence, the idea of nonviolence in the movement of nonviolence and non-cooperation advocated by their greatest national hero Mahatma Gandhi also originated from the benevolence and humanity of Indian religious thoughts. It was from the tenets of Hinduism such as "perseverance in truth", "abstention from killing" and "self-renunciation" that the 'nonviolent' thinking derived, with which Mahatma Gandhi invented the unique path in the struggle for national independence and liberation, and won the final victory and established the Republic of Hindustan.

If we observe the life experience of Mahatma Gandhi closely, we can see clearly that he persisted in using religious tenets through his whole life to instigate people to take part in the struggle against British colonists. For he deemed that "politics will lose its soul without religion". He also strongly believed that the strength of patriotism, the willingness to sacrifice and the national dignity could be unbounded, if aroused by religious thoughts. The reason was they represented the intrinsic elements at the very core of Indian culture with a history of 5000 years and the highest ideal the Indian people pursue. For that reason, he held a firm belief that the religious and moral strength of 'nonviolence' thinking could eventually force the British colonists to correct their errors since they also cherished justice in nature.

Diversity

Diversity stands out as one of the most prominent characteristics of the Indian cultural system. Within this system, there are different cultural elements such as Hellenic culture, Islamic culture, Persian culture, English culture and Chinese culture. The reason for this diversity is multifaceted and the most important factor is the alien cultures brought to India by invaders. For example, the Indian Islamic culture was launched after Babur defeated Sultan Ibrahim Lodi, the ruler of Delhi, in 1526 and founded the Mogul empire. Babur, who had a Mongolian origin and came from Central Asia, was one of the descendants of the Turkish conqueror Timur. The introduction of English culture into India was completed after the British colonists invaded India and imposed colonial rule on it, which lasted for 200 years. Only the spread of Chinese culture into the subcontinent had occurred by peaceful means. Moreover, the friendly cultural exchanges between the two sides have been lasting for several thousand years. This is a matter for renewed collaboration on both sides. As Prof. Ji Xianlin put it, "it's rare in the world history for two countries like China and India to have a history of cultural communications and friendly interactions for at least 2000 years "

Even in Indian pure vernacular cultures, there are different types of vernacular cultures with different characteristics resulting from varying periods, conditions and environments for subsistence and development. They include Vedic culture, Aryan culture, Dravidian culture, Brahmanic culture, Marathi culture, Punjabi culture, Assamese culture, if defined by time period and linguistic area. They include Brahmanic culture, Buddhist culture, Indian Islamic culture, Jain culture, Christian culture, Sikh culture and Bahai culture that rose in the modern times, if defined by religious sects. It is the diversity of Indian culture that exhibits its antiquity, brilliance and glory, making it without parallel in the whole world.

Inclusiveness

Inclusiveness is another salient characteristic of Indian culture that distinguishes it from other cultures. Of all kinds of local cultures, linguistic cultures and religious cultures of India in history, each contains a variety of elements in part from alien cultures. I have experienced it deeply since I started learning Hindi and engaging in the study of Indian culture and South Asian affairs several decades ago. Although all the major languages of the world have loanwords and alien elements, which accords with the law of linguistic development to realize their functions through constant assimilation and creation, Hindi is most salient in this respect. I want to take this as an example to prove the value and universality of the inclusiveness of Indian culture. The constituent elements of Hindi that my colleagues and I have studied are summed up as follows:

Every language has loanwords and alien elements, but those of Hindi are unique. The analysis of the etymology of Hindi shows that Hindi absorbs many words from English, Sanskrit, Persian and Arabic and even a few from Turkish, besides its own derivations.

All these words integrate into the vocabulary of Hindi, perfectly representing the contents of Hindi. If we open a Hindi-Chinese dictionary, we will find that the etymologies of many words are given at the end of the entries, indicating their origins, either from English, or Persian, or Sanskrit, etc. There are also compounds, either made up of a Hindi word and one from a foreign language or composed by two alien words. The reconfiguration of words from different languages not only enriches and enhances the expression of Hindi but also enables it to express meanings that didn't exist in Hindi before. For instance, the word "contract" and the word "separation" are both combinations of Arabic and Persian words so that they are capable of expressing meanings more accurately.

The assimilation of English by Hindi is manifested not only in its vocabulary but also in its absorption and broad use of English grammar and punctuation. English has left a great impact on Hindi, especially modern Hindi. Owing to the influence of English and its absorption and use of English, the capacity of Hindi is further enlarged both in depth and breadth and keeps up with the modern era, thus evolving for a prosperous future. The assimilation can be sorted into two aspects. First, there are many loanwords from English. The linguistic culture brought by the British after they entered India had many words to represent new things with no equivalent in Hindi. Consequently, Indian people had to copy the pronunciations and meanings from English in order to represent things absent or unrecognized in India. Second, there are some paraphrased words and mixed words. Paraphrased words are those created by using Hindi's own linguistic materials and transplanting the meanings of English words according to its word-building rules. Mixed words are those words or phrases that integrate the borrowed components from English with the form of Hindi. Besides English, many other foreign languages also share their contributions to the development and prosperity of Hindi, which can be found if further research is to be carried out.

REGIONALISM OF CULTURE OF A TROPICAL SUBCONTINENT

Being a result of the particular geographic environment and climate, regionalism is the unique characteristic of Indian culture, which some scholars tend to call the "culture of the tropical subcontinent". From a geographic point of view, the Indian subcontinent is just like an isolated island projecting into the Indian Ocean. The geographic separation and scorching weather are the main external factors contributing to the regionalism of Indian culture. Snow covers the Himalayas, the towering 'world roof', all year long and no one would set foot on the tops of these mountains in the winter. Oceans and seas surround India in the east, west and south. The only land which links it to the outside world in the east and west is also blocked by mountains, forests and deserts. People are terrified by the vast virgin forests permeated with noxious mist and miasma and the boundless deserts in which strong winds blow sands and stones day and night, so visitors have no courage to go beyond these limits. The Ganges and the Indus, mother rivers of India, bring benefits to the people, while they often cause serious flooding. Moreover, the tropical and subtropical climate also produces broiling weather and monsoon downpours.

The residents of Indian subcontinent felt insignificant and powerless in the face of the nature, so they held it in more reverence, thus giving birth to the thought that humanity and nature is identical. They imaged hazily that there was a dominating force in the heaven, earth and midair and that humans and everything on earth were nothing but its illusion. This dominating force was later on called 'Brahman'. Gradually, the ideas about "the identity of Brahman-atman" and Self and self were fixed in their minds.

The scorching weather of Indian subcontinent often made Indian people unable to pursue their normal life and work, forcing them to go into the woods or gather under the trees so that they could unfold their endless imaginations about all the phenomena of the nature. As time passed, their imaginations had been enriched and their talents of expression had also grown. The abundance of food and availability of all sorts of tropical and subtropical fruits made it easy for Indian people to eat their fill. So the intellectuals and religious people among them had more time to probe into such questions as the nature of humans, the origin of cosmos, the delicate but concrete relationship between humans and nature or between humans and spiritual world,—all from their unique perspectives. Thus Indian culture has been marked by the characteristics of the culture of tropical subcontinent, and Indian people are famous for their imaginative thinking and eloquence. The works they created are charming, extending their philosophic thoughts aimlessly to rewrite the historical events and the real stories of the heroes in order to mix them with the rich and colorful myths of India. Great poems that are beautiful in rhythm had been compiled and spread wildly. As time passes, it's hard for the later generations to tell the histories from the poems.

Ramayana and Mahabharata, the two most famous epics of India, are among the greatest works of this culture of the tropical subcontinent. Both not only reflect the historical facts of India in that period, but also cover broad fields including philosophy, medicine, literature, carving, music, dance, astrology, geography and meteorology. The epics also spend a large portion of volumes touching upon statecraft such as politics, law, morality and traditions.

VALUES OF INDIAN CULTURE

In recent years, many scholars and experts engaging in studies of cultural values have emerged in China. As a result, quite a few dissertations and works analyzing the values of Chinese and Western cultures have been published. However, those dealing with Indian cultural values are less, not to mention those that expound Indian culture and its values systematically and comprehensively and conduct comparative research about them in international cultural research. So I want to explore this topic to the best of my knowledge in order to receive advice from experts and colleagues.

According to knowledge about cultural values, the patterns, factors and traits of specific values are determined in many aspects such as politics, morality, religion, nation, equality, justice, truth, goodness and beauty. However, they can still be generalized into three major aspects. As Tugalenov, a scholar of the former Soviet Union, put it in his book On the Values of Life and Culture, all the cultural values can be classified into three categories: material values, social and political values and spiritual values. In the following paragraphs, I will use these three criteria to advance my study of the values of Indian culture.

Material Values

The material value on which Indian culture puts emphasis is the perfect devotion/commitment of humans. Though enjoyment of material values is a part of Indian cultural values, it is only a part and cannot represent the ultimate goal the Indian cultural values pursue, that is, to realize the perfect devotion of humans. Most Indians brought up by the traditional

Indian culture care less about the possession and enjoyment of material values: thus there exists a strong national mentality of helping those in distress and aiding those in peril. In India as well as in other countries, it's not surprising to find that a rich person, even a very wealthy one, hands over his fortune for the good of social welfare.

But the difference between India and others lies in the fact that Indian people see it as one way to fulfill their value objectives. It is no doubt that this mentality is linked to such religious thoughts as acquiring merit, doing good, good being rewarded with good and evil with evil. But we can't deny the reality that Indian people pursue spiritual values much more than the material ones. Of course, there are Indians who collect wealth by unfair means or dissipate money without restraint. However most Indians pay little attention to clothing, food, shelter and means of travel and live a plain life. Even senior officials or wealthy people may not certainly seek the enjoyment of modern material life. A number of millionaires, presidents, premiers and ministers eat simple food, live in common houses, wear native clothes and travel by homemade unrefined cars. This is not artificial, but is exactly the spiritual pursuit of Indian people. Most Indians don't think much about possessing their properties after death because they don't believe that man must take money and valuables with him in order to continue his enjoyment. Generally there are no luxuries and treasures buried with the dead after cremation, which is the reason why the majority of Indian cultural relics remain aboveground rather than underground. Another example is Mahatma Ghandi, the leader of the Indian independence movement and the founding father of India. During the Indian struggle for national autonomy and liberation and against British colonial rule, he proposed that Indians weave native cloth themselves, wear native garments, and refuse to use foreign fabrics exported to India by the British. He also led several hundred thousand followers to evaporate brine to make salt. At first glance, it seems that everything Mahatma Ghandi did was just to resist the cruel suppression and rule of British colonists over the Indian people. The ultimate goal of Mahatma Ghandi, however, was the nonviolence as a means and a thinking, that is, he tried to awaken the conscience of the vicious British colonists by demonstrating the self-sacrifice of Indian people, to achieve independence and autonomy of India, and to make Indian and British people live in harmony. Through his whole life, Mahatma Ghandi cared little about personal gain and loss of material interests in his pursuit for material values. He led a strenuous and simple life. He lived just as common people, carrying nothing valuable with him. However, he believed in the law of cause and effect and sought release from the cycle of death and rebirth through realizing the oneness of Brahman-atman.

Social and Political Values

The social and political values of Indian culture are that humans should intend to create a harmonious environment, using the eternal law of the cosmos to normalize their own conducts in order to reach the ultimate stage of oneness with Brahman-atman. On the one hand, India attaches some importance to pragmatic interests and desires. On the other hand, more importantly, it spares no efforts to promote that everyone should persevere in his life and undertake the obligations of his family and his nation for the prosperity of the society and the wellbeing of his posterity rather than personal pursuits and gains. People must follow law and submit to it, complying with the social rules and morals prescribed by the eternal law, which is more than mere civil law and covers a whole range of meanings such as the task and justice of man, human relations and the social order. So the Indian traditional cultural values strongly emphasize that only by dedicating oneself selflessly to the society can his behaviours truly accord with the social and political values and can a harmonious environment be created.

The comprehensive survey of the historical development of the Indian society shows that its social and political values came into being through a strenuous course. In the era of the Upanishads, Indian religious philosophy considered that "karma" was the cause of the round of death and rebirth. So man had to suffer from the round and could not return to Brahman. The only way to eliminate the cause of "karma" was to quit working and stand aloof from worldly affairs. Therefore, it became more and more popular for Indians to sit in meditation and enter into religion in order to cultivate themselves according to religious doctrines.

This trend of thought developed even further and reached its peak with the rise of Buddhism. Buddhism taught people that life was no more than sufferings, the root of which is 'karma". Man can't escape from the round of death and rebirth because of "karma". It's a dead circle that life follows death, and death is at life's heel. Therefore, the only way to extricate oneself from the endless sufferings is to seclude oneself from working, family and society. The attitude of looking down upon fame and gain, power and wealth, and tending to keep distance from the secular world became a big obstacle holding back the productivity of the Indian society and one of the factors eventually leading to the decline of Buddhism in India.

When Hinduism prospered in India, it began to amend the conception of "karma". According to its doctrines, those who dedicate themselves wholly to their work, abide by laws and social norms, and adhere to the eternal law to discipline their behaviours are considered to be free of "karma". Thus, Hinduism changed the utmost way of release from the round of death and rebirth from 'standing aloof from the worldly affairs' to 'joining into the worldly affairs'. The principle of behaviour of Hinduism stressed that man is always content with his lot and is able to control his feeling and get rid of insatiable desire. If he works whole-heartedly, he can set himself free from "karma". The social responsibility and dedication that Hinduism advocates reflects the identity of the social and political values of Indian culture and the nature, which are linked together by the same core contents as benevolence and kindness. Because only by love and benevolence, by loving people and by loving and kindly treating everything on earth can the political values be embodied perfectly. For this reason, Hinduism requires that people should speak, act and work in order to coexist with everything in nature rather than stress blindly on conquering it.

Spiritual Values

The ultimate goal that the spiritual values of Indian culture pursue is to realize the oneness of Brahman-atman, which is the only way for final salvation. India is a religious country. As early as the Vedic era, Indians had a strong belief that some kind of individual personality existed after death, which was considered to be the primitive soul of a human. This belief developed into the thought of heaven at the end of this era. It was said in Atharva Veda that the soul of the dead could reside in heaven, earth and midair, but heaven is the most ideal place. While it was believed in Rig Veda that those people eligible to enter the heaven were sadhus who conducted ascetic practices, soldiers who gave up their lives on the battlefield and devotees who didn't hesitate to sacrifice their properties to Brahman could also enter heaven. Then the conception of 'karma" began to emerge in Atharva Veda, which claimed that man must hold responsibility towards both the good karma and the evil karma on his own, and evil deeds must be punished accordingly. Based on this concept, the idea of the round of death and rebirth came into being. Evildoers must be punished, either being sent to the hell or being transmigrated into such humble things as pig, dog and muck, while those who did good would be rewarded by paradise. It was in the Upanishad era that such issues as the time limit of punishment and reward, soul and salvation were developed and clarified further.

The appearance of the Upanishads had a positive significance to a certain extent because the text was founded on the three major guiding principles of Brahmanism. It was the result of the efforts of some Brahmanic scholars who aspired to seek advanced thoughts to interpret the ultimate meanings of the 'forest treatises', part of the Vedas. These treatises included philosophic thoughts, so they were also called Vedanta philosophy. After it was finalized, the Vedanta philosophy claimed that the dominant in heaven, earth and midair was Brahman. Though invisible and unrevealed as it was, it would appear in every place at any time. The material world and everything in it were just its illusion. Individual soul was essentially one with Brahman. This was the thinking of "the identity of Brahman-atman". Therefore, Hinduism sees the self-realization of the identity of Brahman-atman as the loftiest goal of reaching salvation. But because of "karma" man can't experience and recognize the atman. "Affected by Karma, the atman is unable to return to Brahman to identify with it after death. So man has to suffer from the round of death and rebirth or be reincarnated into a bird, a beast, a worm and a fish." For that matter, Indians consider life to be painful and that they must strive hard to find the way to reach salvation and the identity of Brahma-atman so that the suffering from the round of death and rebirth can be exempted, 'escaped from'. In order to achieve this goal, new paths had been put forward in the Bhagavad Gita, the classic work of Hinduism. They were the path of behaviour, the path of devotion and the path of knowledge.

Path of Behaviour. The believers must abide by the moral norms strictly, devoting themselves to the gods. Actions derive from freedom, so Hinduism encourages people to participate in all kinds of working practices, to love their jobs and to dedicate themselves to their jobs, which quite differs from the Buddhist way of salvation by quitting jobs to eliminate the cause of "karma". As put in the Bhagavad Gita, one whose every undertaking is devoid of the motivation of desires and their objects and who has incinerated all activities in the fire of pure knowledge,—he is the one the spiritually intelligent describe as educated. After giving up attachment to object-driven results, always satisfied, indifferent to external phenomena, he in spite of being engaged in activities does not 'do' anything at all. Bereft of desire, controlled in mind and body, relinquishing all conceptions of proprietorship whereby a person can incur sinful reaction, he performs only sufficient actions to maintain body sustenance.

The "spirit of self-forgetting aloofness of the Indian people", which people in today's India often talk about, is considered to be the ultimate truth they are pursuing, which requires that they exert their efforts to cultivate this spirit in order to work selflessly. This spirit also incarnates the correct values of India that the Indian President Kalam called upon the young people to 'inherit'. Kalam himself is the model practicing these values: he dedicates himself wholly to his work selflessly and remains indifferent to personal gains and losses in his pursuit for the causes of India, be they missile projects or prosperity and strength. So his colleagues described him as a work maniac. For the sake of the missile programs, he pledged to remain a bachelor all his life and joked that he had already married missiles. This is the reason why he is called the "father of missiles" in India. In fact, it is Hinduism itself that has turned the way of release from the round of death and rebirth from aloofness to a joining into worldly affairs and promoting a spirit of 'involved detachment'. Therefore, the great Indian poet Tagore asserted this spirit promotes a 'stage of perfection' which is a combination of philosophic theory and practice. This is also the highest spiritual value modern Indians seek.

Path of Wisdom. Being a Hindu, he must seek truth in rationality and try to realize the identity of soul and Brahman through grasping the experience that "Brahman is atman". He must recognize that the identity of Brahman-atman is the absolute truth, since only Brahman is the absolute existence while all other things are nothing but an illusion. Only through this understanding can he break up the limit of ignorance and eventually reach salvation. The Bhagavad Gita described the importance of the path of wisdom vividly. In the world there is nothing that exists as purifying as transcendental knowledge. One perfected by the science of uniting the individual consciousness with Ultimate Consciousness automatically attains that knowledge in the self in course of time. One with full faith, attentively focused, who has conquered the senses, achieves transcendental knowledge and having achieved transcendental knowledge attains supreme peace. Moreover, the Bhagavad Gita clarified further the importance of knowledge to the people who master it: It is directly related to reaching the highest state of the oneness of atman with Brahman.

The path of wisdom is very popular among Indians today. To most intellectuals, they feel subconsciously the urgency to master knowledge and open the door of wisdom not only for the sake of finding a favourable living and working condition, but also for approaching God and identifying with him.

Path of Devotion. If a Hindu loves a god and submits to him piously in the extreme, this is also a way of gaining the god's favour and reaching salvation. It is an effective way to identify with a god to cherish the god in heart, to do everything for god and to read the name of god silently every minute. For example, Mahatma Gandhi was so pious in his commitment to Rama that, after being shot down by a young Hindu fanatic, he kept murmuring the name of Rama as he used to, until his last moment. His last word, "hay, Rama", was carved on the black gravestone. His commitment to Rama also reflected the piety of Indian people at large. There was one passage spoken out by the god in the Bhagavad Gita, explaining this matter profoundly. "I am equally disposed to all living entitles; there is neither friend nor foe to Me; but those who with loving sentiments render devotional service unto Me, such persons are in Me and I am in them. Even if one committing the most abominable actions renders service only unto Me exclusively without deviation, one is to be considered saintly because one is correctly resolved and properly situated. One swiftly becomes endowed with righteousness and justly obtains everlasting peace. O Arjuna declare it boldly, My devotee never perishes."

'NONVIOLENT' THINKING IN INDIAN CULTURAL VALUES

Nonviolence is the goal and state the Indian cultural values seek to achieve. According to Vedanta philosophy, everything in the world is self deriving from Self, so it should be friendly and equally disposed to others. Everything's true nature is divine and has the true, good and beautiful moral conduct, so people should be kind to and love each other. Moreover, the spirit of friendliness and love ought to be extended to beasts and birds, flowers and plants. Thus, killing is forbidden.

Within the ideological system of Mahatma Gandhi, nonviolent thinking derived from the tenets of Hinduism such as abstention from killing and restraint from harming others' feelings. Nonviolence is love, which means loving everyone and doing more good. He even considered asceticism as the criterion for love. For he always believed that everyone is identical in nature and shares the same humanities as kindness and conscience. He advocated that the nonviolence seekers fully express their inner kindness through self-sacrifice and self-refinement in order to awaken the internal conscience of their enemies, so that they can give up evil and return to good.

The core of 'nonviolent' thinking of Mahatma Gandhi is "perseverance in truth". He believed that the truth was the ultimate reality and source of the cosmos and that everything in the world was no more than its external manifestations. He also presumed that the truth and the god are the law dominating every life in the cosmos. This view of Mahatma Gandhi emphasized that the human internal spirit originated from the same source as that of god, reflecting the divinity in human body. The Indian cultural values believe that people are identical with each other in spiritual nature because god is absolute and indivisible. It is this theory that drove Gandhi to stick to such doctrines as nonviolence and perseverance in truth in the national liberation movement. It needs to be pointed out that Gandhi's thought belongs to historical idealism, which takes truth, goodness and beauty that are abstract and coloured with mysticism as something eternal that goes beyond history and class and as the only way to handle human relations and solve social contradictions. But it also needs to be noted that India is a religious nation and people have strong beliefs in religions. Religion is so popular in India that religious thoughts have penetrated deeply into people's minds and touched every corner of the society. Gandhi succeeded in creating a new ideology that collected the core values of Indian culture completely by combining his view of truth with the idea of nonviolence. Therefore, he was able to mobilize Indian people sufficiently to realize his thinking through arousing the spirit of self-devotion. And his thinking perfected the pursuit of Indian people for spiritual values, leading to the final victory of perseverance in truth and the movement of nonviolence and non-cooperation (with colonialism) and the founding of the Republic of Hindustan.

Although Gandhi's ideas about nonviolence and non-collaboration and perseverance in truth were influenced by Western humanitarianism, it was the spiritual values of Indian culture Gandhi inherited that played the fundamental and decisive role. His theory combined traditional Indian philosophy closely with religion, ethics and social political theories. His ideal was to build a Europe-type society with Indian religion, and adhering to the view of truth and epistemology derived from mystical Indian philosophy and basing its hopes on gods and the identity of humans with God.

BRIEF OUTLINE OF GANDHI'S PHILOSOPHY

What is Gandhian philosophy? It is the religious and social ideas adopted and developed by Gandhi, first during his period in South Africa from 1893 to 1914, and later of course in India. These ideas have been further developed by later "Gandhians", most notably, in India, Vinoba Bhave and Jayaprakash Narayan. Outside of India some of the work of, for example, Martin Luther King Jr. can also be viewed in this light. Understanding the universe to be an organic whole, the philosophy exists on several planes-the spiritual or religious, moral, political, economic, social, individual and collective. The spiritual or religious element, and God, is at its core. Human nature is regarded as fundamentally virtuous. All individuals are believed to be capable of high moral development, and of reform.

The twin cardinal principles of Gandhi's thought are truth and nonviolence. It should be remembered that the English word "truth" is an imperfect translation of the Sanskrit, "satya", and "nonviolence", an even more imperfect translation of "ahimsa". Derived from "sat"-"that which exists"-"satya"contains a dimension of meaning not usually associated by English speakers with the word "truth". There are other variations, too, which we need not go into here. For Gandhi, truth is the relative truth of truthfulness in word and deed, and the absolute truth-the Ultimate Reality. This ultimate truth is God (as God is also Truth) and morality-the moral laws and code-its basis. Ahimsa, far from meaning mere peacefulness or the absence of overt violence, is understood by Gandhi to denote active love-the pole opposite of violence, or "himsa", in every sense. The ultimate station Gandhi assigns nonviolence stems from two main points. First, if according to the Divine Reality all life is one, then all violence committed towards another is violence towards oneself, towards the collective, whole self, and thus "self"-destructive and counter to the universal law of life, which is love. Second, Gandhi believed that ahimsa is the most powerful force in existence. Had himsabeen superior to ahimsa, humankind would long ago have succeeded in destroying itself.

The human race certainly could not have progressed as far as it has, even if universal justice remains far off the horizon. From both viewpoints, nonviolence or love is regarded as the highest law of humankind.

Although there are elements of unity in Gandhi's thought, they are not reduced to a system. It is not a rigid, inflexible doctrine, but a set of beliefs and principles which are applied differently according to the historical and social setting. Therefore there can be no dogmatism, and inconsistency is not a sin. Interpretation of the principles underwent much evolution during Gandhi's lifetime, and as a result many inconsistencies can be found in his writings, to which he readily admitted. The reader of Gandhi's works published by Navajivan Trust will notice that many are prefaced with the following quotation from an April 1933 edition of "Harijan", one of Gandhi's journals. He states straightforwardly: "I would like to say to the diligent reader of my writings and to others who are interested in them that I am not at all concerned with appearing to be consistent. In my search after Truth I have discarded many ideas and learnt many news things.... What I am concerned with is my readiness to obey the call of Truth, my God, from moment to moment, and therefore, when anybody finds any inconsistency between any two writings of mine, if he still has any faith in my sanity, he would do well to choose the later of the two on the same subject."

That there are inconsistencies in Gandhi's writings accords with the fact that the ideas are not a system. In coming to grips with Gandhi's way of thinking it is most important to understand that the perception of truth undergoes an ongoing process of refinement which is evolutionary in nature. In Gandhi's thought the emphasis is on idealism, but on practical idealism. It is rooted in the highest religious idealism, but is thoroughly practical. One label (and almost the only one) Gandhi was happy to have pinned on him was that of "practical idealist". The important principle of compromise is relevant here, as is the acknowledgement that perfect truth and perfect nonviolence can never be attained while the spirit is embodied.

As alluded to above, Gandhian philosophy is certainly considered by Gandhians as a universal and timeless philosophy, despite the fact that on the more superficial level it is set in the Indian social context. They hold that the ideals of truth and nonviolence, which underpin the whole philosophy, are relevant to all humankind. (Recently some have been suggesting that a distinction can be made between the core elements of Gandhi's thought and peripheral elements which, depending on the particular element under consideration, may or may not have timeless relevance.)

Also, it can be universal despite being fundamentally religious, as its religious position stresses not so much the Hindu interpretation of reality as the beliefs which are common to all major religions, and that commonality itself. It holds all religions to be worthy of equal respect and in one sense to be equal. As all are creations of mortal and imperfect human beings, no single religion can embody or reveal the whole or absolute truth.

Gandhian philosophy is also compatible with the view that humankind is undergoing gradual moral evolution. While conflict is seen as inevitable, in fact not always undesirable, violence as the result of conflict is not regarded as inevitable. Simply put, human beings do have the capacity to resolve conflict nonviolently. This might be difficult, but it is not impossible. Liberation from a violent society is seen as requiring many decades or longer-but it is not an imposible ideal. Importantly also, it is not an intellectual doctrine. Gandhi was not an intellectual. Rather, Gandhi's thought was conceived, to a great extent, out of action and as a guide to action, by a man of action. He hesitated to write about anything of which he did not have personal, first-hand experience. In the sense of it being a call to action, Gandhi's thought can also be seen as an ideology.

As a guide to action, Gandhian philosophy is a double-edged weapon. Its objective is to transform the individual and society simultaneously (rather than in sequence, as Marxism describes), in accordance with the principles of truth and nonviolence. The historic task before humankind is to progress towards the creation of a nonviolent political, economic and social order by nonviolent struggle. The social goal was described by Gandhi as Sarvodaya, a term he coined in paraphrasing

John Ruskin's book Unto This Last, meaning the welfare of all without exception. Its political aspect was expressed by the late eminent Gandhian Dr R.R. Diwakar in the following words: "The good of each individual in society consists in his efforts to achieve the good of all." As the foundation of the Gandhian or nonviolent social order is religious or spiritual, economic and political questions are seen from the moral or humanistic perspective. The welfare of human beings, not of systems or institutions, is the ultimate consideration. Materially, it centres on the following concepts and ideals:

- Political decentralisation, to prevent massive concentrations of political power in the hands of too few; rather, to distribute it in the hands of many. The Gandhian political order takes the form of a direct, participatory democracy, operating in a tier structure from the base village-level tier upward through the district and state levels to the national (and international) level.
- Economic decentralisation, to prevent massive concentrations of economic power in the hands of too few, and again, to distribute it in the hands of many. Therefore villages, which are anyway geographically decentralised, become the basic economic units. However, where unavoidable, certain industries may be organised on a more centralised basis, and their ownership and control come under the umbrella of the State.
- The minimisation of competition and exploitation in the economic sphere, and instead, the encouragement of cooperation.
- Production on the basis of need rather than greed, concentrating where India is concerned first on the eradication of poverty (and on the worst extreme of poverty).
- Recognition of the dignity of labour and the greater purity of rural life.
- The practice of extensive self-reliance by individuals, villages, regions and the nation.

- Absence of oppression on the basis of race, caste, class, language, gender or religion.
- A deep respect for mother nature, necessitating an economic system based upon the preservation rather than destruction of the natural environment.

Such concepts clearly represent pillars for a new social order. A theory closely linked to the concept of Sarvodaya, also developed by Gandhi, is that of Trusteeship. Its fundamental objective is to create nonviolent and non-exploitative property relationships. Gandhi believed that the concepts of possession and private property were sources of violence, and in contradiction with the Divine reality that all wealth belongs to all people. However, he recognised that the concept of ownership would not wither easily, nor would the wealthy be easily persuaded to share their wealth. Therefore a compromise was to encourage the wealthy to hold their wealth in trust, to use themselves only what was necessary and to allow the remainder to be utilised for the benefit of the whole society.

It is apparent that Gandhi's philosophy has much in common with several Western philosophies which uphold the ideal of a more just and equitable society. For example, the Gandhian social order has been described as "communism minus violence". (However, Marxists have traditionally rejected Gandhi because of what they regard as his "bourgeois" outlook. Gandhi rejected violent class conflict and the centralisation of political and economic power in the hands of the State as counterproductive to the development of a nonviolent society.)

Nevertheless, Gandhian philosophy, particularly in the Sarvodaya ideal, does contain many socialist sentiments. In fact, such an entity as Gandhian Socialism emerged in theoretical literature during the 1970s and 1980s. Gandhi's thought has been likened also to Utopian Socialism and Philosophical Anarchism, and can be compared with strands of Maoist thought (though not a Western philosophy), and even Western liberal thought. However, Gandhi is incompatible with many aspects of Liberalism and is virtually entirely incompatible with the modern, intensely competitive, ecologically destructive and materialistic capitalism of the West.

As already observed, Gandhi's thought is equally a philosophy of self-transformation. The individual's task is to make a sincere attempt to live according to the principles of truth and nonviolence. Its fundamental tenets are therefore moral. They include-resisting injustice, developing a spirit of service, selflessness and sacrifice, emphasising one's responsibilities rather than rights, self-discipline, simplicity of life-style, and attempting to maintain truthful and nonviolent relations with others.

It should be understood that by simplicity is meant voluntary simplicity, not poverty, which has no element of voluntarism in it. If there is one thing Gandhi does not stand for, it is poverty. A Gandhian should also avoid political office. He or she should remain aloof from formal party politics and equidistant from all political groupings. But this is not to say, and in my view Gandhi does not require, that the individual should remain aloof from all politics.

For often injustice cannot be resisted unless the political power holders and structures are engaged, nonviolently. What was the freedom struggle itself if not a political struggle, against the greatest concentration of political power the world had ever known, the British Empire? In my eyes, there is no particular virtue in attempting to avoid contact with politics. What must be avoided, however, is assumption of political power by a Gandhian (at least this is necessary in the short and medium terms in India), and cooperation with unvirtuous holders of political power on their terms. The ultimate responsibility of a Gandhian is to resist clear injustice, untruth, in conjunction with others or alone.

Resistance should be nonviolent if at all possible. But Gandhi did condone use of violent means in certain circumstances, in preference to submission which he regarded as cowardice and equivalent to cooperation with evil. In relation to the use of violence he stated categorically: "Where there is only a choice between cowardice and violence I would advise violence..." As surprising as it no doubt sounds, Gandhi disliked most not violence, but cowardice and apathy. The eminent peace researcher Johan Galtung has correctly observed that Gandhi preferred first, nonviolent resistance, second, violence in a just cause, and third, meaning least of all, apathy. In general, however, it is held that immoral means, such as violence, cannot produce moral ends, as means are themselves ends or ends in the making.

For the individual self-transformation is attempted with deliberateness rather than with haste. One should not seek to become a Mahatma overnight, because such attempts will surely fail, but to reform oneself over the whole of one's life, as far as one is capable. (Nor should there be any question of superficial imitation of Gandhi.) Gandhi viewed his own life as a process of development undertaken "one step at a time". He saw the need to continually "experiment with truth" (from which he derived the title of his autobiography) in whatever field, in order to come to see the truthful path. Though they were rooted in the highest idealism, the experiments were carried out on a very down-to-earth plane-India's moral, political and social needs as he saw them. Such an approach is available to all at all times. Gandhi believed his own moral and spiritual development to be far from complete at the time of his death. Despite the great heights he had attained, this was indeed true. He had not achieved perfection, as some of those who were close to him have testified. The perception of what is the truthful path is largely a matter for the individual's reason and conscience, which therefore play key roles. The individual should subject each idea to the test of his or her own conscience and reason. Reason and rationality have enormous roles to play in the Gandhian way of thinking. This, I feel, is one of the major Western influences in Gandhi. If there is genuine, sincere disagreement, an idea can be discarded. However, once a principle is accepted a sincere attempt must be made to adhere to it. Ideally there should be harmony between thought, word and action. In this way the outer life becomes a true reflection of the inner, and a mental harmony is also achieved.

The remaining central concept in Gandhi's philosophy is Satyagraha. Defined most broadly (as Gandhi defined it), Satyagraha is itself a whole philosophy of nonviolence. Defined most narrowly, it is a technique or tool of nonviolent action. Because of the intention here to keep this discussion as simple as possible, Satyagraha will be described here in its latter guise. As a technique, Satyagraha was developed by Gandhi in South Africa to give the Indian population there a weapon with which to resist the injustices being perpetrated upon it by the colonial government. But Satyagraha can be practised in any cultural environment-provided the necessary ingredients are present, not least Satyagrah is (those capable of Satyagraha). A Satyagraha campaign is undertaken only after all other peaceful means have proven ineffective. At its heart is nonviolence. An attempt is made to convert, persuade or win over the opponent. It involves applying the forces of both reason and conscience simultaneously. While holding aloft the indisputable truth of his or her position, the Satyagrahi also engages in acts of voluntary self-suffering. Any violence inflicted by the opponent is accepted without retaliation. But precisely because there is no retaliation (which can make the opponent feel his violence is justified), the opponent can only become morally bankrupt if violence continues to be inflicted indefinitely.

Several methods can be applied in a Satyagraha campaign, primarily non-cooperation and fasting. The action is undertaken in the belief in the underlying goodness of the opponent, and in his or her ability to acknowledge the injustice of the action and to cease the injustice, or at least to compromise. Satyagraha in this sense is highly creative. It creates no enemies, hatred or lasting bitterness, but ultimately only mutual regard. After a successful campaign there is not the least hint of gloating, nor is there any desire to embarrass the opponent. The former opponent becomes a friend. There are no losers, only winners. A truthful Satyagraha campaign, though it demands courage, self-discipline and humility on the part of the Satyagrahi, brings to bear tremendous moral pressure on the opponent and can bring about remarkable transformations.

Two factors are absolutely crucial to understand. There can be no Satyagraha in a cause which is not indisputably just and truthful. Nor can there be any element of violence or bitterness in a Satyagraha campaign-it must be conducted in a spirit of genuine nonviolence. Any campaign which is insincere in its spirit of nonviolence, or is not undertaken in a clearly just cause is not Satyagraha as Gandhi meant it. To sum up, Gandhian philosophy is not only simultaneously political, moral and religious, it is also traditional and modern, simple and complex. It embodies numerous Western influences to which Gandhi was exposed, but being rooted in ancient Indian culture and harnessing eternal and universal moral and religious principles, there is much in it that is not at all new. This is why Gandhi could say: "I have nothing new to teach the world. Truth and nonviolence are as old as the hills." Gandhi is concerned even more with the spirit than with the form. If the spirit is consistent with truth and nonviolence, the truthful and nonviolent form will automatically result. Despite its anti-Westernism, many hold its outlook to be ultra-modern, in fact ahead of its time-even far ahead. Perhaps the philosophy is best seen as a harmonious blend of the traditional and modern. The multifaceted nature of Gandhi's thought also can easily lead to the view that it is extremely complex. Perhaps in one sense it is. One could easily write volumes in describing it! Yet Gandhi described much of his thought as mere commonsense. Dr Diwakar sums up Gandhi's thought in a few words: "The four words, truth, nonviolence, Sarvodaya and Satyagraha and their significance constitute Gandhi and his teaching." These are indeed the four pillars of Gandhian thought.

HINDU REFORM MOVEMENTS

Several contemporary groups, collectively termed Hindu reform movements, strive to introduce regeneration and reform to Hinduism. Although these movements are very individual in their exact philosophies they generally stress the spiritual, secular and logical and scientific aspects of the Vedic traditions, creating a form that is egalitarian that does not discriminate based on Jati (caste or subcaste), gender, or race. Thus, most modern Hindu reform movements advocate a return to supposed ancient, egalitarian forms of Hinduism, and view aspects of modern Hinduism, such as discrimination and the caste system, as being corrupt results from colonialism and foreign influence.

Active Hindu communities are to be found in all parts of the world. In particular, countries of the former Soviet Union and Poland have thriving Hindu communities due to the missionary work of the Hare Krishnas. Most of the Hindu movements, with the exception of the Hare Krishna movement, reflect a more Smarta-like ideology. There are groups in India that are actively engaged in getting women and those from socially disadvantaged jatis to become priests of Vedic ritual. One of the foremost movements in breaking the caste system and educating the downtrodden was the Lingayat movement spearheaded by Basavanna in the 12th century in Anubhava Mantapa in Kalyani of Karnataka. The less accessible Vedas were rejected and parallel Vachanas were compiled.

The new movements look up to Swami Vivekananda; Rabindranath Tagore; Ramana Maharshi; Shri Aurobindo (for his *Integral Yoga*); A.C. Bhaktivedanta Swami Prabhupada (founder of the modern Hare Krishna movement); Swami Sivananda, Swami Rama Tirtha; Narayana Guru,Jagadguru Swami Sathyananda Saraswathi, Paramhansa Yogananda; Shrii Shrii Anandamurti. More recently, the work of Maharishi Mahesh Yogi, Sathya Sai Baba, Shirdi Sai Baba, Swami Muktananda, Swami Chinmayananda, Maharishi Dayananda Saraswati, Shriram Sharma Acharya, Sri Sri Ravi Shankar, and Mata Amritanandamayi has inspired millions to create new centres of spiritual development. In the intellectual field, the writings of Ananda Coomaraswamy, Ram Swarup, Sita Ram Goel, Subhash Kak, Frank Morales and David Frawley have been influential.

In social work, Mahatma Gandhi, Vinoba Bhave, Baba Amte and Shrii Shrii Anandamurti have been most important. Sunderlal Bahuguna created the *chipko* movement for the preservation of forestlands according to the Hindu ecological ideas. The Rashtriya Swayamsevak Sangh or RSS was founded by Keshav Baliram Hegdewar in 1925. The goal was to unite Hindus, make them rise over their caste differences and work to achieve a Hindu Rashtra; the ideology of the Sangh, closely associated with political Hinduism, came to be known as Hindutva.

In Indonesia several movements favour a return to Hinduism in Java, Sumatra, Kalimantan, and Sulawesi. Balinese Hinduism, known as Agama Hindu Dharma, has witnessed great resurgence in recent years. Shrii Prabhat Rainjan Sarkar (founder of Ananda Marga) initiated a new renaissance in the Indian world of samgeet.

INDIAN SOCIO-RELIGIOUS REFORM MOVEMENTS

Hindu reform movements in India materialized in different periods to purify the religion and also to eliminate the evil rituals practised by the Hindus. Some movements even aimed at erasing the caste discriminations in Hindu society. The most influential and prominent Hindu reform movements in India included the formation of the organization like the the Brahmo Samaj, Arya Samaj, Manav Dharma Sabha, Paramahansa Mandali, Prarthana Samaj, etc. Most of these organizations were started during the British period and made huge impacts on the then Indian society. The Brahmo Samaj was probably the most influential and significant organization which propelled the Hindu reform movements in India to a great extent. Brahmo Samaj was started and led by Raja Ram Mohan Roy in the year 1828. The Brahmo Samaj propagated the concept of worshipping one God; ideas like omnipresence of the omnipotent found a divine dimension amidst the teaching of the Brahmo Samaj. Brahmo Samaj also raised their voice against the evil rituals like Sati, child marriage, etc. and supported the movement for widow remarriage.

The Arya Samaj was another remarkable organization which further supported the Hindu reform movement to gain its desired contour. Dayananda Saraswati started and led the Arya Samaj. The Shuddhi movement was one of the most important features of Arya Samaj. The Aryas developed this ritual to readmit the lower caste Hindus, who were converted into Islam or Christianity. The Arya Samaj also actively opposed all the evil rituals practised in Hinduism and supported the cause of women education. The Samaj established educational institutions for providing education to the women at various levels as well. The Manav Dharma Sabha was an influential organization in the Hindu reform movement that started in Surat on 22nd June, 1844. Mehtaji Durgaram Manchharam was one of the prominent figures of this organization. During the 1830s, he became a prominent leader among the educated Gujaratis and formed a group that included the personalities like Dadoba Panderung Tarkhad, Dinmani Shankar, Dalpatram Bhagubai and Damodar Das. The main reason behind the foundation of Manav Dharma Sabha was the conversion of a

Parsi student, Nasarwanji Manakji to Hinduism. After a huge debate and controversy that continued for twenty days, Manakji was recanted and readmitted to the Parsi community. However, the event encouraged Durgaram, Dadoba and a few of their friends to establish the Manav Dharma Sabha. The Manav Dharma Sabha rejected 'the existence of ghosts, their exorcism by means of incantations, the evils of early marriage and the bar against remarriage of high caste Hindu widows'. The Sabha also challenged magicians and the reciters of incantations to demonstrate their skills. Though they criticised the caste system, they did not take any direct action against this institution. However, the Manav Dharma Sabha began to shatter in 1846 and its functions were ceased in 1852.

However, one of the prominent organizations in shaping the Hindu reform movements in India was the Paramahansa Mandali. The foundation of this organization was closely linked to the acculturative Manav Dharma Sabha and Dadoba Panderung was the leader of the Paramahansa Mandali. While living in Surat, he got influenced by the ideals of Manav Dharma Sabha and was also actively involved activities of the Sabha. He carried with him the ideals of Manav Dharma Sabha to Bombay and he outlined his own doctrines in Dharma Vivechan (A Discussion of the Unity of Man), which was written in 1843. Dadoba and a few of his friends founded the radical socio-religious society, named Paramahansa Mandali in 1849. The Mandali spoke against the caste system and followed two major principles. The principles were that, the Mandali would not attack any religion and would reject any religion which claimed that it had 'the infallible record of God's revelation to man'. The Mandali also rejected the caste system, idols, orthodox rituals and Brahmanical authority.

Established with an objective to change the religious and social life of Maharashtra, the Prarthana Samaj is considered as one of the major institutions in delineating the progress of Hindu reform movements in India. The Samaj drew its inspiration from the Paramahansa Mandali and was also influenced by Keshab Chandra Sen. Sen's visit to Bombay in 1867 generated considerable enthusiasm among the English-educated elite of Maharashtra. Being influenced by the ideals of Keshab Chandra Sen, Dr Atmaram Panderung and a few others established a new organisation named Prarthana Samaj (Prayer Society) in 1867. Many members of the Samaj were directly involved with the Paramahansa Mandali and they carried the ideology of the society with them. The Prarthana Samaj showed a syncretistic acceptance of all religions. It was committed to worship the one God and to seek the truth in all religions and the Samaj also wished to avoid sectarian conflict in their pursuit of morality and truth. The Samaj believed that no created being or object that has been worshipped by any sect should be ridiculed or condemned. The Prarthana Samaj also attempted to provide education to all classes of the society and wished to end the ban on widow remarriage. They claimed to abandon all caste restrictions, to abolish child marriage and also to encourage the education of women.

The Veda Samaj in South India was another striking formation which further propelled the Hindu reform movement in India. Founded in 1864 by Sridharalu Naidu and Keshab Chandra Sen in Madras, the Veda Samaj accepted the theistic ideals of the Brahmo Samaj. The Samaj considered marriage and the funeral rituals as 'matters of routine, destitute of all religious significance'. They also strongly spoke for 'discarding all sectarian views, of gradually abandoning caste distinctions, of tolerating the view of strangers and never offending anyone's feelings'. Opposing polygamy and child marriage and campaigning for widow remarriage were some of the most important features of Veda Samaj movement.

The Hindu reform movement in India was started mainly due to the conflict between the Brahmins and non-Brahmins in Indian society. The Brahmins always enjoyed a higher status than the other castes in the society and the movements were mainly formed to end this dominance. Eliminating the evil practices like Sati, child marriage, dowry, polygamy, etc. were also some of the other prominent objectives of the Hindu reform movements in India.

AMBEDKARITE BASIS FOR RELIGIOUS REFORM

The most immediate context for these proposals is the justification Ambedkar gives to them immediately afterwards.

He explains that there is no difference between the role of a Hindu priest and any other "profession". Like a doctor or a lawyer, a priest performs necessary functions in the community and is called upon when needed. The state regulates other professions with examinations and certification awarded solely on merit; why should religion be any different? From this alone, we can see that Ambedkar does not perceive religion as a manner of tradition, and that he would be unimpressed by arguments that Hinduism has been practiced a certain way for 3000 years, so the tradition must be continued in the same form. On the contrary, Ambedkar sees religion as a profession like medicine and law that is constantly improving and fits itself to the needs of the people. This attitude is summarized by his famous statement to a Mahar conference: "Religion is for man, and not man for religion." In this belief he was not alone, nor was he the first: Ludwig Feuerbach had cast Christianity in a similar light a century earlier in Das Wesen des Christentums when he called its "true" essence "anthropological".

Rodney Starke and Roger Finke are only echoing these words of Ambedkar and Feuerbach when they present as a "new paradigm" their economic theory of religion. According to Starke and Finke, rather than religious adherence being an "opium" used by the few to brainwash the many, individuals make choices of religious attitude "guided by their preferences and tastes... follow[ing] the dictates of reason in an effort to achieve their desired goals." It is hard to say whether this is a universal paradigm, but Ambedkar saw its appeal and political application. He considered the "new paradigm" a turning point in the development of modern civilization: "Man in the antique world did not call upon his maker to be righteous to him. Such is this... Revolution in Religion." He saw "equality and human dignity" as laws that would hold stronger and truer for modern Indians than the law of caste.

Consider the paradigm Ambedkar was pitted against. In the Manusmriti, Manu states that "castes are inherited by birth and they cannot be given up." Following this tradition, one's ability to make choices based on "preference and taste" is highly limited; questions of how one makes a living, where one worships, and who one is allowed to eat with cannot be decided based on personal convictions, but must adhere to the unchanging law of caste. When Ambedkar makes the distinction in this speech between the fearmongering of the "priestly class" and the desires and needs of the people, he is looking to the "new", anthropological paradigm as the model which subverts these traditionalist claims. In short, Ambedkar's rebuttal to traditionalism opened the door to both Hindu reform and, eventually, conversion to Buddhism.

The Hindu Code Bill

While Ambedkar is famous for his Buddhist movement and authorship of the Indian Constitution, another of his great struggles was not directly related to either of these subjects. From April 1947 to October 1951, a period inclusive of the entire debate over the Constitution, he pushed for the passage of a revised Hindu Code which he authored and sponsored. The debate over this code occupies over 1300 pages of the official edition of Ambedkar's writings, and it was the prolonged ambivalence of the government over the reform of the Hindu Code which eventually drove Ambedkar to resign as law minister of India. The Hindu Code is an aspect of Indian law dating to the 18th century, when the British were compelled to codify unwritten traditions in India based on a combination of British law and inaccurate English translations of Persian translations of prehistoric religious texts.

While India is a secular nation and does not have religious courts, there is a great variation in matters of family law. During the Hindu Code debate, Ambedkar justified the British system as follows: "This country is inhabited by very many communities. Each one has its special laws and merely because the State desired to assume a secular character it should withdraw itself from regulating the lives of the various communities, undoubtedly would result in nothing but chaos and anarchy." It is clear that Ambedkar supported the regulation of such aspects of private life as marriage, separation, inheritance, adoption, and funerals, and on this principle at least he was not playing favourites, as the bill applied the same rules to Hindus and Buddhists.

Ambedkar had a strong belief in establishing equality and human rights through European-style legality, which was part of the reason he was chosen to author the Indian Constitution despite his anti-authoritarian streak. His plan for the Hindu Code, reflecting this belief, was ambitious and consequential. The bill would have legalized divorce, permitted intercaste marriage and adoption, standardized property ownership across the wide diversity of local traditions, and allotted a much larger inheritance to daughters and widows than the prior norm. The intent of these reforms can be easily gathered from the lengthy debate on the bill: to render all Hindus equal in the eye of the law, including Dalits and women, and to bring the practice of divorce under the auspices of the Indian justice system rather than leaving it to be worked out by the parties involved. He and his supporters justified these changes, not by asserting that Hinduism itself needed reform, but by claiming that they were returning to the standard of Hindu texts.

We see in the Hindu Code Bill an intermediary stage between using internal and external pressure to reform Hinduism. Obviously, the bill changes the traditional relationship between Hinduism and the law: with its passage, Hindu families affected by divorce or intercaste marriage would no longer be able to sue on the grounds that their religion had been disrespected. But Ambedkar's wording of the bill also allowed Hindu power structures to remain in place. Because the original draft applied to all Indians who were not Muslim, Parsi, or Christian, it did not encourage Dalits to convert away from Hinduism to obtain additional legal rights. Rather, Ambedkar aimed to bring the same legal rights to all Indians that he wanted for his own supporters; the bill was written with the human rights interests of even the most conservative Brahmin in mind. In his defences of the bill, too, Ambedkar shows an acceptance of what he saw as some problematic aspects of Hinduism. Instead of objecting to the textual basis of Hinduism itself, he engages Hindus on their own terms, citing the Dayabhag, Kautilya, Parashara Smrti, and Brhaspati Smrti.

However, Ambedkar's Untouchable birth and participation in the Dalit civil rights movement was not exactly appealing to the conservatives who sought such justifications. The fact that the same man who had burnt the Manusmirti was now proposing radical changes to the existing system of Hindu law led to an ugly debate where he was accused of attempting to pollute the law with "a spirit of supreme contempt for anything Hindu" and even of "aim[ing] at the utter demolition of the structure of Hindu society". It is remarkable that he introduced the bill in the first place, and even moreso that he pursued its adoption for four years. In less capable hands the bill would have been abandoned, but Ambedkar made sure this happened. Although the controversy did not die down after his resignation, the bills eventually passed with most of the reforms intact.

The Hindu Code Bill legitimatized Ambedkar's legalistic approach to bringing about social change, and gave weight to the "new paradigm" of valuing the desires of common people over the demands of the Brahmins. It also asserted the ability of the state to make its own decisions on matters of family law rather than bowing to religious authorities. Finally, the actual reform accomplished gave under represented groups such as Dalits and women new legal rights, which could be seen as a movement by government towards Ambedkar's goals. However, compared to his proposed reforms in The Annihilation of Caste, the consequences of this bill on the structure of Hinduism were relatively minimal. This bill was clearly not equivalent to what Ambedkar was trying to accomplish with this propositions.

Hinduism and Indianness

The Hindutva movement, which has been active since the early 20th century, promotes defence of Hinduism as a national policy for India. Although not all Indians are Hindus and not all Hindus are Indians, Hindu nationalists appeal to tradition and authority to argue that support for Hinduism is the mark of a true patriot. They are assisted by the close link between the words for "Hindu" and "Indian" in many Indian languages (e.g., Hindustan for India). If he honestly aimed to reform Hinduism, therefore, Ambedkar would not have been able to get very far without an authentically Indian authority to appeal to. In a 1954 speech, shortly before his death, Ambedkar said that "positively, my social philosophy may be said to be enshrined in three words: liberty, equality, and fraternity." Understanding the obvious implication of this trifecta, he added, "Let no one, however, say that I have borrowed my philosophy from the French Revolution." He goes on to explain how Buddha interpreted the relationship between these three ideals. But if he recognized the origin of this phrase, then he clearly was referencing the French Revolution, and more generally Enlightenment principles. It is curious that Buddha, whom he calls his "master" in this speech, is only an interpreter for the French motto. In his other writings, Ambedkar uses "liberty, equality and fraternity" as the three chief signs of humane and just religion: they represent to him everything that Hinduism is not. Is this a sign that he held European values more highly than Indian values, and wished to make over India in the image of Europe? Certainly this has been an active strain of criticism about his life's work, and the debate over the Hindu Code bill was largely a question of Indianness versus international opinion.

The proposed reforms for Hinduism play into this argument easily, because they seem to be partially an attempt to rewrite Hinduism from scratch in order to model it after Christianity. Rather than a diverse bundle of contradictory sacred texts, which different strains of Hinduism honour in different orders and ways, Ambedkar would have a group compile "one and only one standard book of Hindu Religion" which would become the only legal text for teaching Hinduism in the country. He does not mention the word "Bible", but the parallel is obvious. Meanwhile, he would eliminate the caste distinctions which render all Brahmins priests by birth, and instead outlaw preaching or holding ceremonies without accreditation, and allow any Hindu to become a priest if they pass an examination. This resembles the method by which some sects of Christianity accredit priests.

However, a closer look reveals some clear discrepancies with how Western nations treat religion, and suggests that Ambedkar was modelling his ideal Hinduism on his understanding of Buddhism. The Buddha and His Dhamma is his "one standard book", specifically written to encourage a single orthopraxy and the elimination of "not-dhamma" popular beliefs, and in this aspiration it resembles Theravada Buddhism. In Ambedkar's Buddhism, we find a set of open standards for the priesthood similar to those laid out in The Annihilation of Caste: the Sangha is free of all barriers of caste, sex, and status, and monks are certified by oral examination. This, too, accurately reflects how Theravada is practiced in Southeast Asian countries, with the exception that the nun's lineage died out in the medieval era.

Additionally, and more bizarrely to Western eyes, the state plays a large role in the proposed reform. The priest is required to be "the servant of the State", the number of priests will be fixed by the state, and the state will draw up an examination which all priests will be required to pass. This system does not seem to be a blueprint for a religion so much as an parallel agency to the Indian Civil Service, the immense administrative and education bureaucracy mentioned by Ambedkar. Since the separation of church and state was an issue long since settled by Ambedkar's time, he could not be said to be drawing on any contemporary Western source. Rather, these reforms must point deeper, to Ambedkar's understanding of the nature of Hinduism itself.

Hinduism as Non-Religion

If our understanding is correct, then Ambedkar imagined an egalitarian Hindu reform which would ground it in Buddhism, and enforce this reform across the nation by law. This would be an ambitious program indeed. But doesn't regulating religiousness undermine one's capacity for free expression, the entire basis of the "new paradigm"? Ambedkar's statement of personal philosophy, given many years after this speech, reaffirms this : "Law is secular, which anybody may break while fraternity or religion is sacred which anybody must respect." This statement portrays religion as a matter of voluntary association ("fraternity") which could not be manufactured by the law. There is the possibility that Ambedkar had completely reversed his position on Hinduism after going through the ordeal of the Hindu Code Bill and preparing for his own conversion to Buddhism. Even if that is the case, how do we resolve the initial contradiction? The answer is in

Ambedkar's conception of Hinduism, and this answer may also supply us with a resolution for some of the remaining problems with his proposed reforms. Ambedkar, deriving his understanding of religion from Max Muller, recognized that "in all ancient Society, Law and Religion were one." He therefore recognized the Manusmriti as a "Code of Laws", but not as a "book of Religion" in the modern sense, because it did not fulfill his requirements for modern religion—namely, it lacks social utility, justice, and the "fraternity" associated above with religion, not to mention equality and liberty. He wrote that "what Hindus call Religion is really Law", a statement that seems clear enough given his legal background and legalistic critique of Hinduism, but appended a clear denunciation of claims to religious status: "Frankly, I refuse to call this code of ordinances, as Religion."

In Ambedkar's perception, the Manusmriti must be reread, not as an expression of transcendental order, but as a Draconian and fundamentally unjust code of laws originating in the mind of the "hireling" Manu in order to serve "the interests of a class... whose title to being supermen was not to be lost even if they lost their virtue." This condemnation mirrors the description of the modern priestly class as one that " recognizes no duties [and] knows only of rights and privileges." By placing the Manusmriti in historical context and reevaluating it as a self-serving tract, Ambedkar delegitimizes and desanctifies. Of course, just because it is a legal system that favours one group over another does not necessarily mean it is uninspired. The legal system of the Quran is justified today as being the direct command of God, and likely some Brahmins would defend the Manusmriti with a similar argument. In response, Ambedkar points to the less than divine origins of the book, as a production of a minor class of guru, to show that rather than deserving the protection of "religious freedom", it ought to be treated as a legal text and regulated in that way.

It is not difficult to see the connection from this line of argument directly to Ambedkar's proposals for Hindu reform. In these proposals, Ambedkar is minimizing the theological implications of reform in order to focus in on legal changes. If the role a Brahmin plays in a village is that of a sort of rogue lawyer, rather than a metaphysical teacher, it is easier to understand why he cannot be allowed to enforce his laws without earning and receiving the approval of a government authority. Such unjust laws as those in the Manusmriti, too, could not possibly be certified for enforcement in a democratic nation; it is better to set up a single law-book, which regulates the behaviour of local lawyers, and does not allow gross contradictions from town to town. When he says that "to my mind there is nothing revolutionary in this", he means that he is only applying the same standards to Hinduism as he would to his own profession as lawyer and legislator.

Was Ambedkar justified in this reductionist view of Hinduism? I am inclined to agree with Professor Zelliot that his proposals are "legalistic". However, they are certainly not "naïve" in the sense of unsophisticated or lacking understanding of Hinduism. Rather, they show that Ambedkar has read the Manusmriti and determined its legal structure, and is providing in his speech an analysis of the bare minimum reform needed to provide legal equality to the Dalits if they were to remain Hindus. If any of his reforms were ignored, Brahmins would retain the capability to enforce the unjust law of caste, and the Dalits would be no better off than where they started.

Protections in the Constitution

Ambedkar inserted into his drafts of the Indian constitution a concern for the rights of traditionally unprotected and oppressed people, similar to what we find in the Hindu Code Bill and his critiques of Hinduism. Not only does it categorically abolish untouchability, establish an officer to monitor "scheduled castes and scheduled tribes", and outlaw religious and caste discrimination, but the preamble declares that the establishment of justice, liberty, and equality is the very purpose of the Republic of India. The preamble is echoed in section 38, which reads that "the state shall strive to promote the welfare of the people by securing and protecting as effectively as it can a social order in which justice, social, economic and political, shall inform all the institutions of the national life." Given the opportunity to write the Constitution, Ambedkar turned it into a vehicle for social justice and an affirmation of some of his lifelong values. In recent years, rather than ignoring these sections of the Constitution, the Indian government has endeavoured to expand on them. The single officer appointed for the sake of Dalit rights in the initial Constitution was amended in 1990 to become a "National Commission". The provision in the Constitution to monitor the condition of socially backward classes (such as the Criminal Tribes) also became a full-scale Commission in 1992.

The structure of the Indian Constitution shows the successful application of Ambedkar's legal ideas to a universal context. Here, he did not have any competing authority which required him to defend his political philosophy: Hinduism was not a social institution especially familiar with constitutions, and the main debate during the adoption of the Constitution was over the inclusion of "emergency powers".

Ambedkar's proposals for Hinduism, although they conflict with the Western conception of "religious freedom", reflect his modern and humanistic values with respect to religion as a practice. They are linked to his belief that "religion was made for man" and betray a skeptical analysis of unjust power structures. The Hindu Code Bill, which changed the nature of the state's relationship with Hinduism, the Constitution, which promoted social justice, and the structure of the Buddhist movement he initiated at the end of Ambedkar's life reflect elements of the reforms he laid down here.

Still, would Ambedkar really have expected reform-minded Hindus to pick up on his line of argument and begin pressing for complete government control over their own religion? Given the tone of his message, I do not believe that he thought anything of the sort. Perhaps he purposefully exaggerated the extent to which his reforms would have to be enforced in order to demonstrate how hopeless the situation was for Dalits. By the time this speech was made, Ambedkar had already given up on satyagraha as a means of social change, burned the Manusmriti, and quarrelled with Gandhi over the subject of Untouchability. He seems to express a personal skepticism in the possibility for meaningful internal change when he ends his speech by saying, "I will not be with you. I have decided to change." Rather than preparing for battle, he is already bowing out of the discussion. If he could have conceived of a more reasonable approach to Hindu reform, he more likely would already have begun pushing for that reform himself in the public sphere, rather than offering it as a suggestion to others. Instead, I believe that Ambedkar used this list of reforms as a rhetorical device to accurately summarize the insurmountable extent of the caste problem in Hinduism.

SOCIAL WORK FOR SOCIAL JUSTICE: TEN PRINCIPLES

Human Dignity

Dignity of the human person is the ethical foundation of a moral society. The measure of every institution is whether it threatens or enhances the life and dignity of the human person. Social workers respect the inherent dignity and worth of all individuals. Social workers treat each person in a caring, respectful manner mindful of individual differences and cultural and ethnic diversity. Social workers seek to promote the responsiveness of organizations, communities and social institutions to individuals' needs and social problems. Social workers act to prevent and eliminate domination of, exploitation of, and discrimination against any person or group on any basis.

Dignity of Work and the Rights of Workers

In a marketplace where profit often takes precedence over the dignity and rights of workers, it is important to recognize that the economy must serve the people, not the other way around. If the dignity of work is to be protected, the basic rights of workers must be respected – the right to productive work, to decent and fair wages, to organize and join unions, to private property and to economic initiative. Social workers challenge injustice related to unemployment, workers' rights and inhumane labour practices. Social workers engage in organized action, including the formation of and participation in labour unions, to improve services to clients and working conditions.

Community and the Common Good

All individuals by virtue of their human nature have social needs. Human relationships enable people to meet their needs and provide an important vehicle for change. *The family*, in all its diverse forms, *is the central social institution that must be supported and strengthened. The way in which society is organized – in* education, *economics, politics,* government – *directly affects human dignity and the common good.* Social workers promote the general welfare and development of individuals, families and communities. Social workers seek to strengthen relationships among people at all levels to promote the well being of all.

Solidarity

We are our brother's and sister's keeper. We are one human family, whatever our national, racial, ethnic, economic, and ideological differences. An ethic of care acknowledging our interdependence belongs in every aspect of human experience including the family, community, society and global dimensions. Social workers understand that relationships between and among people are an important vehicle for change. Social workers engage people as partners in the helping process and seek to strengthen relationships among people to promote well being at all levels.

Rights and Responsibilities

People have a right and a responsibility to participate in society and to work together toward the common good. *Human dignity is protected and healthy community can be achieved only if human rights are protected and responsibilities are met.* Accordingly, every person has a fundamental *right to things necessary for human decency. Corresponding to these rights are responsibilities to family, community and society.* Social workers, mindful of individual differences and diversity, respect and promote the right of all individuals to self-determination and personal growth and development. Social workers provide education and advocacy to protect human rights and end oppression. Social workers empower individuals/groups to function as effectively as possible.

Stewardship

It is incumbent upon us to recognize and protect the value of all people and all resources on our planet. While rights to personal property are recognized, these rights are not unconditional and are secondary to the best interest of the common good especially in relation to the right of all individuals to meet their basic needs. Stewardship of resources is important at all levels/settings: family, community, agency, community and society. Social workers strive to ensure access to needed information, services and resources; equality of opportunity; and meaningful participation for all people. Social workers promote the general welfare of people and their environments.

Priority for the Poor and Vulnerable

A basic moral test of any community or society is the way in which the most vulnerable members are faring. In a society characterized by deepening divisions between rich and poor, the needs of those most at risk should be considered a priority. Social workers advocate for living conditions conducive to the fulfilment of basic human needs and to promote social, economic, political, and cultural values and institutions that are compatible with the realization of social justice. Social workers pursue change with and on behalf of vulnerable and oppressed individuals and groups to: address poverty, unemployment, discrimination and other forms of social injustice; expand choice and opportunity; and promote social justice.

Governance/Principle of Subsidiarity

Governance structures in all levels / settings have an imperative to promote human dignity, protect human rights, and build the common good. While the principle of subsidiarity calls for the functions of government to be performed at the lowest level possible in order to insure for self-determination and empowerment, higher levels of government have the responsibility to provide leadership and set policy in the best interest of the common good. Social workers engage in social and political action in order to promote equality, challenge injustice, expand opportunity and empower individuals, families and groups to participate in governance structures at all levels.

Participation

All people have a right to participate in the economic, political and cultural life of society. Social justice and human dignity require that all people be assured a minimum level of participation in the community. It is the ultimate injustice for a person or a group to be excluded unfairly. Social workers strive to ensure access to equal opportunity and meaningful participation for all. Social workers empower individuals and groups to influence social policies and institutions and promote social justice. Social workers advocate for change to ensure that all people have equal access to the resources and opportunities required to meet basic needs and develop fully.

Promotion of Peace

In light of the human dignity and worth of all and the ethical imperatives of solidarity and stewardship, we are called to promote peace and non-violence at all levels – within families, communities, society and globally. *Peace is the fruit of justice and is dependent upon the respect and cooperation between peoples and nations.* Social workers promote peace and the general welfare of society from local to global levels.

SOCIAL JUSTICE AND PEOPLE OF FAITH

Social justice is a central social work value (NASW, 2000). Although no single, agreed-on conceptualization of social justice exists (Sterba, 1999), the construct has been associated with a wide variety of populations and perspectives. For instance, the intersection between social justice and race, gender, age, disability, sexual orientation, and class has been widely discussed (Thompson, 2002). More recently, the literature has featured examinations of social justice and international adoptions (Hollingsworth, 2003), probation services, Tibetan immigrants (Nassar, 2002), mental health (Sheppard, 2002), late-fife care (Johnson, 2002), marginalized South Asian children (O'Kane, 2002), and education for undocumented families (Belanger, 2001).

Largely absent from the social work literature on social justice, however, has been any similar discussion of religion. An examination of Social Work Abstracts using the keywords "religion" or "spirituality" and "social justice" revealed no articles designed to equip social workers to challenge social injustice in the area of religion, a finding consistent with studies indicating that most social workers have received little, if any, content on religion and spirituality during their graduate educations.

The paucity of literature represents a significant oversight given the growing professional interest in religion and spirituality. The extant research has suggested that most social workers are interested in addressing religion in their practices, underscoring the need for material on social justice. Furthermore, and perhaps most important, social workers have an ethical duty to address religiously based social injustice. Therefore, this article represents an initial step in helping social workers challenge social injustice on behalf of what some refer to as "people of faith" individuals who adhere to the mainstream tenets of their respective faith traditions. In keeping with the Code of Ethics's injunctions, I have adopted a transnational perspective.

DEFINING SOCIAL JUSTICE: A HUMAN RIGHTS FRAMEWORK

As implied earlier, social justice is a highly contested construct. Although the term is widely used, there is little agreement regarding what the concept signifies or how it should be operationalized (Reisch, 2002). Observers have noted that a wide variety of types, perspectives, and conceptualizations (Sterba, 1999) of social justice exist.

One method that has been used to anchor the construct is human rights, with some commentators reporting that this understanding is gaining ground as a framework for understanding social justice. Within this framework, human rights are commonly defined as those characteristics that are necessary for us to live as human beings. Human rights flow from the fact that all human beings have inherent dignity and worth. As these rights are grounded in the human condition, they are universal, applying equally to all human beings around the world, independent of their recognition in law. Social justice is exhibited by working to ensure that human rights are respected, nationally and internationally.

In keeping with the contested nature of social justice, the human rights framework is not without critics. Perhaps the most significant criticism has come from postmodern conceptualizations of social justice (Sterba, 1999). Lyotard (1979/1984) defined postmodernism as the rejection of meta-narratives and the accompanying idea of universals. Consequently, constructs that apply to all individuals, such as human rights, are no longer tenable. Conceptualizations of social justice are individual, local, and particular—a multiplicity of justices exist as opposed to any single, universal understanding of justice. In keeping with this line of thought, human rights have been criticized as an expression of Western values, and implementing these values in Western and particularly non-Western cultures is, at best, a dubious enterprise and, at worst, an unethical implosion of culturally foreign values (Pateman, 1998).

Others have noted, however, that postmodernism's rejection of universal conceptualizations is inconsistent as postmodernists themselves resort to the use of universals to describe their own version of social justice. Furthermore, although respect for autonomy and for cultural diversity are central social work values, a number of social work authors have expressed difficulty with the idea that absolutely any culturally sanctioned behaviour is acceptable, that no minimal standards of conduct apply universally. As has been noted, to reject universalism is to accept the idea that there is no place for widely affirmed basic rights, such as freedom from torture (George). In other words, without philosophical acknowledgment of universalism, it is impossible to say that people in every nation, across cultures, should not be subjected to torture.

In light of the criticisms that have been advanced against the idea of human rights, some have suggested adopting a limited number of basic rights that are widely supported (George, 1999). Although most rights theorists agree that certain rights are inherent in the human condition, they disagree about the extent and scope of these rights. Some individuals posit the existence of a limited number of rights (Feinberg, 1973), around which a substantial degree of consensus typically exists, and others argue for broader conceptualizations that tend to inspire more controversy (West, 1998). One way to maximize respect for autonomy and cultural diversity is to adopt a more limited conceptualization of human rights that is widely affirmed.

6

Western History of Ideologies for Social Change

WOMEN'S LABOUR ORGANISATIONS IN BRITISH INDIA

Women's Labour Organisations in British India put in a lot of effort for the improvement of women's working situation in India, especially in the factories. However, they fell short of actually bringing about these changes as they were working along international norms, and trying to implement international standards of change which were not quite suitable for the Indian situation. Women's Labour Organisations in British India emerged in response to the plight of the women in the workforce, particularly in factories and mines. The various women's organisations developed their interest in female factory workers in response to the enquiries of the Royal commission and the enquiries of the International Labour Organisation (ILO). For a long time the women's organisations focused on issues such as civil rights, education, and the social environment. They assumed that women, except for the most unfortunate, were economic dependants. Most women belonging to women's organizations seemed unaware that a significant percentage of women supported themselves and their families.

Whitley Committee Report

While touring India in 1929, the Whitley Committee asked women's organizations to prepare proposal describing their activities among workers. The Bombay Provincial Women's

Council had been interested in the welfare of women workers for some time, so they complied with the request. While they were preparing these reports it stimulated their interest and enthusiasm for a discussion of the economic and social conditions of working women. After the publication of the Report of the Whitley Committee the National Council of Women in India formed a study committee on labour and the Bombay Council scheduled a three-day conference on women and labour. This conference was designed to enlighten their members about the labour issues and bridge the gap between themselves and women labourers.

WORKS OF THE ALL INDIA WOMEN'S CONFERENCE

During this time, the All India Women's Conference (AIWC) decided to broaden its scope of activities to include social issues and appointed a number of sub-committees. By 1931 the AIWC had instituted a sub-committee on labour, begun visiting mills, and sent out questionnaires to gather data on conditions in the factories. Both the Bombay Council and the AIWC approved of the Whitley Report's recommendations for reduced hours of work, women inspectors and medical practitioners, maternity benefits, and prohibition of women working below ground in the mines.

The Mumbai Council's programs touched the lives of real working women. They set up regional centres offering medical services, sewing lessons, and literacy classes. They also arranged for piecework for the wives and children of labourers. Lectures and entertainment, sometimes for audiences of 800 women, were arranged at the mills. Mumbai mill owners appreciated their work, contributing 40 percent of the Council's annual budget by 1939. Factory women showed up in large numbers to consult with medical personnel, listen to lectures, and attend literacy classes-adequate proof that they valued these services. The AIWC concentrated on legislation. They asked the government to appoint a female representative to the ILO and by 1935 were officially reporting to this body. ILO interests became their interests and the measures undertaken by the ILO stimulated them into action. As a downside of this, they became oblivious to the real issues and concerns of women labourers. The importance of the international connection becomes evident in AIWC demands for social insurance, maternity benefits, and other measures to improve working conditions. By and large they ignored Rajkumari Amrit Kaur's warning that special legislation had already caused employers to lay off women and hire men.

IMPACT OF LEGISLATION FOR WOMEN

The legislation of labour fixed the maximum hours of work, forbade women from nightly duties, prohibited child labour, and made maternity benefits, compulsory. Unfortunately, when bids were made to implement these rules, the consequences were upsetting. Women in conspicuous numbers were fired, and men were hired to replace them. Many women workers, finding that no options were left for them, adjusted laws in such a way, that the outcome was just the reverse of what was desired. For example, work-hours were reduced to give women time for rest. For women, desperate to survive the fight for existence, limited work-time yielded inadequate money. Thus even in their leisure time, they sought part-time employment in other factories. Naturally, this work for unearthly hours was bound to take a toll on their health. Maternity leave, devised to maintain and care for pregnant mothers turned out to be an obstruction for those who required work in order to live their lives. The state of these women was deplorable. The role of women in labour movements has been largely ignored. Nevertheless, women's presence in strikes and labour disturbances, as strike breakers and as labour leaders, was noted from the 1920s. Prominent women such as Maniben Kara, Ushabai Dange and Parvati Bhore in Mumbai and Santosh Kumari Devi and Prabhabati Debi in Kolkata, became leaders of trade unions and represented both women and men to management. Other accounts have noted women's presence at the head of demonstrations in the 1928-29 Mumbai textile strike and commented on their militancy.

Drawbacks of the Women's Labour Organisations

The women's organizations ignored practical evidence that new regulations were not improving the conditions of work for women and continued to support the ILO demand that international standards should be extended to Indian women. There were a few middle-class women who attempted to learn about the conditions of factory women. Maniben Kara tried to do social work among these women and concluded that her efforts were futile. She joined the labour unions but since only 1 percent of their membership was female, her work was with men. Legislative norms codified by the ILO started functioning in India during the lull period of world economy. However legislation could never decrease the rate of women's employment in the factory sectors. Number of factory employees, incorporating even those of the textile factories and jute mills, reached the optimum pedestals of 16.5 percent in 1927 and descended to 15 percent in 1932.

Though the women's labour organisations did much to improve the situation of the working women in ways that they felt would be beneficial, they fell short of the required level of change. This was because of their inability to understand the problems of the women they claimed to represent. The fact was that the Indian situation differed significantly from the European scene. However, no steps were taken to determine what Indian women workers wanted.

Social Darwinism

Social Darwinism is a term used for various late nineteenth century ideologies which, while often contradictory, exploited ideas of survival of the fittest. It especially refers to notions of struggle for existence being used to justify social policies which make no distinction between those able to support themselves and those unable to support themselves. While the most prominent form of such views stressed competition between individuals in free market capitalism, it is also associated with ideas of struggle between national or racial groups. In sociology it has been defined as a theory of social evolution which asserts that "There are underlying, and largely irresistible, forces acting in societies which are like the natural forces that operate in animal and plant communities. One can therefore formulate social laws similar to natural ones. These social forces are of such a kind as to produce evolutionary progress through the natural conflicts between social groups. The best-adapted and most successful social groups survive these conflicts, raising the evolutionary level of society generally (the 'survival of the fittest')." The term has very rarely been used as a self description. The term first appeared in Europe in 1877, and around this time it was used by sociologists opposed to the concept. The term was popularized in the United States in 1944 by the American historian Richard Hofstadter who used it in the ideological war effort against fascism to denote a reactionary creed which promoted competitive strife, racism and nationalism. Before Hofstadter's work the use of the term in English academic journals was quite rare. The term "social darwinism" has rarely been used by advocates of the supposed ideologies or ideas; instead it has almost always been used (pejoratively) by its opponents.

The term draws upon the common use of the term *Darwinism*, which has been used to describe a range of evolutionary views, but in the late 19th century was applied more specifically to natural selection as first advanced by Charles Darwin to explain speciation in populations of organisms. The process includes competition between individuals for limited resources, popularly but inaccurately described by the phrase "survival of the fittest", a term coined by sociologist Herbert Spencer. While the term has been applied to the claim that Darwin's theory of evolution by natural selection can be used to understand the social endurance of a nation or country, social Darwinism commonly refers to ideas that predate Darwin's publication of *On the Origin of Species*. Others whose ideas are given the label include the 18th century clergyman Thomas Malthus, and Darwin's cousin Francis Galton who founded eugenics towards the end of the 19th century.

Theories and Origins

The term Darwinism had been coined by Thomas Henry Huxley in his April 1860 review of *On the Origin of Species*, and by the 1870s it was used to describe a range of concepts of evolutionism or development, without any specific commitment to Charles Darwin's own theory. The first use of the phrase "social Darwinism" was in Joseph Fisher's 1877 article on *The History of Landholding in Ireland* which was published in the *Transactions of the Royal Historical Society*. Fisher was commenting on how a system for borrowing livestock which had been called "tenure" had led to the false impression that the early Irish had already evolved or developed land tenure;

These arrangements did not in any way affect that which we understand by the word " tenure," that is, a man's farm, but they related solely to cattle, which we consider a chattel. It has appeared necessary to devote some space to this subject, inasmuch as that usually acute writer Sir Henry Maine has accepted the word " tenure " in its modern interpretation, and has built up a theory under which the Irish chief " developed " into a feudal baron. I can find nothing in the Brehon laws to warrant this theory of social Darwinism, and believe further study will show that the Cain Saerrath and the Cain Aigillue relate solely to what we now call chattels, and did not in any way affect what we now call the freehold, the possession of the land. – *Fisher 1877.*

Despite the fact that social Darwinism bears Charles Darwin's name, it is also linked today with others, notably Herbert Spencer, Thomas Malthus, and Francis Galton, the founder of eugenics. In fact, Spencer was not described as a social Darwinist until the 1930s, long after his death.

Darwin himself gave serious consideration to Galton's work, but considered the ideas of "hereditary improvement" impractical. Aware of weaknesses in his own family, Darwin was sure that families would naturally refuse such selection and wreck the scheme. He thought that even if compulsory registration was the only way to improve the human race, this illiberal idea would be unacceptable, and it would be better to publicize the "principle of inheritance" and let people decide for themselves.

In *The Descent of Man, and Selection in Relation to Sex* of 1882 Darwin described how medical advances meant that the weaker were able to survive and have families, and commented on the effects of this, while cautioning that hard reason should not override sympathy, and considering how other factors might reduce the effect: Thus the weak members of civilized societies propagate their kind. No one who has attended to the breeding of domestic animals will doubt that this must be highly injurious to the race of man. It is surprising how soon a want of care, or care wrongly directed, leads to the degeneration of a domestic race; but excepting in the case of man himself, hardly any one is so ignorant as to allow his worst animals to breed.

The aid which we feel impelled to give to the helpless is mainly an incidental result of the instinct of sympathy, which was originally acquired as part of the social instincts, but subsequently rendered, in the manner previously indicated, more tender and more widely diffused. Nor could we check our sympathy, even at the urging of hard reason, without deterioration in the noblest part of our nature. The surgeon may harden himself whilst performing an operation, for he knows that he is acting for the good of his patient; but if we were intentionally to neglect the weak and helpless, it could only be for a contingent benefit, with an overwhelming present evil.... We must therefore bear the undoubtedly bad effects of the weak surviving and propagating their kind; but there appears to be at least one check in steady action, namely that the weaker and inferior members of society do not marry so freely as the sound; and this check might be indefinitely increased by the weak in body or mind refraining from marriage, though this is more to be hoped for than expected.

WESTERN CULTURE

Western culture (sometimes equated with Western civilization or European civilization) refers to cultures of European origin. Roots of the Western civilization may be traced back to 9000 BC, when the first great cultures grew out of agricultural cores in South-West Asia, China, India, Mexico, and Peru. The Westernmost of this Old World's agricultural cores, the area around the headwaters of the Euphrates, Tigris, and Jordan Rivers in South-West Asia, spread outwards across Europe. Western culture in its strictly European geographical range began with the Greeks, was enlarged and strengthened by the Romans, reformed and modernized by the fifteenth-century Renaissance and Reformation, and globalized by successive European empires that spread the European ways of life and education between the sixteenth and twentieth centuries. European Culture developed with a complex range of philosophy, medieval scholasticism and mysticism, Christian and secular humanism. Rational thinking developed through a long age of change and formation with the experiments of enlightenment, naturalism, romanticism, science, democracy, and socialism. With its global connection, European culture grew with an all-inclusive urge to adopt, adapt, and ultimately influence other trends of culture. The term "Western culture" is used very broadly to refer to a heritage of social norms, ethical values, traditional customs, religious beliefs, political systems, and specific artifacts and technologies. Specifically, Western culture may imply:

- a Graeco-Roman Classical and Renaissance cultural influence, concerning artistic, philosophic, literary, and legal themes and traditions, the cultural social effects of migration period and the heritages of Celtic, Germanic, Romanic, Iberians, Slavic and other ethnic groups (especially from the Islamic world), as well as a tradition of rationalism in various spheres of life, developed by Hellenistic philosophy, Scholasticism, Humanisms, the Scientific Revolution and Enlightenment, and including, in political thought, widespread rational arguments in favour of freethought, human rights, equality and democratic values averse to irrationality and theocracy.
- a Biblical-Christian cultural influence in spiritual thinking, customs and either ethic or moral traditions, around Post-Classical Era.
- Western European cultural influences concerning artistic, musical, folkloric, ethic and oral traditions, whose themes have been further developed by Romanticism.

The concept of western culture is generally linked to the classical definition of the Western world. In this definition, Western culture is the set of literary, scientific, political, artistic and philosophical principles which set it apart from other cultural spheres. Much of this set of traditions and knowledge is collected in the Western canon. The term has come to apply to countries whose history is strongly marked by European immigration or settlement, such as the Americas, and Australasia, and is not restricted to Western Europe. Some tendencies that define modern Western societies are the existence of political pluralism, prominent subcultures or countercultures (such as New Age movements), increasing cultural syncretism resulting from globalization and human migration.

Terminology

From its very beginnings in Mesopotamia and then ancient Greece, the East-West distinction has been somewhat difficult to define with precision. The Greeks were not so different from their Eastern neighbours for example. In the Middle Ages, where Islam was contrasted to the West, it is of the Islamic Near East, having, since the time of Alexander the Great, been Hellenized, ruled by Rome and Constantinople and part of the Orthodox communion, was as much under the influence of Byzantine and Biblical-Christian history as "Christendom". In addition, much of Southern and Eastern Europe had fallen under Islamic rule at various times during the Middle Ages. In the later 20th to early 21st century, with the advent of increasing globalism, it has become more difficult to determine which individuals fit into which category, and the East–West contrast is sometimes criticized as relativistic and arbitrary.

Globalism has, especially since the end of the cold war, spread western ideas so widely that almost all modern countries or cultures are to some extent influenced by aspects of western culture which they have absorbed. Recent stereotyped Western views of "the West" have been labelled *Occidentalism*, paralleling Orientalism, the term for the 19th century stereotyped views of "the East". Geographically, "The West" today would normally be said to include Catholic and Protestant Europe as well as the overseas territories belonging to the Anglosphere, the Hispanidad, the Lusofonia or the Francophonie.

History

Western culture is neither homogeneous nor unchanging. As with all other cultures it has evolved and gradually changed over time. All generalities about it have their exceptions at some time and place. The organisation and tactics of the Greek Hoplites differed in many ways from the Roman legions. The polis of the Greeks is not the same as the American superpower of the 21st century. The gladiatorial games of the Roman Empire are not identical to present-day football. The art of Pompeii is not the art of Hollywood. Nevertheless, it is possible to follow the evolution and history of the West, and appreciate its similarities and differences, its borrowings from, and contributions to, other cultures of humanity. Concepts of what is *the West* arose out of legacies of the Western Roman Empire and the Eastern Roman Empire. Later, ideas of the west were formed by the concepts of Christendom and the Holy Roman Empire. What we think of as Western thought today is generally defined as Greco-Roman and Judeo-Christian culture, and includes the ideals of the Renaissance and the Enlightenment.

The Classical West

In Homeric literature, and right up until the time of Alexander the Great, for example in the accounts of the Persian Wars of Greeks against Persians by Herodotus, we see the paradigm of a contrast between the West and East. Nevertheless the Greeks felt they were civilized and saw themselves (in the formulation of Aristotle) as something between the wild barbarians of most of Europe and the soft, slavish Easterners. Ancient Greek science, philosophy, democracy, architecture, literature, and art provided a foundation embraced and built upon by the Roman Empire as it swept up Europe, including the Hellenic World in its conquests in the 1st century BC. In the meantime however, Greece, under Alexander, had become a capital of the East, and part of an empire. The idea that the later Orthodox or Eastern Christian cultural descendants of the Greek-speaking Eastern Roman empire, are a happy mean between Eastern slavishness and Western barbarism is promoted to this day, for example in Russia, creating a zone which is both Eastern and Western depending upon the context of discussion.

For about five hundred years, the Roman Empire maintained the Greek East and consolidated a Latin West, but an East-West division remained, reflected in many cultural norms of the two areas, including language. Although Rome, like Greece, was no longer democratic, the idea of democracy remained a part of the education of citizens, as if the emperors were a temporary emergency measure. Eventually the empire came to be increasingly officially split into a Western and Eastern part, reviving old ideas of a contrast between an advanced East, and a rugged West. In the Roman world one could speak of three main directions; North (Celtic tribes and Parthians), the East (lux ex oriente), and finally South which implied danger, historically via the Punic wars (Quid novi ex Africa?) The West was peaceful – it contained only the Mediterranean.

With the rise of Christianity in the midst of the Roman world, much of Rome's tradition and culture were absorbed by the new religion, and transformed into something new, which would serve as the basis for the development of Western civilization after the fall of Rome. Also, Roman culture mixed with the pre-existing Celtic, Germanic and Slavic cultures, which slowly became integrated into Western culture starting, mainly, with their acceptance of Christianity.

The Medieval West

The Medieval West was at its broadest the same as Christendom, including both the "Latin" or "Frankish" West, and the Orthodox Eastern part, where Greek remained the language of empire. More narrowly, it was Catholic (Latin) Europe. After the crowning of Charlemagne, this part of Europe was referred to by its neighbours in Byzantium and the Moslem world as "Frankish".

After the fall of Rome much of Greco-Roman art, literature, science and even technology were all but lost in the western part of the old empire, centered around Italy, and Gaul (France). However, this would become the centre of a new West. Europe fell into political anarchy, with many warring kingdoms and principalities. Under the Frankish kings, it eventually reunified and evolved into feudalism. Charlemagne was crowned Emperor of the Romans by the Pope in 800. His reign is associated with the Carolingian Renaissance, a revival of art, religion, and culture through the medium of the Catholic Church. Through his foreign conquests and internal reforms, Charlemagne helped define both Western Europe and the Middle Ages. He is numbered as Charles I in the regnal lists of France, Germany (where he is known as Karl der Große), and the Holy Roman Empire. The re-establishment of a Western "Roman" imperium challenged the status of the Eastern Roman Emperor in Constantinople and strained relations between Eastern and Western Europe. Much of the basis of the post-Roman cultural world had been set before the fall of the Empire, mainly through the integrating and reshaping of Roman ideas through Christian thought. The Greek and Roman paganism had been completely replaced by Christianity around the 4th and 5th centuries, since it became the official State religion following the baptism of emperor Constantine I. Roman Catholic Christianity and the Nicene Creed served as a unifying force in Western Europe, and in some respects replaced or competed with the secular authorities. Art and literature, law, education, and politics were preserved in the teachings of the Church, in an environment that, otherwise, would have probably seen their loss. The Church founded many cathedrals, universities, monasteries and seminaries, some of which continue to exist today. In the Medieval period, the route to power for many men was in the Church.

In a broader sense, the Middle Ages, with its tension between Greek reasoning and Levantine monotheism was not confined to the West but also stretched into the old East, in what was to become the Islamic world. The philosophy and science of Classical Greece was largely forgotten in Western and Northern Europe after the collapse of the Western Roman Empire, other than in isolated monastic enclaves (notably in Ireland, which had become Christian but which was never conquered by Rome). Although the Eastern Emperor Justinian (the last Emperor to speak Latin as a first tongue) closed the Academy in AD 529 (a date that is often cited as the end of Antiquity), the learning of Classical Antiquity was better preserved in the Byzantine Eastern Roman Empire, whose capital at Constantinople stood for another millennium, before being captured by the Ottoman Turks. Justinian's Corpus Juris Civilis Roman civil law code was preserved in the East and Constantinople maintained trade and intermittent political control over outposts such as Venice in the West for centuries. Classical Greek learning was also subsumed, preserved and elaborated in the rising Islamic world, which gradually supplanted Roman-Byzantine control over the Mediterranean, Middle East, North Africa, Iberia and even Greece itself-becoming a dominant cultural-political force in those regions. Thus, from the margins of the Roman world much of the learning of classical antiquity was slowly reintroduced to Western Europe in the centuries following the collapse of the Western Roman Empire. Irish missionaries such as St Columba propagated Christianity and latin learning in Western Europe during the Early Medieval Period and Byzantine Greeks and Islamic Arabs reintroduced texts from Antiquity to Western Europe during the Late Middle Ages and Renaissance of the 12th century.

The rediscovery of the Justinian Code in Western Europe early in the 10th century rekindled a passion for the discipline of law, which crossed many of the re-forming boundaries between East and West. Eventually, it was only in the Catholic or Frankish west, that Roman law became the foundation on which all legal concepts and systems were based. Its influence can be traced to this day in all Western legal systems (although in different manners and to different extents in the common (England) and the civil (continental European) legal traditions). The study of canon law, the legal system of the Catholic Church, fused with that of Roman law to form the basis of the refounding of Western legal scholarship. The ideas of civil rights, equality before the law, equality of women, procedural justice, and democracy as the ideal form of society were principles which formed the basis of modern Western culture.

The West actively encouraged the spreading of Christianity, which was inexorably linked to the spread of Western culture. Owing to the influence of Islamic culture and Islamic civilization — a culture that had preserved some of the knowledge of ancient Mesopotamia, Egypt, India, Persia, Greece, and Rome— in Islamic Spain and southern Italy, and in the Levant during the Crusades, Western Europeans translated many Arabic texts into Latin during the Middle Ages. Later, with the fall of

Constantinople and the Ottoman conquest of the Byzantine Empire, followed by a massive exodus of Greek Christian priests and scholars to Italian towns like Venice, bringing with them as many scripts from the Byzantine archives as they could, scholars' interest for the Greek language and classic works, topics and lost files was revived. Both the Greek and Arabic influences eventually led to the beginnings of the Renaissance. From the late 15th century to the 17th century, Western culture began to spread to other parts of the world by intrepid explorers and missionaries during the Age of Discovery, followed by imperialists from the 17th century to the early 20th century.

The Modern Era

Coming into the modern era, the historical understanding of the East-West contrast-as the opposition of Christendom to its geographical neighbours-began to weaken. As religion became less important, and Europeans came into increasing contact with far away peoples, the old concept of Western Culture began a slow evolution towards what it is today. The Early Modern "Age of Discovery" in the 15th, 16th and 17th centuries faded into the "Age of Enlightenment" continuing into the 18th, both characterized by the military advantages coming to Europeans from their development of firearms and other military technologies. The "Great Divergence" became more pronounced, making the West the bearer of science and the accompanying revolutions of technology and industrialisation. Western political thinking also eventually spread in many forms around the world. With the early 19th century "Age of Revolution" the West entered a period of World empires, massive economic and technological advance, and bloody international conflicts continuing into the 20th century. Religion in the meantime has waned considerably in Western Europe, where many are agnostic or atheist. Nearly half of the populations of the United Kingdom (44-54%), Germany (41-49%), France (43-54%) and the Netherlands (39-44%) are non-theist. However, religious belief in the United States is very strong, about 75-85% of the population, as also happens in most of Latin America.

As Europe discovered the wider world, old concepts adapted. The Islamic world which had formerly been considered "the

Orient" ("the East") more specifically became the "Near East" as the interests of the European powers for the first time interfered with Qing China and Meiji Japan in the 19th century. Thus, the Sino-Japanese War in 1894–1895 occurred in the "Far East", while the troubles surrounding the decline of the Ottoman Empire simultaneously occurred in the "Near East". The "Middle East" in the mid-19th century included the territory east of the Ottoman empire but West of China, i.e. Greater Persia and Greater India, but is now used synonymously with "Near East".

Politics

Despite the Western empires in the past, concepts of democracy and an emphasis on freedom has been seen as distinguishing Western peoples from non-western neighbours. In the Middle Ages and early modern times, the concept of a separation of Church and state developed, allowing for the development of more distinctive political norms, such as the doctrine of the separation of powers, which make modern Western democracy distinct from democracy in general.

In comparison to many other cultures in the world, western cultures tend to emphasize the individual. Much of this respect for difference and individual liberties remain, however, still theoretical, in many ways, among mainstream society, when the individual factor encounters a strong opposition from social customs and consensus, and thus resists to be accepted or understood. This situation, has tended to change among most progressive sectors of society, as a consequence of the many social and counter-cultural movements that the last decades have come to see. Creativity and the expression of the individual is commonly encouraged in Western culture. New subcultures, art and technology constantly emerge. Furthermore, capitalism which is found in almost every western country, supports a highly individualistic ideology.

The forms of government usually adopted in western societies, as a part of a wider, nowadays ruling social-economical liberal capitalist structure, are multi-party parliamentary or presidential (also 'congressional') systems selected by universal suffrage (a right first extended to include women in Australasia at the close of the 19th century), frequently referred to as *figurative* democracy, which favours some sort of majority consensus when coming to adopt collective decisions.

WIDESPREAD INFLUENCE

Elements of Western culture have had a very influential effect on other cultures worldwide. People of many cultures, both Western and non-Western, equate *modernization* (adoption of technological progress) with *westernization* (adoption of Western culture). Some members of the non-Western world have suggested that the link between technological progress and certain harmful Western values provides a reason why much of "modernity" should be rejected as being incompatible with their vision and the values of their societies. These types of argument referring to imperialism and stressing the importance of freedom from it and the relativist argument that different cultural norms should be treated equally, are also present in Western philosophy.

What is generally uncontested, is that much of the technology and social patterns which make up what is defined as "modernization" were developed in the Western world.

Music, Art, Story-telling and Architecture

Some cultural and artistic modalities are also characteristically Western in origin and form. While dance, music, visual art, story-telling, and architecture are human universals, they are expressed in the West in certain characteristic ways.

The symphony has its origins in Italy. Many important musical instruments used by cultures all over the world were also developed in the West; among them are the violin, piano, pipe organ, saxophone, trombone, clarinet, and the theremin. The solo piano, symphony orchestra and the string quartet are also important performing musical forms.

The ballet is a distinctively Western form of performance dance. The ballroom dance is an important Western variety of dance for the elite. The polka, the square dance, and the Irish step dance are very well-known Western forms of folk dance. Historically, the main forms of western music are European folk, choral, classical, country, rock and roll, hip-hop, and electronica.

While epic literary works in verse such as the Mahabarata and Homer's Iliad are ancient and occurred worldwide, the novel as a distinct form of story telling only arose in the West in the period 1200 to 1750. Photography and the motion picture as a technology and as the basis for entirely new art forms were also developed first in the West. The soap opera, a popular culture dramatic form originated in the United States first on radio in the 1930s, then a couple of decades later on television. The music video was also developed in the West in the middle of the twentieth century. Important western architectural motifs include the Doric, Corinthian, and Ionic columns, and the Romanesque, Gothic, Baroque, and Victorian styles are still widely recognised, and used even today, in the West. Much of Western architecture emphasises repetition of simple motifs, straight lines and expansive, undecorated planes. A modern ubiquitous architectural form that emphasizes this characteristic is the skyscraper, first developed in New York and Chicago.

Oil painting is said to have originated by Jan van Eyck, and perspective drawings and paintings had their earliest practitioners in Florence. In art, the Celtic knot is a very distinctive Western repeated motif. Depictions of the nude human male and female in photography, painting and sculpture are frequently considered to have special artistic merit. Realistic portraiture is especially valued. In Western dance, music, plays and other arts, the performers are only very infrequently masked. There are essentially no taboos against depicting God, or other religious figures, in a representational fashion. Many forms of popular music have been derived from African-Americans, and their innovations of jazz and blues serve as the basis from which much of modern popular music was derived. folklore and music during 20th and 19th centuries, initially by themselves, but later played and further developed together with White & Black Americans, British people, and Westerners in general. These include jazz, blues and rock music (that in a wider sense include the rock and roll and heavy metal genres), rhythm and blues, funk, techno as well as the ska and reggae genres from Jamaica. Several other related or derived styles were developed and introduced by western pop culture such as pop, metal and dance music.

Sport

Since Classical Antiquity, sport has been an important facet of Western cultural expression. A wide range of sports were already established by the time of Ancient Greece and the military culture and the development of sports in Greece influenced one another considerably. Sports became such a prominent part of their culture that the Greeks created the Olympic Games, which in ancient times were held every four years in a small village in the Peloponnesus called Olympia. Baron Pierre de Coubertin, a Frenchman, instigated the modern revival of the Olympic movement. The first modern Olympics were held at Athens in 1896. The Romans built immense structures such as the Colisseum in Rome to house their festivals of sport. The Romans exhibited a passion for blood sports, as in the infamous Gladiatorial battles which pitted contestants against one another in a fight to the death. The Olympic Games revived many of the sports of Classical Antiquity-such as Graeco-Roman wrestling, discus and javelin.

The sport of Bullfighting is a traditional spectacle of Spain, Portugal, southern France and some Latin American countries which traces its roots to prehistoric bull worship and sacrifice and is often linked to Rome, where many human-versus-animal events were held. Bullfighting spread from Spain to its Central and South American colonies, and in the 19th century to France, where it developed into a distinctive form in its own right. Jousting and hunting were popular sports in the Western Europe of the Middle Ages, and the aristocratic classes of Europe developed passions for leisure activities. A great number of the popular global sports were first developed or codified in Europe. The modern game of golf originated in Scotland, where the first written record of golf is James II's banning of the game in 1457, as an unwelcome distraction to learning archery. The Industrial Revolution which began in Britain in the 18th Century brought increased leisure time, leading to more time for citizens to attend and follow spectator sports, greater participation in athletic activities, and increased accessibility. These trends continued with the advent of mass media and global communication. The bat and ball sport of cricket was first played in England during the 16th century and was exported around the globe via the British Empire. A number of popular modern sports were devised or codified in Britain during the 19th Century and obtained global prominence-these include Ping Pong, modern tennis, Association Football, Netball and Rugby.

Football (also known as soccer) remains hugely popular in Europe but has grown from its origins to be known as the "world game". Similarly, sports such as cricket, rugby and netball were exported around the world, particularly among countries in the Commonwealth of Nations, thus India and Australia are among the strongest cricketing nations, while victory in the Rugby World Cup has been shared among the Western Nations of New Zealand, Australia, South Africa, France and England.

Australian Rules Football, an Australian variation of football with similarities to Gaelic football and rugby evolved in the British colony of Victoria in the mid-19th century. The United States also developed unique variations of English sports. English migrants took antecedants of baseball to America during the colonial period. The history of American football can be traced to early versions of rugby football and association football. Many games known as "football" were being played at colleges and universities in the United States in the first half of the 19th century American football resulted from several major divergences from rugby, most notably the rule changes instituted by Walter Camp, the "Father of American Football". Basketball was invented in 1891 by James Naismith, a Canadian physical education instructor working in Springfield, Massachusetts in the United States. From these American origins, basktball has grown to be on of the great international participation sports.

Professionalism in sport in the West became prevalent during the 20th Century, further adding to the increase in sport's popularity, as sports fans began following the exploits of professional athletes through radio, television, and the internet—all while enjoying the exercise and competition associated with amateur participation in sports.

Scientific and Technological Inventions and Discoveries

A feature of Western culture is its focus on science and technology, and its ability to generate new processes, materials and material artifacts. It was the West that first developed steam power and adapted its use into factories, and for the generation of electrical power. The electrical motor, dynamo, transformer, and electric light, and indeed most of the familiar electrical appliances, were inventions of the West. The Otto and the Diesel internal combustion engines are products whose genesis and early development were in the West. Nuclear power stations are derived from the first atomic pile constructed in Chicago in 1942.

Communication devices and systems including the telegraph, the telephone, radio, television, communication and navigation satellites, mobile phone, and the Internet were all invented by Westerners. The pencil, ballpoint pen, CRT, LCD, LED, photograph, photocopier, laser printer, ink jet printer, plasma display screen and world wide web were also invented in the West. Ubiquitous materials including concrete, aluminum, clear glass, synthetic rubber, synthetic diamond and the plastics polyethylene, polypropylene, PVC and polystyrene were invented in the West. Iron and steel ships, bridges and skyscrapers first appeared in the West. Nitrogen fixation and petrochemicals were invented by Westerners. Most of the elements, were discovered and named in the West, as well as the contemporary atomic theories to explain them.

The transistor, integrated circuit, memory chip, and computer were all first seen in the West. The ship's chronometer, the screw propeller, the locomotive, bicycle, automobile, and aeroplane were all invented in the West. Eyeglasses, the telescope, the microscope and electron microscope, all the varieties of chromatography, protein and DNA sequencing, computerised tomography, NMR, x-rays, and light, ultraviolet and infrared spectroscopy, were all first developed and applied in Western laboratories, hospitals and factories. In medicine, vaccination, anesthesia, and all the pure antibiotics were created in the West. The method of preventing Rh disease, the treatment of diabetes, and the germ theory of disease were discovered by Westerners. The eradication of that ancient scourge, smallpox, was led by a Westerner, Donald Henderson. Radiography, Computed tomography, Positron emission tomography and Medical ultrasonography are important diagnostic tools developed in the West.

Other important diagnostic tools of clinical chemistry including the methods of spectrophotometry, electrophoresis and immunoassay were first devised by Westerners. So were the stethoscope, electrocardiograph, and the endoscope. Vitamins, hormonal contraception, hormones, insulin, Beta blockers and ACE inhibitors, along with a host of other medically proven drugs were first utilised to treat disease in the West. The double-blind study and evidence-based medicine are critical scientific techniques widely used in the West for medical purposes.

In mathematics, calculus, statistics, logic, vector, tensor and complex analysis, group theory and topology were developed by Westerners. In biology, evolution, chromosomes, DNA, genetics and the methods of molecular biology are creatures of the West. In physics, the science of mechanics and quantum mechanics, relativity, thermodynamics, and statistical mechanics were all developed by Westerners. The discoveries and inventions by Westerners in electromagnetism include Coulomb's law (1785), the first battery (1800), the unity of electricity and magnetism (1820), Biot–Savart law (1820), Ohm's Law (1827), and the Maxwell's equations (1871). The atom, nucleus, electron, neutron and proton were all unveiled by Westerners.

In finance, double entry bookkeeping, the limited liability company, life insurance, and the charge card were all first used in the West. Westerners are also known for their explorations of the globe and space. The first expedition to circumnavigate the Earth (1522) was by Westerners, as well as the first to set foot on the South Pole (1911), and the first human to land on the moon (1969). The landing of robots on Mars (2004) and on an asteroid (2001), and the Voyager explorations of the outer planets (Uranus in 1986 and Neptune in 1989) were all achievements of Westerners.

Themes and Traditions

Western culture has developed many themes and traditions, the most significant of which are:

- Greco-Latin classic letters, arts, architecture, philosophical and cultural tradition, that include the influence of preeminent authors such as Plato, Aristotle, Homer, Herodotus, and Cicero, as well as a long mythologic tradition
- A tradition of the importance of the rule of law which has its roots in Ancient Greece.
- The Catholic and Protestant Christian cultural tradition and ethic.
- Secular humanism, rationalism and Enlightenment thought, as opposed to traditionally preeminent Catholicism and Protestant Christianity, religious and moral doctrines in lifestyle. Though such opposition has not fully ended, it set the basis for a new critical attitude and open questioning of religion, favouring freethinking and questioning of the church as an authority, which resulted in open-minded and reformist ideals inside, such as liberation theology, which partly adopted these currents, and secular and political tendencies such as laicism, agnosticism, materialism and atheism.
- Widespread usage of terms and specific vocabulary borrowed, based or derived from Greek and Latin roots or etymologies for almost any field of arts, science and human knowledge, becoming easily understandable and common to almost any European language, and being a source for inventing internationalized neologisms for nearly any purpose. It is not rare for full loan Latin phrases or expressions, such as *in situ*, *grosso modo* or *tempus fugit*, to be in usage, many of them giving name to artistic or literatic concepts or currents. The usage of such roots and phrases is standardized in giving official scientific names for biological species (such as *Homo sapiens* or *Tyrannosaurus rex*). This shows a reverence for these languages, called classicism.
- Generalized usage of some form of the Latin or Greek

alphabet. The latter includes the standard cases of Greece and other derived forms, such as Cyrillic, the case of those Slavic Eastern countries of Christian Orthodox tradition, historically under the Byzantine and later Russian czarist or Soviet area of influence. Other variants of it are encountered for Gothic and Coptic alphabets, that historically substituted older scripts, such as Runic, and Demotic or Hieroglyphic systems.

- Scholasticism.
- Renaissance arts and letters.
- Natural law, human rights, constitutionalism, parliamentarism (or presidentialism) and formal liberal democracy in recent times — prior to the 19th century, most Western governments were still monarchies.
- A large influence, in modern times, of many of the ideals and values developed and inherited from Romanticism
- Several subcultures (sometimes deriving into urban tribes) and countercultural movements, such as hippie lifestyle or New Age, that have left several influences on contemporary mainstream or subcultural tendencies (some of them, especially in the mainstream, can become merely aesthetic).

SCIENTIFIC CHARITY (CHARITY ORGANIZATION SOCIETIES)

Scientific charity built on Americans' notion of self-reliance, limited government, and economic freedom. Proponents of scientific charity shared the poorhouse advocates' goals of cutting relief expenses and reducing the number of able-bodied who were receiving assistance, as well as the moral reformers' goal of uplifting people from poverty through discipline and religious education via private charity. In this model, individuals responded to charity and the government stayed out of the economic sphere. Individuals were seen as rational actors who freely made decisions based on their own self-interest and who were responsible for how they fared economically. Scientific charity fit well with the post–Civil War concept of social

Darwinism, which held that humans were in competition and the strong survived and thrived while the weak did not. Not surprisingly, Charity Organization Societies were generally opposed to unions.

Two of the leading advocates for Charity Organization Societies were Josephine Lowell and S. Humphrey Gurteen. Lowell, who was from a radical abolitionist family, believed that idleness was a major cause of poverty, and she advocated giving those who requested relief a labour test (such as breaking stones or chopping wood) before they received private charity. During her life, she developed several principles to guide her social reform work.

One of her key principles was that "charity must tend to develop the moral nature of those it helps." Lowell opposed both local government relief and almsgiving (individual giving directly to the poor) since she felt this practice did not morally uplift the people and created dependency. She felt that charity agents and visitors could provide a personal relationship conducive to helping needy individuals instead of treating them as "cases." Lowell thought "that each case must be dealt with radically and a permanent means of helping it to be found, and that the best way to help people is to help them to help themselves."

Gurteen provided many practical ideas to implement organized Charity Organization Societies. Gurteen's plan was to have various groups already providing services to the poor coordinate their efforts.

There would be a central office that served as a charity clearinghouse where "friendly visitors" (COS agents) involved in investigating the poor would meet to compare notes to determine who was worthy of relief and who was an imposter. This collaboration would result in a complete registry of every person in the city who was receiving public or private assistance. The goal of this organized approach was to stop providing relief to the undeserving poor but continue to provide the deserving poor with the assistance to solve their own problems. Gurteen believed that COS would end outdoor relief, stop pauperism, and reduce poverty to its lowest possible level.

CHARITY ORGANIZATION SOCIETY

The Charity Organization Societies also called the Associated Charities was a private charity that existed in the late 19th and early 20th centuries as a clearing house for information on the poor. The society was mainly concerned with distinction between the deserving poor and undeserving poor. The society believed that giving out charity without investigating the problems behind poverty created a class of citizens that would always be dependent on alms giving. The society originated in Elberfeld, Germany and spread to Buffalo, New York around 1877. The conviction that relief promoted dependency was the basis for forming the Societies. Instead of offering direct relief, the societies addressed the cycle of poverty. Neighbourhood charity visitors taught the values of hard work and thrift to individuals and families. The COS set up centralized records and administrative services and emphasized objective investigations and professional training. There was a strong scientific emphasis as the charity visitors organized their activities and learned principles of practice and techniques of intervention from one another. The result led to the origin of social casework. Gradually, over the ensuing years, volunteer visitors began to be supplanted by paid staff.

Charity Organization Societies were made up of charitable groups that used scientific philanthropy to help poor, distressed or deviant persons. The Societies considered themselves more than just alms givers. Their ultimate goal was to restore as much self-sufficiency and responsibility as an individual could manage. Through their activities, the Societies tended to be aware of the range of social services available in their communities. They thus became the primary source of information and referral for all services. Through these referrals, a Society often became the central agency in the social services of its community. For instance, the Charity Organization Society of Denver, Colorado, the forerunner of the modern United Way of America, coordinated the charitable activities of local Jewish, Congregational and Catholic groups. Its work under the leadership of Frances Wisebart Jacobs ranged from work with tuberculosis patients to the care and education of young children and was funded in part by direct assistance from the city itself.

The Charity Organization Society movement can be compared to the settlement house movement which emphasized social reform rather than personal problems as the proper focus of charity.

Britain's Charity Organisation Society

In Britain, the Charity Organisation Society led by Helen Bosanquet and Octavia Hill was founded in London in 1869 and supported the concept of self help and limited government intervention to deal with the effects of poverty. The organisation claimed to use "scientific principles to root out scroungers and target relief where it was most needed". The Charity Organisation Society was renamed Family Welfare Association in 1946 and still operates today as Family Action, a registered family support charity.

THE ROLE OF DEVELOPMENT SKILLS IN SOCIAL WORK PRACTICE

In this article our perspective is to discuss the intensification and perspectives of development work in the social sector in Finland and the question of social work skills in relation to the development in practice. Within the last decades Finland has experienced far reaching changes in relation to development work and social planning. What are the implications of this development for the master's degree programmes in social work? This forms the context in which we as members of the team of social work educators have been planning our social work curriculum in Pori which has started in autumn 2004. The Department of Pori was founded in 2004 as part of the Faculty of Social Sciences at the University of Tampere. The department offers master's degree programmes in social work as well as in social policy and sociology. The City of Pori, which is located on the western coast of Finland, represents a new location of social work teaching in Finland. Instead of a single university Pori has the Pori University Consortium , in which five different Finnish universities and different fields are presented with 2400 students and 190 staff members.

The Pori University Consortium has expressly regional targets. The many-sided development and raising the competitive potential of the Satakunta region by increasing the academic know-how are the reasons why the city of Pori promotes university education. The Department of Pori at Tampere University gives high priority to questions of welfare services and working life. This follows the development plan the city of Pori has been supporting through different projects and the funding of the professorship on welfare services for five years. In this context the education of qualified social workers (master in social work) and experts in welfare services is a new challenge.

TRENDS OF DEVELOPMENT WORK IN THE FINNISH SOCIAL SECTOR

The discussion of development work in the social sector has been very active during the last decade in Finland. The concept of development work can be defined in relation to social planning. We understand development work as a new trend of state politics to promote social welfare affairs. It represents a different orientation for example compared to centralized social planning politics which were very much the case during the 1960's and 1970's. On the other hand development work can be understood as an instrument of steering when new practices and services are needed and new social problems emerge.

If we look back we can see that the entire concept of development work has changed. It has become more difficult to define the whole concept because it has become wider and more blurred. The idea of development work as specialized work towards new products, processes or practices has changed. Instead development work has become an everyday practice which happens everywhere. Almost everything can be understood as development work. The idea of development work as a way to search for innovations also changes when development work is taken more as a tool for political and administrative steering. In the Finnish context the municipalities are responsible for organizing and developing social services at the local level – e.g. fitting the demands of laws and national standards to the local practices . The municipalities have also an active role in identifying social problems and finding innovative solutions. During the 1990's projects have become a very widely used tool of development work. They are used as a way to promote change and innovations – but at the same time they are used to fund basic work which is organized in a project-mode.

In the social sector the strong role of the state and the whole public sector has always been characteristic in Finland. This means that the organization, directions and funding comes mostly from the state. Inside this strong state control we find different periods of how social planning and development work have been organized. Past decades can be described as a pendulum of state direction. Next we give a description of the main trends of these periods.

Centralized Steering and Control

The period from the early 1970's to 1993 can be characterized as a time of growing state welfare in Finland. Especially the 1970's can be described as a period of strong and centralized steering and planning ideology. During this period laws and norms together with economic and resource steering were the main state instruments to direct and at the same time to develop the social sector. The state social planning was accompanied by strong control by the state. The economic and resource steering was strongly connected to the detailed local plans which were a prerequisite to get state funding. Besides the law the most visible form of normative steering were different regulations and official instructions the Finnish National Board of Social Welfare used to give. These regulations were followed by all municipalities. The planning and development work happened mainly at the top level (central government) of the system and the instructions distributed were the same for all municipalities. Local development happened under strong state direction and control.

Deregulation and Local Self-determination

In Finland like in other western countries during the 1980's the discussion of decentralization of decision making, responsiveness to citizens and a service attitude by the administration increased. In practice this meant different deregulation projects and the abolition of norms. In the Finnish case after 1993 the steering and control functions of the state were severely reduced. On the one hand this happened by the closing of the National Board of Social Welfare. It was replaced by the National Research and Development Centre for Welfare and Health with a new kind of orientation. This change meant the weakening of normative steering and replacing it by steering through information as a new instrument for indirect steering and development. An emphasis on quality, horizontal learning, benchmarking etc. was introduced and implemented.

On the other hand the role of the state was weakened by the state subsidy reform in 1993 which enhanced the independence of the local governments. The leading idea was to strengthen the decision-making of the municipalities and enhance efficiency and profitability by granting them one total sum of state money to organize all the services. It was understood that the situations and the circumstances in the municipalities in different parts of the country varied. So the municipalities had a free hand and they were in charge of the organisation of services as they best fitted to the local situations. At the same time municipalities got the responsibility for the local development work. So the use of economic steering instruments changed dramatically and the municipal boards got a new role in decision making. The 1990s economic recession in Finland coincided with the process of weakening the state direction of social affairs. At the local level this meant that development work was almost totally cut in many municipalities. Additionally welfare services were very much narrowed. The great idea of local democracy as a tool of development turned to the democratic cutting down of local welfare services.

Characteristic of the 1990's situation in Finland was the unbalanced regional development. In this situation some municipalities or groups of them kept active as so-called forerunner or visionary municipalities (Kokko 2002, 58) and some municipalities totally dropped out of development work and tried to manage and pursue only their compulsory duties. At the same time non-governmental organisations became one significant actor of development projects. The development model of this deregulation period could be described as a disjointed-model. Political dissatisfaction with this situation of deregulation and the absence of steering tools led to new attempts to grant special services in social welfare. The new so-called earmarked state subsidies were directed to most critical services like child protection, work with mentally disabled, mental health work and welfare for substance abusers. (Heikkilä 2004.)

The disappearance of the traditional planning culture made room for a new kind of project culture as a forum for development during the 1990's. New funding possibilities e.g. through EU-programs encouraged different local actors to co-operate and to start and develop project work. The volume of the different development projects has been so huge that it led to project chaos and also to a sense of exhaustion with projects at the local level. A step forward was the attempt of local actors to combine different development projects to larger entities.

STATE-PROMOTED DEVELOPMENT NETWORKS

At the beginning of the 2000's the relation of steering and development is again re-conceptualised. There seems spread a longing for the old social planning approach and a search for new instruments as well. It has been said that the closing of the National Boards on Social Welfare and Health at the beginning of the 1990's was a mistake. A new kind of regulation and control seems to be required after the decade of decentralization and deregulation. Another discussion concerning the instruments of steering has lately been concentrated on strengthening the fundamental and social rights of citizens which are grounded in the constitution. The main elements of this new philosophy of steering are adequate state funding, the right of citizens to obtain services, and minimum standards for the quality of services.

Besides these discussions the state has launched new large development programs in the field of social and welfare affairs as well as in other fields of the public sector. Development programs can be seen as a new instrument of strategic management besides other more traditional instruments like management by results and planning. The orientation of development work in the context of the 2000's has changed again. We could call the 2000's the network-decade or the companionship-decade. The organization of the development work is somehow again state directed. Now the state very strongly directs the special funding for the development work done in different networks. This means that different companionships or networks of municipalities are necessary to get funding for larger development projects. The third sector as well as the Universities with social work programmes and the Polytechnics with social services programmes are integrated into the local and regional development work. This establishes a new form of co-operation between research, education and the field of practice which is a dominant feature of changes taking place also in the other Nordic countries.

The new development work model is embedded in the National Development Project for Social Services in Finland . Finland has launched this programme to reform its social services during 2003-2007. The purpose is to enhance the entire comprehensive service system. Along with the national programme to reform health care, this programme is one of the most important projects of the present government. A key issue is to improve the availability and quality of services. Besides these programmes the state has also launched new structures for development work. 2001 saw the opening of eight regional Social and welfare centres of expertise which cover the whole of Finland. The task of these centres is to network in their county areas and promote development work by bringing together different actors from practice, education and research. The structure and tasks of these centres are based on law and they are funded by the state. An example of the resources for this new kind of development work are government grants to the joint projects, for example of regional development units in specific fields.

We have outlined the main phases of the Finnish development during the last decades. The last one, the network model, represents a new orientation, which is very much promoted by the state. In this phase the practice does not equal the theoretical model. There are lively networks, networks that are forming and networks which ought to be organized. A critical question is if this networking is the best way to organize services and promote development. Co-operation takes much time, it is not always the most effective way to organize things. Also the basic level municipal social work and social services may stay outside the development done in special settings. This model has many possibilities but it can also restrict different new efforts and lead to over-standardisation. Compared to the top-down –model the direction of social planning is now no longer clear. The best or most important knowledge is no longer accumulated at the top level. Instead local practices and networks are important fields for knowledge production, leading to good practices and development. The direction of the steering by information does not happen only centrally from the top down. Instead local networks are steering themselves and other equals by means of information dissemination. They control and evaluate their own practices and negotiate to different directions. In this situation we could at least ask if we are moving closer to so called-knowledge intensive organizations which are more familiar in the business world.

DEVELOPMENT SKILLS AND SOCIAL WORK EDUCATION

Social work education in Finland has a diverse history beginning from the late 1800's. During the past decades different (lower and higher) degrees provided the qualification of professional social worker. The period before the 2nd World War was the time for first steps in social work education with different short courses and early stages of vocational training. After the 2nd Worl War, during the 1940's the vocational training of professional social workers was launched. Bachelor-level training was established although parallel to this there existed still different short courses due to the shortage of workers in the field. The scope of this education was to train social welfare officials with a good knowledge of law according to the requirements of municipalities. In a process that started already in the 1960's social work developed as an academic dicipline. At first it happened as a part of social policy programmes. Since the year 2000 social work has been an independent academic dicipline at six universities .

At present we are beginning a new historical phase. Since August 1st 2005 Finland has a new competence law (Laki 272/ 2005), which prescribes the educational qualifications for different tasks in social work and social services. According to this new law the qualification for a professional social worker is the master degree in social work as a major subject or master degree in another major subject and social work as minor subject which are together comparable to studies in social work as a major subject. This new law follows the practice of social work education established since 1999 in Finland.

How does practice reflect this competence law? In the field the educational background of professional social workers varies. There is variation at first because of the different training generations of social workers. Secondly there is variation because of the shortage of educated professional social workers; someone has to do the job and municipalities are forced to hire non-qualified substitutes.

Social Work as a Context of Development Skills

Historically and roughly speaking social work has two traditions: (1) client or case work and group work orientation and (2) structural social work and community work orientation. The first operates mainly with individuals and groups in their surroundings. The latter operates at political and policy level to change contexts, environments and social structures. Traditionally in Finland social work practice has operated mainly within the first one and with secondary emphasis on the local community policy level. Hence management, leadership and development skills have not been emphasised within the field of social work. A requirement for these skills was strongly brought about with the growth of the network-model in the social sector. Today it is seen that development and management work pervades all social work areas: individual, community and structural matters. It has to do with organizing and managing services and processes. Assessment and development processes both in individual life situations and structural matters are core functions of social work.

In Finnish social work education two major topics are emphasized: professional skills in the direct work with client and scientific research skills. There are several reasons for this. Client work skills e.g. social work methods, interaction skills, group work skills and community work skills are needed to operate as a social worker in municipal, governmental and civic society organisations and settings. As a university subject among other subjects in the social sciences social work education emphasizes also research skills. Majoring in social work is compatible to other social science subjects. Holders of Masters of Social Work possess basic knowledge and skills to work as a researcher in a research institution or in a university department or other research settings and to practice post graduate studies.

New challenges for social work education have been raised in many contemporary discussions and processes. The reform of the degree structure in 2005 in Finland following the European Bologna process has set new challenges for education. Among others one task for broader consideration is the focus on skills for the working life. Beside the Bologna process social work educators have faced other expectations also. These expectations have several sources.

Firstly Finland experienced a deep recession and cost cuts in the 1990's. Accordingly there was a shortage of social work development and leadership skills.

Secondly towards the 2000's several actors including the Ministry of Social Affairs and Health, the Ministry of Education and the Union of Professional Social Workers emphasised development and leadership skills in the social sector. And thirdly there is a vivid discussion over the administrative planning and reform model in the social sector in the direction of New Public Management, the provider-purchaser split, network skills and process management.

There have been some educational responses to these expectations. Universities have improved curriculum contents. Different educational institutes produced separate leadership education programmes and extension studies. Some polytechnics constructed higher degree programs and universities created professional licentiate studies and developed post graduate degree study courses on the matter. Also in the Pori team we deliberated how to respond to the demands for wide expertise and field experience: How to educate project work skills, development skills and leadership skills alongside with client work and research skills?

Structure of the Master Degree in Social Work

We present the Finnish structure of social work education. According to the Bologna process Finland follows the two-cycle degree system since 1.8.2005. Despite this two-cycle system we take new students to the universities straight to the master programmes and they are assumed to take both the bachelor and master level degree.

We have some special master programmes too but there is no intake to the bachelor studies only. On the bachelor programme the studies consist of basic studies and intermediate studies of social work. In addition there are common studies for social scientists, language studies and studies in minor subjects. The master programme concentrates on deepening the knowledge and skills in the main subject. Master thesis studies form about half of the whole master studies.

The content of social work major studies can be divided into four main themes which run through both the bachelor and masters programmes. The first one is social work theory. The second one consists of different fields of social work and of organizational questions. The third theme is professional skills in social work and the fourth is research methods and research skills in social work. We see these four fields as the principal elements of the social work programmes in Finland. In practice there is some variation and different emphasis in the social work programmes at six different Finnish universities.

Social Work Skills in the Pori Curriculum

Social work professional skills are taught at all educational levels. At the basic level there is an introductory course to social work skills called Openings to social work profession (3 credits). This first year course reflects self-knowledge through group work and interactive methods. At the intermediate level the emphasis is on client, case and group work skills. There are several courses on professional social work skills mainly during the second year of the bachelor studies. The courses are Introduction to Social Law, Practical Skills of Social Work, Methods of Practical Social Work, Seminar of Practical Skills and Practice Education (all together 20 credits).

At the master level the focus is on the development and management of social work processes and social services in organisations including supporting multidisciplinary studies (15 credits). The aims are to advance theoretical knowledge and to develop practice skills by combining the development skills studies and ongoing development process in an organization. Students participate in ongoing development projects for two months. Development practice can be divided into three phases: planning, implementing and evaluating. Students participate in one or several phases of an ongoing development work in practice and they are supervised by a university teacher and a practice teacher. They report the phase of the ongoing development project and reflect on theoretical elements concerning the ongoing process. As a part of their practical training the students report also their individual involvements in three phases: planning, implementing and evaluating. The development project and the students' reports are discussed in a joint seminar.

WHAT IS A CLINICAL SOCIAL WORKER?

Clinical social workers must have a master's or doctorate degree in social work, with an emphasis on clinical experience. They must undergo a supervised clinical field internship and have at least 2 years of postgraduate supervised clinical social work employment. Clinical social workers are approved providers in most insurance and managed care plans, and practice in the following settings:

- Private practice
- Medical facilities (e.g., hospitals)
- Mental health clinics
- Child welfare agencies
- Schools
- Community organizations
- Places of employment.

Clinical social workers may be licensed by the state in which they practice. Requirements are prescribed by state law and include education, supervision, experience, and a written examination.

SOCIAL ECOLOGICAL MODEL

The Social Ecology Model, also called Social Ecological Perspective, is a framework to examine the multiple effects and interrelatedness of social elements in an environment. SEM can provide a theoretical framework to analyze various contexts in multiple types of research and in conflict communication. Social ecology is the study of people in an environment and the influences on one another (Hawley, 1950). This model allows for the integration of multiple levels and contexts to establish the *big picture* in conflict communication. Research that focuses on any one level underestimates the effects of other contexts. SEM is primarily a qualitative research model to conduct field observations; however, it has and can also be utilized in experimental settings.

History

There are several adaptations of the Social Ecological Model; however, the initial and most utilized version is Urie Bronfenbrenner's (1977, 1979) *Ecological Systems Theory* which divides factors into four levels: macro-, exo-, meso-, and micro-, which describe influences as intercultural, community, organizational, and interpersonal or individual. Traditionally many research theorists have considered only a dichotomy of perspectives, either micro (individual behaviour) or macro (media or cultural influences). Bronfenbrenner's perspective (1979) was founded on the person, the environment, and the continuous interaction of the two. This interaction constantly evolved and developed both components. However, Bronfenbrenner realized it was not only the environment directly affecting the person, but that there were layers in between, which all had resulting impacts on the next level. His research began with the primary purpose of understanding human development and behaviour. Bronfenbrenner's work was an extension from Kurt Lewin's (1935) classic equation showing that behaviour is a function of the person and the environment.

Bronfenbrenner (1979) considered the individual, organization, community, and culture to be nested factors, like Russian dolls. Each echelon operates fully within the next larger sphere. Although Bronfenbrenner first coined the phrase

Ecological Systems Theory, it is necessary to mention that Amos H. Hawley (1950) conducted a significant amount of research in this field as well, along with many other philosophers, including his colleague, R. D. McKenzie. Hawley's work on the "interrelatedness of life" in his book, *Human Ecology* (1950), was grounded in Charles Darwin's writings on the "web of life".

Conceptual Framework

SEM is essentially a *Systems Theory* approach to understanding development that occurs in various spheres due to actions in different systems. There are many effects that occur from cross-level influences and relationships between and among levels that SEM addresses. Relationships include parallels or isomorphisms and discontinuities or cross-level effects. The single direction arrows indicate cross-level effects, whereas the circular arrows indicate isomorphisms or discontinuities.

SPHERES OF INFLUENCE

Micro-

Microsystems consist of individual or interpersonal features and those aspects of groups that comprise the social identity (Gregson, 2001) which may include roles that a person plays (i.e. mother, father, sister, brother, child, etc.) or characteristics they have in common. These interpersonal attributes are strong as to how an individual perceives oneself. These qualities and factors can be learned, as in membership to a group, but many are ingrained (e.g., ethnicity, gender). In the interpersonal sphere, there are also many components of the individual, including psychological and cognitive factors, like personality, knowledge, beliefs (Gregson, 2001). The individual in his or her own microsystem is constantly shaped, not only by the environment, but by any encounter or other individual they come in contact with. This *shaping* is well explored in child development, as it would be unreasonable to believe a child is solely a product of the societal environment. There are multiple, simultaneous influences in child behaviour and learning including culture, school, teacher, parental support and education level, involvement in extracurricular activities, etc. Examples of microsystems outside the self also include groups of friends, family, unorganized athletics, or social clubs.

Meso-

Mesosystems are the organizational or institutional factors that shape or structure the environment within which the individual and interpersonal relations occur (Gregson, 2001). These aspects can be rules, policies, and acceptable business etiquette within a more formal organization. There are some organizations that foster entirely different atmospheres than other corporations, i.e. Google, where employees may wear pajamas to the office. The organizational component is especially influential with younger, more impressionable employees, as it helps to shape the ethics and expectations of a typical organization for these individuals. Examples include schools, companies, churches, and sports teams. Mesosystems are essentially the norm forming component of a group or organization, and the individual is an active participant in this group or organization. Bronfenbrenner (1979) also claimed that the richer the medium for communication in this system, the more influential it is on the microsystem.

Exo

Exosystems refer to the community level influence, including fairly established norms, standards, and social networks (Gregson, 2001). There will likely be many organizations and interpersonal relationships that compose the community, and this web of organizations and relationships creates the community. The community is larger than the meso-; however, it is considerably smaller than the respective nation or culture it composes. The community level in a geographic sense, for example, may be Midwestern or Iowan, while the next level up (macro) would be an American. However, it does not have to be associated with any physical or spatial relationships. Another example could be membership in special interest groups or political affiliations. Exosystems are essentially any setting which affects the individual, although the individual is not required to be an active participant (Bronfenbrenner, 1979).

Macro-

Macrosystems are the cultural contexts (Bronfenbrenner, 1979), not solely geographically or physically, but emotionally and ideologically. These influences are more easily seen than the other factors, mainly due to the magnitude of the impact. Examples of significant intercultural effects include Communism, Western culture, Military, Islam, and Christianity. For instance, the macrosystem of Communism is a Marxist philosophy that believes that wealth should be shared in the macrosystem. A Communist country, such as Cuba (exo), governs and regulates the environment within which corporations (meso) and society or individuals (micro) exist. Media plays a significant role on all levels, as it communicates information and assists in the development of expectations for all individuals in the respective culture.

Isomorphisms & Discontinuities

Isomorphisms are parallels in the impact on one level and the resulting impact on another level (Oetzel, Ting-Toomey, & Rinderle, 2006). Researchers studying isomorphic models expect to see an equal effect in both magnitude and direction when at least one influence level shifts. Discontinuities are essentially the antonym of isomorphisms. A discontinuity is an effect on one level or group which produces an unequal, potentially in the opposite direction, impact on at least one more level.

CROSS-LEVEL EFFECTS

Top-down Effects

The consideration of top-down effects (McLeroy et al., 1988; Stokols, 1996) establishes that environmental effects shape individual behaviour. The nested factors are essentially influenced by the external influences that embody these factors. Community and organizational factors often determine how individuals will respond in crisis situations. There is a program called OK-FIRST, which is an outreach project of the Oklahoma Climatological Survey and the Oklahoma Mesonet to educate the community and public officials to help individuals respond in the appropriate way during a weather-related risk. Ethnicity and historical relationships also shape individual conflict behaviour. This is obviously true in many situations observed in the conflict in the Middle East. The media additionally plays a significant role in reinforcing these stereotypes. Top-down effects are essentially the most prominent of any of the social ecological components.

Bottom-up Effects

Bottom-up effects describe how individuals or community affect higher levels, as in how individuals form alliances or coalitions to accomplish personal goals. There is also an impact in cultures due to global corporations' presence in some countries. For instance, Google China has increased the accessibility of information to reach a wider audience in a Communist nation. Guerrero and La Valley (2006) recognize emotions are caused by feelings (i.e. anger, guilt, jealousy, greed, etc.) and that these feelings impact events likely to occur. The psychological instability of the shooter in the Virginia Tech incident demonstrates microcosms affecting macrocosms.

Interactive Effects

Interactive effects are interdependent and occur simultaneously at multiple levels. For instance in culturally diverse workgroups, there would likely be conflicts between group members, interaction effects in completing the goal of workgroup for the organization, and some learning at the individual level. Another excellent question from Oetzel, Ting-Toomey, & Rinderle (2006) is what role does technology play in cultures, organizations, community, and interpersonal conflicts? McLeroy et al. noted that the "ecological perspective implies reciprocal causation between the individual and the environment" which essentially defines interactive effects.

Empirical Studies

Stanford Prison Experiment In Zimbardo's experiment in 1971, they randomly assigned subjects to be either prison guards or prisoners. This *prison* was actually a basement at Stanford University, and the subjects were actually volunteers who responded to a newspaper advertisement. Essentially the study was conducted to observe the interpersonal dynamics in a prison environment. The individuals immediately began to take their respective roles very seriously, almost as a self-fulfilling prophecy. The prisoners rioted, and the guards hassled and intimidated the prisoners to *maintain* order. Applying the Social Ecological Model, top-down and interactive effects created groups that were very unlike the individuals within the mesosystems. It is difficult to believe that all of the individuals involved in the study were truly sadistic or rebellious prior to the experiment.

Milgram Experiment Stanley Milgram's studies were conducted in 1961-1962 at Yale on subjects that answered a newspaper advertisement. The objective of his research was to observe the power of authority in following orders (Milgram, 1963). This experiment was conducted in response to the beginning of the Eichmann trials. Adolf Eichmann was a high ranking officer of the Nazi Party. He was on trial for war crimes and crimes against humanity. Was he simply following orders? In Milgram's experiment the subjects were assigned to the role as the "teacher" and were required to administer a shock to the "student" to facilitate learning. The "teacher" was ordered to administer increasing and almost fatal electric shocks to the "student" whenever they proved an incorrect response. The experimenter sat in the same room as the "teacher" and observed the learning process.

In actuality, the "student" was actually a researcher and no real electric shock was ever administered. These studies demonstrated that individuals can easily be persuaded to inflict harm if they are ordered to do so. These individuals were a product of the mesosystems they participated in.

SEM Applications in Multiple Contexts

Below are only a few of the abundant contexts in which the SEM could be applied. SEM applied to a problem or situation can provide a vivid, detailed snapshot or framework to analyze the inputs on various levels and the resulting impacts.

Corporate Ethics

In the midst of corporate scandals, many conflicts are implicit, while some are explicit. The existence of multiple stakeholders, including company leadership, employees, shareholders, and customers has tended to blur the corporate mission and increase conflict. There are many interactive and cross-level effects when observing a corporation from an external perspective. Many corporations feel as though their duty is to create financial value for the shareholders, while they still have a responsibility to the customers. In some industries, it is difficult to discern when the loyalty is shifted too far towards shareholders or employees in lieu of the customers. The operating environment (or what other companies were doing) had created some of the ambiguity in corporate ethics in the late 1990's. There was obviously a requirement for a higher prevalence of regulatory authorities and consumer advocacy groups (consumer protection) due to some inappropriate and unethical decisions. The decision to require Sarbanes-Oxley compliance is an excellent example of how individuals and organizations created a need for increased regulation in a bottom-up approach.

Economics

Geographic or environmental determinism, conceived by Ellsworth Huntington, is an economic theory that is highly dependent on the ecological environment and geography. Essentially from a top-down approach, the environment dictates a considerable amount to the lifestyle of the individual and the economy of the country. If the region is mountainous or arid and there is little land for agriculture, the country typically will not prosper as much as another country. The theory fundamentally states economics, human habits, and cultural characteristics are shaped by geography. In Neoclassical economics, output is a function of natural resources, human resources, capital resources, and technology (Alfred Marshall, 1890). Technology is a direct effect of an entrepreneurial mind or individual. This would indicate that there are also bottom-up effects in economics.

Risk Communication

When a natural disaster or risk occurs, what is the best way to ensure the safety of all individuals which may potentially be affected? The SEM could assist the researcher to analyze the timing of when the information is received and identify the receivers and stakeholders. This situation is an environmental influence that may be very far reaching. The individual's education level, understanding, and affluence may dictate what information he or she receives and processes and through which medium. If the information receiver actually alters the context of the message and medium to communicate more appropriately with the individual stakeholders, this would be a bottom-up effect.

Health

There are many ecological factors that potentially improve or harm a personal's physical health. To prevent illnesses, a person should avoid an environment in which they may be more susceptible to contracting a virus or where there immune system would be weakened. This also includes possibly removing oneself from a workgroup or organization if there are breathing or inhalation risks (i.e. toxic pollutants, passive smoking) or avoiding a sick coworker. Some environments are particularly conducive to health benefits. Surrounding yourself with physically fit people will potentially motivate you to become more active, diet, or work out at the gym. The government banning trans fat may have a positive top-down effect on the health of all individuals in that state or country. There have been many studies done on obesity prevention, and everything from access to parks and playgrounds to cultural norms to self-efficacy affect the tendency for an individual to become obese.

Political Conflict

The act of politics is making decisions, and playing politics is all about appeasing all the parties involved while still reaching the ultimate goal. A decision may be required of an individual, organization, community, or country. A decision a congressman makes affects anyone in his or her jurisdiction. If one makes decision not to vote for the President of the United States, one has given oneself no voice in the election. If many other individuals choose not to voice their opinion and/or vote, they have inadvertently allowed a majority of others to make the decision for them. On the international level, if the leadership of the U.S. decides to occupy a country in the Middle East, it not only affects the leadership. It also affects U.S. service members, their families, and the communities they come from. If the U.S. is spending money on a political conflict, the value of the U.S. dollar may be adversely affected. There are multiple cross-level and interactive effects of a decision. As the action of one jihadist may potentially disrupt the lives of hundreds of service members, their respective families, the unit to which they belong, the community, and the nation.

ECOLOGICAL SYSTEMS THEORY

Ecological Systems Theory, also called Development in Context or Human Ecology theory, specifies four types of nested environmental systems, with bi-directional influences within and between the systems.

Urie Bronfenbrenner is generally regarded as one of the world's leading scholars in the field of developmental psychology. His Ecological Systems Theory holds that development reflects the influence of several environmental systems, and it identifies five environmental systems:

- *Micro system:* The setting in which the individual lives. These contexts include the person's family, peers, school, and neighbourhood. It is in the micro system that the most direct interactions with social agents take place; with parents, peers, and teachers, for example. The individual is not a passive recipient of experiences in these settings, but someone who helps to construct the settings.
- *Mesosystem:* Refers to relations between microsystems or connections between contexts. Examples are the relation of family experiences to school experiences, school experiences to church experiences, and family experiences to peer experiences. For example, children whose parents have rejected them may have difficulty developing positive relations with teachers.
- *Exosystem:* Involves links between a social setting in which the individual does not have an active role and the individual's immediate context. For example, a husband's or child's experience at home may be influenced by a mother's experiences at work. The mother might receive a promotion that requires more

travel, which might increase conflict with the husband and change patterns of interaction with the child.

- *Macrosystem:* Describes the culture in which individuals live. Cultural contexts include developing and industrialized countries, socioeconomic status, poverty, and ethnicity.
- *Chronosystem:* The patterning of environmental events and transitions over the life course, as well as sociohistorical circumstances. For example, divorces is one transition. Researchers have found that the negative effects of divorce on children often peak in the first year after the divorce. By two years after the divorce, family interaction is less chaotic and more stable. As an example of sociohistorical circumstances, consider how the opportunities for women to pursue a career have increased during the last thirty years."

The person's own biology may be considered part of the microsystem; thus the theory has recently sometimes been called "Bio-Ecological Systems Theory." Per this theoretical construction, each system contains roles, norms and rules which may shape psychological development. For example, an inner-city family faces many challenges which an affluent family in a gated community does not, and vice versa. The inner-city family is more likely to experience environmental hardships, such as teratogens and crime. On the other hand the sheltered family is more likely to lack the nurturing support of extended family.

Since its publication in 1979, Bronfenbrenner's major statement of this theory, *The Ecology of Human Development* has had widespread influence on the way psychologists and others approach the study of human beings and their environments. As a result of his groundbreaking work in "human ecology", these environments — from the family to economic and political structures — have come to be viewed as part of the life course from childhood through adulthood. Bronfenbrenner has identified Soviet developmental psychologist Lev Vygotsky and German-born psychologist Kurt Lewin as important influences on his theory.

Bronfenbrenner's work provides one of the foundational elements of the Ecological counselling Perspective, as espoused by Robert K. Conyne, Ellen Cook, and the University of Cincinnati Counselling Program. There are many different theories related to human development. The ecological theory emphasizes environmental factors as playing the major role to development. This theory does in fact vary from culture to culture.

WHAT IS JUDEO-CHRISTIANISM?

Judeo-Christianism is an ideology which seeks to impose Judeo-Christian religious values on Europe. Judeo-Christians seek to destroy the freedom of conscience: they want the state to enforce a single, homogenous Judeo-Christian culture. Typically, they want the Judeo-Christian culture constitutionally specified, as the sole national culture. They also tried to alter the (now-abandoned) European Constitution in the same way.

Judeo-Christianism is similar to Islamism, which it so often opposes. The religious basis is different, but the goals and tactics are often equivalent. Both are ideologies, and seek a specific transformation of society. Both are by definition political. Some Jews regard Judaism as a private religion. Some Christians regard Christianity as a private religion. 'Judeo-Christian values' on the other hand, exist *only* in the context of state and society. There is no private Judeo-Christian belief. There is, as yet, no 'Judeo-Christian religion'. The religious foundation of the ideology derives from two separate religions. Without *both* these religions, Judeo-Christianism would not exist. The Dutch populist Geert Wilders is a typical exponent of Judeo-Christianism. He has proposed re-writing Article 1 of the Dutch Constitution, to declare that national values are 'Judeo-Christian'. (Its present version forbids discrimination, although it has no direct application in law). Wilders has often restated this proposal, and now demands that all other EU countries should adopt similar constitutional provisions. He sees this as the legal foundation for repressive measures against non-Judeo-Christian elements. His prime targets are Islam, Islamic institutions, and Muslims, but he also suggests measures against "cultural relativists". For instance, he proposed legislation against halal meat: not the Muslims who ate it would be guilty of a criminal offence, but those who served or sold it.

Wilders' suspicion of multiculturalists and relativists derives from his view that Europe is threatened with total Islamisation, which would transform it into 'Eurabia'. Continent-wide state enforcement of 'Judeo-Christian values' is, in his view, the appropriate response. Most Judeo-Christians share this historical perspective, and this fundamental rejection of Islam in Europe. However, their response is a mirror image of the scenario they claim to oppose. They advocate forced conversion to Judeo-Christianism, instead of forced conversion to Islam. Since Judeo-Christians seek to destroy the freedom of conscience, and to transform Europe into a religious-conservative museum continent, political repression of Judeo-Christianism is historically necessary, and morally legitimate. Part of that repression would be inevitably directed against the Jewish and Christian religions, which are the source of the ideology.

The visible presence of the Judeo-Christian heritage, to which the ideology appeals, should be limited. A European programme for the selective closure of churches and synagogues would be necessary. Some are recognised historical monuments, but many have no architectural value, and are little used anyway. Certainly, no new churches and synagogues should be built (given the number existing already, they are simply not needed).

Christian and Jewish schools should be closed-unless they explicitly disown Judeo-Christian values, undertake not to teach them, and allow supervision of this undertaking. Political parties which advocate Judeo-Christian values should be banned. That would include the new anti-Islam populists like Wilders PVV, but also some older Christian and christian-democrat parties. Public advocacy of state enforcement of Judeo-Christian values should be criminalised. That would cover any demands for them to be legally and/or constitutionally specified, or to be made a requirement for employment, or for access to any service. (It would not preclude statements of personal adherence to these values).

Of course, some of these measures are drawn from the repertoire of populists like Wilders...

"... we will have to close down all Islamic schools for they are fascist institutions, to prevent any further indoctrination of young children with an ideology of violence and hatred.... we will have to close down all radical and forbid the construction of any new mosques, there is enough Islam in Europe."

That is logical enough: Wilders and other Judeo-Christians mirror the Islamism, which they claim to oppose. Measures designed to limit the effects of one religious-political ideology, will probably work for another. It is not a game of tit-for-tat, but a question of logic: how to deploy the state's powers, against such an ideology. There is no need to re-invent the wheel.

HUMANISM

Humanism is an attitude of thought which gives primary importance to human beings. Its outstanding historical example was Renaissance humanism from the fourteenth to sixteenth centuries, which developed from the rediscovery by European scholars of classical Latin and Greek texts. As a reaction against the religious authoritarianism of Medieval Catholicism, it emphasized human dignity, beauty, and potential, and affected every aspect of culture in Europe, including philosophy, music, and the arts. This humanist emphasis on the value and importance of the individual influenced the Protestant Reformation, and brought about social and political change in Europe.

There was another round of revival of humanism in the Age of Enlightenment in the seventeenth and eighteenth centuries as a reaction against the newly prevalent dogmatic authoritarianism of Lutheranism, Calvinism, Anglicanism, and the Counter-Reformation from around the end of the sixteenth century to the seventeenth century. During the last two centuries, various elements of Enlightenment humanism have been manifested in philosophical trends such as existentialism, utilitarianism, pragmatism, and Marxism. Generally speaking, Enlightenment humanism was more advanced than Renaissance humanism in its secular orientation, and produced atheism, Marxism, as well as secular humanism. Secular humanism, which denies God and attributes the universe entirely to material forces, today has replaced religion for many people.

Secular humanism, in its neglect of God the source of human values, risks an impoverishment of meaning. Yet humanism is an inevitable reaction to theism when it is authoritarian and dogmatic. For human beings created in the image of God, the values of humanism express human beings' God-given nature. Hence, while secular humanism is antithetical to theism, religious humanism and theism are complementary.

HUMANISM IN RENAISSANCE AND ENLIGHTENMENT

Renaissance humanism was a European intellectual and cultural movement which began in Florence, Italy, in the last decades of the fourteenth century, rose to prominence in the fifteenth century, and spread throughout the rest of Europe in the sixteenth century. The term "humanism" itself was coined much later, in 1808, by German educator F.J. Niethammer to describe a program of study distinct from science and engineering; but in the fifteenth century, the term *"umanista,"* or *"humanist,"* was current, meaning a student of human affairs or human nature. The movement developed from the rediscovery by European scholars of many Greek and Roman texts. Its focus was on human dignity and potential and the place of mankind in nature; it valued reason and the evidence of the senses in understanding truth. The humanist emphasis upon art and the senses marked a great change from the contemplation on the biblical values of humility, introspection, and meekness that had dominated European thought in the previous centuries. Beauty was held to represent a deep inner virtue and value, and an essential element in the path towards God.

Renaissance humanism was a reaction to Catholic scholasticism which had dominated the universities of Italy, and later Oxford and Paris, and whose methodology was derived from Thomas Aquinas. Renaissance humanists followed a cycle of studies, the *studia humanitatis* (studies of humanity), consisting of grammar, rhetoric, poetry, history, and moral philosophy, based on classical Roman and Greek texts. Many humanists held positions as teachers of literature and grammar or as government bureaucrats. Humanism affected every aspect of culture in Europe, including music and the arts. It profoundly influenced philosophy by emphasizing rhetoric and a more literary presentation and by introducing Latin translations of Greek classical texts which revived many of the concepts of ancient Greek philosophy.

The humanist emphasis on the value and importance of the individual was not necessarily a total rejection of religion. According to historians such as Nicholas Terpstra, the Renaissance was very much characterized with activities of lay religious co-fraternities with a more internalized kind of religiosity, and it influenced the Protestant Reformation, which rejected the hierarchy of the Roman Catholic Church and declared that every individual could stand directly before God. Humanist values also brought about social and political change by acknowledging the value and dignity of every individual regardless of social and economic status. Renaissance humanism also inspired the study of biblical sources and newer, more accurate translations of biblical texts.

Humanist scholars from this period include the Dutch theologian Erasmus, the English author Thomas More, the French writer Francois Rabelais, the Italian poet Francesco Petrarch, and the Italian scholar Giovanni Pico della Mirandola.

Enlightenment Humanism

The term, "Enlightenment humanism," is not as well known as "Renaissance humanism." The reason is that the relationship of humanism to the Enlightenment has not been as much clarified by historians than that between humanism and the Renaissance. But, there actually existed humanism in the Enlightenment as well, and quite a few historians have related humanism to the Enlightenment. Enlightenment humanism is characterized by such key words as autonomy, reason, and progress, and it is usually distinguished from Renaissance humanism because of its more secular nature. While Renaissance humanism was still somewhat religious, developing an internalized type of religiosity, which influenced the Protestant Reformation, Enlightenment humanism marked a radical departure from religion.

The Enlightenment was a reaction against the religious dogmatism of the late sixteenth and seventeenth centuries. The religious dogmatism of that time in Europe had been developed in three domains: 1) Protestant scholasticism by Lutheran and Calvinist divines, 2) "Jesuit scholasticism" (sometimes called the "second scholasticism") by the Counter-Reformation, and 3) the theory of the divine right of kings in the Church of England. It had fueled the bloody Thirty Years' War (1618-1648) and the English Civil War (1642-1651). The Enlightenment rejected this religious dogmatism. The intellectual leaders of the Enlightenment regarded themselves as a courageous elite who would lead the world into progress from a long period of doubtful tradition and ecclesiastical tyranny. They reduced religion to those essentials which could only be "rationally" defended, i.e., certain basic moral principles and a few universally held beliefs about God. Taken to one logical extreme, the Enlightenment even resulted in atheism. Aside from these universal principles and beliefs, religions in their particularity were largely banished from the public square.

Humanism after the Enlightenment

After the Enlightenment, its humanism continued and was developed in the next two centuries. Humanism has come to encompass a series of interrelated concepts about the nature, definition, capabilities, and values of human persons. In it refers to perspectives in philosophy, anthropology, history, epistemology, aesthetics, ontology, ethics, and politics, which are based on the human being as a point of reference. Humanism refers to any perspective which is committed to the centrality and interests of human beings. It also refers to a belief that reason and autonomy are the basic aspects of human existence, and that the foundation for ethics and society is autonomy and moral equality. During the last two centuries, various elements of humanism have been manifested in philosophical views including existentialism, utilitarianism, pragmatism, personalism, and Marxism.

Also in the area of education, the late nineteenth century educational humanist William T. Harris, who was U.S. Commissioner of Education and founder of the *Journal of*

Speculative Philosophy, followed the Enlightenment theory of education that the studies that develop human intellect are those that make humans "most truly human." His "Five Windows of the Soul" (mathematics, geography, history, grammar, and literature/art) were believed especially appropriate for the development of the distinct intellectual faculties such as the analytical, the mathematical, and the linguistic. Harris, an egalitarian who worked to bring education to all children regardless of gender or economic status, believed that education in these subjects provided a "civilizing insight" that was necessary in order for democracy to flourish.

Modern Humanist Movements

One of the earliest forerunners of contemporary chartered humanist organizations was the Humanistic Religious Association formed in 1853 in London. This early group was democratically organized, with male and female members participating in the election of the leadership and promoted knowledge of the sciences, philosophy, and the arts.

Active in the early 1920s, Ferdinand Canning Scott Schiller considered his work to be tied to the humanist movement. Schiller himself was influenced by the pragmatism of William James. In 1929, Charles Francis Potter founded the First Humanist Society of New York whose advisory board included Julian Huxley, John Dewey, Albert Einstein, and Thomas Mann. Potter was a minister from the Unitarian tradition and in 1930, he and his wife, Clara Cook Potter, published *Humanism: A New Religion.* Throughout the 1930s, Potter was a well-known advocate of women's rights, access to birth control, civil divorce laws, and an end to capital punishment.

Raymond B. Bragg, the associate editor of *The New Humanist,* sought to consolidate the input of L. M. Birkhead, Charles Francis Potter, and several members of the Western Unitarian Conference. Bragg asked Roy Wood Sellars to draft a document based on this information which resulted in the publication of the *Humanist Manifesto* in 1933. It referred to humanism as a religion, but denied all supernaturalism and went so far as to affirm that: "Religious humanists regard the universe as self-existing and not created." So, it was hardly religious humansim; it was rather secular humanism. The *Manifesto* and Potter's book became the cornerstones of modern organizations of secular humanism. They defined religion in secular terms and refused traditional theistic perspectives such as the existence of God and his act of creation.

In 1941, the American Humanist Association was organized. Noted members of The AHA include Isaac Asimov, who was the president before his death, and writer Kurt Vonnegut, who also was president before his death.

Secular and Religious Humanism

Secular humanism rejects theistic religious belief, and the existence of God or other supernatural being, on the grounds that supernatural beliefs cannot be supported rationally. Secular humanists generally believe that successful ethical, political, and social organization can be accomplished through the use of reason or other faculties of man. Many theorists of modern humanist organizations such as American Humanist Association hold this perspective. Religious humanism embraces some form of theism, deism, or supernaturalism, without necessarily being allied with organized religion. The existence of God or the divine, and the relationship between God and human beings is seen as an essential aspect of human character, and each individual is endowed with unique value through this relationship. Humanism within organized religion can refer to the appreciation of human qualities as an expression of God, or to a movement to acknowledge common humanity and to serve the needs of the human community. Religious thinkers such as Erasmus, Blaise Pascal, and Jacques Maritain hold this orientation.

Assessment

As long as human beings were created in the image of God, their values and dignity are to be respected. But history shows that they were very often neglected even in the name of God or in the name of an established religious institution like church. So, it was natural that Renaissance humanism occurred in the fourteenth century as a reaction against the religious authoritarianism of Medieval Catholicism. If the Renaissance was a humanist reaction, there was also a faith-oriented reaction, which was the Protestant Reformation. Hence, Medieval Catholicism is said to have been disintegrated into two very different kinds of reactions: Renaissance and Reformation. In the late sixteenth and seventeenth centuries, there was again religious authoritarianism, which arose from among Lutheranism, Calvinism, Anglicanism, and the Counter-Reformation. Therefore, Enlightenment humanism naturally emerged as a movement against it, and its more faith-oriented counterpart was Pietism. Enlightenment humanism was more advanced in its secular orientation than Renaissance humanism, and its tradition even issued in atheism and Marxism. Today, so-called secular humanism constitutes a great challenge to established religion.

Secular humanism, in its neglect of God the source of human values, risks an impoverishment of meaning. Yet, humanism is an inevitable reaction to theism when it is authoritarian and dogmatic. For human beings created in the image of God, the values of humanism express human beings' God-given nature. Hence, while secular humanism is antithetical to theism, religious humanism and theism are complementary. As the American theologian Reinhold Niebuhr said, a "new synthesis" of Renaissance and Reformation is called for.

HUMANISM TO PROTESTANT REFORMATION

In Europe, the 16th century was a great century of change on many sides. The major change had occurred in religion. During the Dark Ages, before the Renaissance the dominant religion in the world especially in Europe was Roman Catholicism. Together with the Renaissance, Europe became a secular place. The humanist approach evolved in these days which support "to promote the development of human capacities and to open new possibilities for mankind" (The New Knowledge, n.d.). Enlightenment period began to raise questions about everything in the world including the Church. This led to the Protestant Reformation, so this meant the first big division in religion and also it was the messenger of religious wars. Europeans had to face off with this reality that they had to "make a choice – to be Catholic or Protestant". All of these events had occurred as a consequence of humanist approach that was influenced on Protestant Reformation. Humanism firstly awakened the consciousness of individual power, creativity and realizing the natural world then gave rise to the scientific explorations, secondly by the help of this achievements humanism helped believers.

In conclusion, 16th century Europeans saw big changes in social and religious life. Humanism firstly arose in Italy: in Milan, Florence, Venice, Roma and Pisa which had a common point to have potent economic forces. In addition to the explorations of natural world the help of science, the wish to have a secular, more personal and spiritual religion which created by humanism also prepared the way to the Protestant Reformation.) and this approach was created by the humanism and the works of humanists. Humanists were not unbelievers but they did not want the religion as a "prime dominating". When people started to understand the Bible texts more precisely, they recognized the necessity of an immediate reformation in the Church; many rejected the dogmatic official doctrines created by the church and started to look for different approaches with new methods. The Enlightenment period was initiated by this struggle. Consequently, Protestant Reformation started to respond the need for a more personal, tolerant and spiritual religion which separates from the government and serves for salvation and can "touch the believer directly, in the heart". The reason for this leading role of Europe was the situation which gave rise for evolving and enhancing new ideas easily. As a result of this examination, Protestant Reformation took its part in history. However, Catholic Church did not think any reformation as a respond for this unwilling situation, thus the Protestant Reformation began. "Human ability to control over nature or to shape society according to its needs and desires" lead to the belief of man was the creator of his own destiny (Humanism, n. Humanism took its meaning from the Latin word humanitas which is used to refer a certain type of education that allowed people "to explore the whole range of knowledge, including the sciences and mathematics, in order to develop their full potential". In those days the dominated factor on people"tms life was religion, they depended on the

Church to educate and to explain the world so in this point of view it is not surprising to see that the Church chose the way of avoiding ideas that didn't obey to its teachings and dogmas and in progressive situations the Church implemented the persecution for those enlightened people who had new ideas and thought a lot according to the Church.

PROTESTANT REFORMATION

The Protestant Reformation, also called the Protestant Revolt or simply The Reformation, was the European Christian reform movement that established Protestantism as a constituent branch of contemporary Christianity. It was led by Martin Luther, John Calvin and other Protestants. The self-described "reformers" (who "protested") objected to the doctrines, rituals and ecclesiastical structure of the Roman Catholic Church, and created new national Protestant churches. The Catholics responded with a Counter Reformation, led by the Jesuit order, which reclaimed large parts of Europe, such as Poland. In general, northern Europe, with the exception of Ireland and pockets of Britain, turned Protestant, and southern Europe remained Catholic, while fierce battles that turned into warfare took place in the centre. The largest of the new denominations were the Anglicans (based in England), the Lutherans (based in Germany and Scandinavia), and the Reformed churches (based in Germany, Switzerland, the Netherlands and Scotland). There were many smaller bodies as well. The most common dating begins in 1517 when Luther published *The Ninety-Five Theses*, and concludes in 1648 with the Treaty of Westphalia that ended years of European religious wars.

Religious Situation in Europe

The Protestant Reformation began as an attempt to reform the Roman Catholic Church, carried out by Western European Catholics who opposed what they perceived as false doctrines and ecclesiastic malpractice — especially the teaching and the sale of indulgences or the abuses thereof, and simony, the selling and buying of clerical offices — that the reformers saw as evidence of the systemic corruption of the Church's Roman hierarchy, which included the Pope. Both issues were dealt with in an altogether different manner by the Roman Catholic Church during the Counter-Reformation.

Martin Luther's spiritual predecessors included John Wycliffe and Jan Hus, who likewise had attempted to reform the Roman Catholic Church. The Protestant Reformation began on 31 October 1517, in Wittenberg, Saxony, where Martin Luther nailed his *Ninety-Five Theses on the Power and Efficacy of Indulgences* to the door of the Castle Church, in Wittenberg, the theses debated and criticized the Church and the Pope, but concentrated upon the selling of indulgences and doctrinal policies about purgatory, particular judgment, Mariology (devotion to Mary, Jesus's Mother), the intercession of and devotion to the saints, most of the sacraments, the mandatory clerical celibacy, including monasticism, and the authority of the Pope. In the event, other religious reformers, such as Ulrich Zwingli, soon followed Martin Luther's example.

Moreover, the reformers soon disagreed among themselves and divided their movement according to doctrinal differences — first between Luther and Zwingli, later between Luther and John Calvin — consequently resulting in the establishment of different and rival Protestant Churches (denominations), such as the Lutheran, the Reformed, the Puritans, and the Presbyterian. Elsewhere, the religious reformation causes, processes, and effects were different; Anglicanism arose in England with the English Reformation, and most Protestant denominations derive from the Germanic denominations. The reformers also accelerated the development of the Catholic Counter-Reformation of the Roman Catholic Church.

History and Origins

All mainstream Protestants generally date their doctrinal separation from the Roman Catholic Church to the 16th century, occasionally called the *Magisterial Reformation*, because the ruling magistrates supported them; unlike the *Radical Reformation*, which the State did not support. Older Protestant churches, such as the Unitas Fratrum (Unity of the Brethren), Moravian Brethren (Bohemian Brethren) date their origins to Jan Hus in the early 15th century. As it was led by a Bohemian noble majority, and recognized, for a time, by the Basel

Compacts, the Hussite Reformation was Europe's first Magisterial Reformation. One hundred years later, in Germany the protests erupted simultaneously, whilst under threat of Islamic Ottoman invasion [1], which especially distracted the German princes responsible for military defence.

Corruption

Unrest due to the Great Schism of Western Christianity (1378–1416) excited wars between princes, uprisings among the peasants, and widespread concern over corruption in the church. The first of a series of disruptive and new perspectives came from John Wycliffe at Oxford University, then from Jan Hus at the University of Prague. The Roman Catholic Church officially concluded this debate at the Council of Constance (1414–1417). The conclave condemned Jan Hus, who was executed by burning in spite of a promise of safe-conduct. Wycliffe was posthumously burned as a heretic. The Council of Constance confirmed and strengthened the traditional medieval conception of church and empire. It did not address the national tensions, or the theological tensions which had been stirred up during the previous century. The council could not prevent schism and the Hussite Wars in Bohemia. Martin Luther was shocked by the corruption of the clergy on a trip to Rome in 1510. Sixtus IV (1471–1484) was the first Pope to impose a license on brothels and a special tax on priests who kept a mistress. He also established the practice of selling indulgences to be applied to the dead, thereby establishing a virtually infinite source of revenue. Pope Alexander VI (1492–1503) was one of the most controversial of the Renaissance Popes. He fathered seven children, including Lucrezia and Cesare Borgia, by at least two mistresses. Fourteen years after his death, the corruption of the papacy that Pope Alexander VI exemplified – particularly the sale of indulgences – prompted Luther to nail a summary of his grievances on the door of a church at Wittenberg in Germany and launch the Protestant Reformation.

16th Century

The protests against the corruption emanating from Rome began in earnest when Martin Luther, an Augustinian monk at the university of Wittenberg, called in 1517 for a reopening of the debate on the sale of indulgences and the authority to absolve sin and remit one from purgatory. Luther's dissent marked a sudden outbreak of a new and irresistible force of discontent. The Reformers made heavy use of inexpensive pamphlets (using the relatively new printing press) so there was swift movement of both ideas and documents, including *The Ninety-Five Theses*.

Parallel to events in Germany, a movement began in Switzerland under the leadership of Ulrich Zwingli. These two movements quickly agreed on most issues, as the recently introduced printing press spread ideas rapidly from place to place, but some unresolved differences kept them separate. Some followers of Zwingli believed that the Reformation was too conservative, and moved independently toward more radical positions, some of which survive among modern day Anabaptists. Other Protestant movements grew up along lines of mysticism or humanism (cf. Erasmus), sometimes breaking from Rome or from the Protestants, or forming outside of the churches. After this first stage of the Reformation, following the excommunication of Luther and condemnation of the Reformation by the Pope, the work and writings of John Calvin were influential in establishing a loose consensus among various groups in Switzerland, Scotland, Hungary, Germany and elsewhere.

The Reformation foundations engaged with Augustinianism. Both Luther and Calvin thought along lines linked with the theological teachings of Augustine of Hippo. The Augustinianism of the Reformers struggled against Pelagianism, a heresy that they perceived in the Roman Catholic Church of their day. In the course of this religious upheaval, the German Peasants' War of 1524–1525 swept through the Bavarian, Thuringian and Swabian principalities, leaving scores of Catholics slaughtered at the hands of Protestant bands, including the Black Company of Florian Geier, a knight from Giebelstadt who joined the peasants in the general outrage against the Roman Catholic hierarchy. Martin Luther, however, condemned the revolt, thus contributing to its eventual defeat. Some 100,000 peasants were killed. Even though Luther and Calvin had very similar theological teachings, the relationship between their followers turned quickly to conflict. Frenchman Michel de Montaigne told a story of a Lutheran pastor who declared over dinner that he would rather hear a hundred masses than take part in one of Calvin's sacraments.

The political separation of the Church of England from Rome under Henry VIII, beginning in 1529 and completed in 1536, brought England alongside this broad Reformed movement. However, religious changes in the English national church proceeded more conservatively than elsewhere in Europe. Reformers in the Church of England alternated, for centuries, between sympathies for Roman Catholic traditions and Protestantism, progressively forging a stable compromise between adherence to ancient tradition and Protestantism, which is now sometimes called the via media.

Martin Luther, John Calvin, and Ulrich Zwingli are considered Magisterial Reformers because their reform movements were supported by ruling authorities or "magistrates". Frederick the Wise did not support Luther, who was a professor at the university he founded, but he protected him by hiding Luther in Wartburg Castle in Eisenach. Frederick the Wise was a very devout Roman Catholic, but only protected Luther in hopes of obtaining greater political autonomy from the Church. Zwingli and Calvin were supported by the city councils in Zurich and Geneva. Since the term "magister" also means "teacher", the Magisterial Reformation is also characterized by an emphasis on the authority of a teacher. This is made evident in the prominence of Luther, Calvin, and Zwingli as leaders of the reform movements in their respective areas of ministry. Because of their authority, they were often criticized by Radical Reformers as being too much like the Roman Popes. For example, Radical Reformer Andreas Karlstadt referred to the Wittenberg theologians as the "new papists".

The Central Issue: Free Will

In his work, *Luther: Right or Wrong?*, Fr. McSoreley pinpoints with laser precision the true and abiding reason for the Reformation, according to Luther himself: What was the central issue of Luther's protest? With unmistakable clarity Luther himself answers this question in the closing paragraph of *De servo arbitrio* (1525), his powerful reply to the long-awaited attack made by Desiderius Erasmus in *De libero arbitrio* (1524). Fully confident that he has refuted Erasmus, Luther offers him a singular word of consolation:

"Moreover, I give you hearty praise and commendation on this further account – that you alone, in contrast with all others, have attacked the real thing, that is, the essential issue. You have not wearied me with those extraneous issues about the papacy, purgatory, indulgences and such like-trifles, rather than issues-in respect of which almost all to date have sought my blood (though without success); you, and you alone, have seen the *hinge* on which all turns [*cardo rerum*], and aimed for the *vital spot*. For that I heartily thank you...."

Not the doctrines of the papacy, purgatory or indulgences, but the *doctrine of the freedom of the will* was the real issue –the *res ipsa* of Luther's reformation protest! This was not merely an isolated, passing statement. Already in 1520, in the *Assertio omnium articulorum M. Lutheri per bullam Leonis X, novissimam damnatorum*, Luther signaled out the thirty-sixth article – the one in which he defends the thesis that the free will, after Adam's fall, is a name devoid of content (*res de solo titulo; eyn eytteler name*) – as the *real issue of his reformation*. Again he speaks of the other questions about the papacy, councils and indulgences as "trifles" (*nugae*) but explicitly insists that this article is the *most important point of his doctrine*. Did Luther change his mind after 1525 about the importance of his doctrine of the unfree will? It seems unlikely that he did. Twelve years after he wrote *De servo arbitrio*, Luther could still write to Wolfgang Capito (July 9, 1537), in reference to the forthcoming publication of his collected works: "I consider none of my books to be worthwhile, except perhaps *De servo arbitrio* and the Catechism."

Humanism to Protestantism

The frustrated reformism of the humanists, ushered in by the Renaissance, contributed to a growing impatience among reformers. Erasmus and later figures like Martin Luther and

Zwingli would emerge from this debate and eventually contribute to another major schism of Christendom. The crisis of theology beginning with William of Ockham in the 14th century was occurring in conjunction with the new burgher discontent. Since the breakdown of the philosophical foundations of scholasticism, the new nominalism did not bode well for an institutional church legitimized as an intermediary between man and God. New thinking favored the notion that no religious doctrine can be supported by philosophical arguments, eroding the old alliance between reason and faith of the medieval period laid out by Thomas Aquinas.

The major individualistic reform movements that revolted against medieval scholasticism and the institutions that underpinned it were humanism, devotionalism, and the observantine tradition. In Germany, "the modern way" or devotionalism caught on in the universities, requiring a redefinition of God, who was no longer a rational governing principle but an arbitrary, unknowable will that cannot be limited. God was now a ruler, and religion would be more fervent and emotional. Thus, the ensuing revival of Augustinian theology, stating that man cannot be saved by his own efforts but only by the grace of God would erode the legitimacy of the rigid institutions of the church meant to provide a channel for man to do good works and get into heaven. Humanism, however, was more of an educational reform movement with origins in the Renaissance's revival of classical learning and thought. A revolt against Aristotelian logic, it placed great emphasis on reforming individuals through eloquence as opposed to reason. The European Renaissance laid the foundation for the Northern humanists in its reinforcement of the traditional use of Latin as the great unifying language of European culture.

The polarization of the scholarly community in Germany over the Reuchlin (1455–1522) affair, attacked by the elite clergy for his study of Hebrew and Jewish texts, brought Luther fully in line with the humanist educational reforms who favored academic freedom. At the same time, the impact of the Renaissance would soon backfire against traditional Roman Catholicism, ushering in an age of reform and a repudiation of much of medieval Latin tradition. Led by Erasmus, the humanists condemned various forms of corruption within the church, forms of corruption that might not have been any more prevalent than during the medieval zenith of the church. Erasmus held that true religion was a matter of inward devotion rather than outward symbols of ceremony and ritual. Going back to ancient texts, scriptures, from this viewpoint the greatest culmination of the ancient tradition, are the guides to life. Favoring moral reforms and de-emphasizing didactic ritual, Erasmus laid the groundwork for Luther.

Humanism's intellectual anti-clericalism would profoundly influence Luther. The increasingly well-educated middle sectors of Northern Germany, namely the educated community and city dwellers would turn to Luther's rethinking of religion to conceptualize their discontent according to the cultural medium of the era. The great rise of the burghers, the desire to run their new businesses free of institutional barriers or outmoded cultural practices, contributed to the appeal of humanist individualism. To many, papal institutions were rigid, especially regarding their views on just price and usury. In the North, burghers and monarchs were united in their frustration for not paying any taxes to the nation, but collecting taxes from subjects and sending the revenues disproportionately to the Pope in Italy.

These trends heightened demands for significant reform and revitalization along with anticlericalism. New thinkers began noticing the divide between the priests and the flock. The clergy, for instance, were not always well-educated. Parish priests often did not know Latin and rural parishes often did not have great opportunities for theological education for many at the time. Due to its large landholdings and institutional rigidity, a rigidity to which the excessively large ranks of the clergy contributed, many bishops studied law, not theology, being relegated to the role of property managers trained in administration. While priests emphasized works of religiosity, the respectability of the church began diminishing, especially among well educated urbanites, and especially considering the recent strings of political humiliation, such as the apprehension of Pope Boniface VIII by Philip IV of France, the "Babylonian Captivity", the Great Schism, and the failure of conciliar reformism. In a sense, the campaign by Pope Leo X to raise funds to rebuild St. Peter's Basilica was too much of an excess by the secular Renaissance church, prompting high-pressure indulgences that rendered the clergy establishments even more disliked in the cities.

Luther borrowed from the humanists the sense of individualism, that each man can be his own priest (an attitude likely to find popular support considering the rapid rise of an educated urban middle class in the North), and that the only true authority is the Bible, echoing the reformist zeal of the conciliar movement and opening up the debate once again on limiting the authority of the Pope. While his ideas called for the sharp redefinition of the dividing lines between the laity and the clergy, his ideas were still, by this point, reformist in nature. Luther's contention that the human will was incapable of following good, however, resulted in his rift with Erasmus finally distinguishing Lutheran reformism from humanism.

Lutheranism Adopted by the German Princes

Luther affirmed a theology of the Eucharist called Real Presence, a doctrine of the presence of Christ in the Eucharist which affirms the real presence yet upholding that the bread and wine are not "changed" into the body and blood; rather the divine elements adhere "in, with, and under" the earthly elements. He took this understanding of Christ's presence in the Eucharist to be more harmonious with the Church's teaching on the Incarnation. Just as Christ is the union of the fully human and the fully divine (cf. Council of Chalcedon) so to the Eucharist is a union of Bread and Body, Wine and Blood. According to the doctrine of real presence, the substances of the body and the blood of Christ and of the bread and the wine were held to coexist together in the consecrated Host during the communion service. While Luther seemed to maintain the perpetual consecration of the elements, other Lutherans argued that any consecrated bread or wine left over would revert to its former state the moment the service ended. Most Lutherans accept the latter. A Lutheran understanding of the Eucharist is distinct from the Reformed doctrine of the Eucharist in that Lutherans affirm a real, physical presence of Christ in the

Eucharist (as opposed to either a "spiritual presence" or a "memorial") and Lutherans affirm that the presence of Christ does not depend on the faith of the recipient; the repentant receive Christ in the Eucharist worthily, the unrepentant who receive the Eucharist risk the wrath of Christ.

Luther, along with his colleague Philipp Melanchthon, emphasized this point in his plea for the Reformation at the *Reichstag* in 1529 amid charges of heresy. But the changes he proposed were of such a fundamental nature that by their own logic they would automatically overthrow the old order; neither the Emperor nor the Church could possibly accept them, as Luther well knew. As was only to be expected, the edict by the Diet of Worms (1521) prohibited all innovations. Meanwhile, in these efforts to retain the guise of a Catholic reformer as opposed to a heretical revolutionary, and to appeal to German princes with his religious condemnation of the peasant revolts backed up by the Doctrine of the Two Kingdoms, Luther's growing conservatism would provoke more radical reformers.

At a religious conference with the Zwinglians in 1529, Melanchthon joined with Luther in opposing a union with Zwingli. There would finally be a schism in the reform movement due to Luther's belief in real presence—the real (as opposed to symbolic) presence of Christ at the Eucharist. His original intention was not schism, but with the *Reichstag* of Augsburg (1530) and its rejection of the Lutheran "Augsburg Confession", a separate Lutheran church finally emerged. In a sense, Luther would take theology further in its deviation from established Roman Catholic dogma, forcing a rift between the humanist Erasmus and Luther. Similarly, Zwingli would further repudiate ritualism, and break with the increasingly conservative Luther.

Aside from the enclosing of the lower classes, the middle sectors of northern Germany, namely the educated community and city dwellers, would turn to religion to conceptualize their discontent according to the cultural medium of the era. In northern Europe, Luther appealed to the growing national consciousness of the German states because he denounced the Pope for involvement in politics as well as religion. Moreover, he backed the nobility, which was now justified to crush the

Great Peasant Revolt of 1525 and to confiscate church property by Luther's Doctrine of the Two Kingdoms. This explains the attraction of some territorial princes to Lutheranism, especially its Doctrine of the Two Kingdoms. However, the Elector of Brandenburg, Joachim I, blamed Lutheranism for the revolt and so did others. In Brandenburg, it was only under his successor Joachim II that Lutheranism was established, and the old religion was not formally extinct in Brandenburg until the death of the last Roman Catholic bishop there, Georg von Blumenthal, who was Bishop of Lebus and sovereign Prince-Bishop of Ratzeburg.

With the church subordinate to and the agent of civil authority and peasant rebellions condemned on strict religious terms, Lutheranism and German nationalist sentiment were ideally suited to coincide. Though Charles V fought the Reformation, it is no coincidence either that the reign of his nationalistic predecessor Maximilian I saw the beginning of the movement. While the centralized states of western Europe had reached accords with the Vatican permitting them to draw on the rich property of the church for government expenditures, enabling them to form state churches that were greatly autonomous of Rome, similar moves on behalf of the Reich were unsuccessful so long as princes and prince bishops fought reforms to drop the pretension of the secular universal empire.

THE REFORMATION OUTSIDE GERMANY

Switzerland

Zwingli: Parallel to events in Germany, a movement began in Switzerland under the leadership of Huldrych Zwingli. These two movements quickly agreed on most issues, as the recently introduced printing press spread ideas rapidly from place to place, but some unresolved differences kept them separate. Some followers of Zwingli believed that the Reformation was too conservative, and moved independently toward more radical positions, some of which survive among modern day Anabaptists. Other Protestant movements grew up along lines of mysticism or humanism (cf. Erasmus), sometimes breaking from Rome or from the Protestants, or forming outside of the churches.

John Calvin

Following the excommunication of Luther and condemnation of the Reformation by the Pope, the work and writings of John Calvin were influential in establishing a loose consensus among various groups in Switzerland, Scotland, Hungary, Germany and elsewhere. Geneva became the unofficial capital of the Protestant movement, led by the Frenchman Calvin, until his death (when Calvin's ally, William Farel, assumed the spiritual leadership of the group).

The Reformation foundations engaged with Augustinianism. Both Luther and Calvin thought along lines linked with the theological teachings of Augustine of Hippo. The Augustinianism of the Reformers struggled against Pelagianism, a heresy that they perceived in the Roman Catholic Church of their day. Ironically, even though both Luther and Calvin had very similar theological teachings, the relationship between Lutherans and Calvinists evolved into one of conflict.

Scandinavia

All of Scandinavia ultimately adopted Lutheranism over the course of the 16th century, as the monarchs of Denmark (who also ruled Norway and Iceland) and Sweden (who also ruled Finland) converted to that faith.

In Sweden the Reformation was spearheaded by Gustav Vasa, elected king in 1523. Friction with the pope over the latter's interference in Swedish ecclesiastical affairs led to the discontinuance of any official connection between Sweden and the papacy from 1523. Four years later, at the Diet of Västerås, the king succeeded in forcing the diet to accept his dominion over the national church. The king was given possession of all church property, church appointments required royal approval, the clergy were subject to the civil law, and the "pure Word of God" was to be preached in the churches and taught in the schools—effectively granting official sanction to Lutheran ideas.

Under the reign of Frederick I (1523–33), Denmark remained officially Roman Catholic. But though Frederick initially pledged to persecute Lutherans, he soon adopted a policy of protecting Lutheran preachers and reformers, of whom the most famous was Hans Tausen. During his reign, Lutheranism made significant inroads among the Danish population. Frederick's son, Christian, was openly Lutheran, which prevented his election to the throne upon his father's death. In 1536, the authority of the Roman Catholic bishops was terminated by national assembly. The next year, following his victory in the Count's War, he became king as Christian III and continued the reformation of the state church with assistance of Johannes Bugenhagen.

England

Church of England

The separation of the Church of England (or Anglican Church) from Rome under Henry VIII, beginning in 1529 and completed in 1536, brought England alongside this broad Reformation movement; however, religious changes in the English national church proceeded more conservatively than elsewhere in Europe. Reformers in the Church of England alternated, for centuries, between sympathies for Roman Catholic tradition and more reformed principles, gradually developing into a tradition which is considered a middle way (via media) between the Roman Catholic and Protestant traditions.

The English Reformation followed a different course from the Reformation in continental Europe. There had long been a strong strain of anti-clericalism, and England had already given rise to the Lollard movement of John Wycliffe, which played an important part in inspiring the Hussites in Bohemia. Lollardy was suppressed and became an underground movement so the extent of its influence in the 1520s is difficult to assess. The different character of the English Reformation came rather from the fact that it was driven initially by the political necessities of Henry VIII.

Henry had once been a sincere Roman Catholic and had even authored a book strongly criticizing Luther, but he later found it expedient and profitable to break with the Papacy. His wife, Catherine of Aragon, bore him only a single child, Mary. As England had recently gone through a lengthy dynastic conflict, Henry feared that his lack of a male heir might jeopardize his descendants' claim to the throne. However, Pope Clement VII, concentrating more on Charles V's "sack of Rome", denied his request for an annulment. Had Clement granted the annulment and therefore admitted that his predecessor, Julius II, had erred, Clement would have given support to the Lutheran assertion that Popes replaced their own judgement for the will of God.

King Henry decided to remove the Church of England from the authority of Rome. In 1534, the Act of Supremacy made Henry the Supreme Head of the Church of England. Between 1535 and 1540, under Thomas Cromwell, the policy known as the Dissolution of the Monasteries was put into effect. The veneration of some saints, certain pilgrimages and some pilgrim shrines were also attacked. Huge amounts of church land and property passed into the hands of the Crown and ultimately into those of the nobility and gentry. The vested interest thus created made for a powerful force in support of the dissolutions.

There were some notable opponents to the Henrician Reformation, such as Thomas More and Bishop John Fisher, who were executed for their opposition. There was also a growing party of reformers who were imbued with the Zwinglian and Calvinistic doctrines now current on the Continent. When Henry died he was succeeded by his Protestant son Edward VI, who, through his empowered councillors (with the King being only nine years old at his succession and not yet sixteen at his death) the Duke of Somerset and the Duke of Northumberland, ordered the destruction of images in churches, and the closing of the chantries. Under Edward VI the reform of the Church of England was established unequivocally in doctrinal terms.

Yet, at a popular level, religion in England was still in a state of flux. Following a brief Roman Catholic restoration during the reign of Mary 1553–1558, a loose consensus developed during the reign of Elizabeth I, though this point is one of considerable debate among historians. Yet it is the so-called "Elizabethan Religious Settlement" to which the origins of Anglicanism are traditionally ascribed. The compromise was uneasy and was capable of veering between extreme Calvinism on the one hand and Catholicism on the other, but compared to the bloody and chaotic state of affairs in contemporary France, it was relatively successful until the Puritan Revolution or English Civil War in the 17th century.

Puritan Movement

The success of the Counter-Reformation on the Continent and the growth of a Puritan party dedicated to further Protestant reform polarized the Elizabethan Age, although it was not until the 1640s that England underwent religious strife comparable to that which its neighbours had suffered some generations before. The early *Puritan movement* (late 16th-17th centuries) was Reformed or Calvinist and was a movement for reform in the Church of England. Its origins lay in the discontent with the Elizabethan Religious Settlement. The desire was for the Church of England to resemble more closely the Protestant churches of Europe, especially Geneva. The Puritans objected to ornaments and ritual in the churches as idolatrous (vestments, surplices, organs, genuflection), which they castigated as "popish pomp and rags". They also objected to ecclesiastical courts. They refused to endorse completely all of the ritual directions and formulas of the *Book of Common Prayer*; the imposition of its liturgical order by legal force and inspection sharpened Puritanism into a definite opposition movement.

The later Puritan movement were often referred to as dissenters and nonconformists and eventually led to the formation of various reformed denominations. The most famous and well-known emigration to America was the migration of the Puritan separatists from the Anglican Church of England, who fled first to Holland, and then later to America, to establish the English colonies of New England, which later became the United States.

These Puritan separatists were also known as "the Pilgrims". After establishing a colony at Plymouth (which would become part of the colony of Massachusetts) in 1620, the Puritan pilgrims received a charter from the King of England which legitimized their colony, allowing them to do trade and commerce with merchants in England, in accordance with the principles of mercantilism. This successful, though initially quite difficult, colony marked the beginning of the Protestant presence in America (the earlier French, Spanish and Portuguese settlements had been Roman Catholic), and became a kind of oasis of spiritual and economic freedom, to which persecuted Protestants and other minorities from the British Isles and Europe (and later, from all over the world) fled to for peace, freedom and opportunity. The Pilgrims of New England disapproved of Christmas and celebration was outlawed in Boston from 1659 to 1681. The ban was revoked in 1681 by Sir Edmund Andros, who also revoked a Puritan ban against festivities on Saturday night. However it wasn't until the mid-19th century that celebrating Christmas became fashionable in the Boston region.

The original intent of the colonists was to establish spiritual Puritanism, which had been denied to them in England and the rest of Europe to engage in peaceful commerce with England and the native American Indians and to Christianize the peoples of the Americas.

Scotland

The Reformation in Scotland's case culminated ecclesiastically in the re-establishment of the church along reformed lines, and politically in the triumph of English influence over that of France. John Knox is regarded as the leader of the Scottish reformation The reformation parliament of 1560, which repudiated the pope's authority, forbade the celebration of the mass and approved a Protestant Confession of Faith, was made possible by a revolution against French hegemony under the regime of the regent Mary of Guise, who had governed Scotland in the name of her absent daughter Mary, Queen of Scots (then also Queen of France).

The Scottish reformation decisively shaped the Church of Scotland and, through it, all other Presbyterian churches worldwide. A spiritual revival also broke out among Roman Catholics soon after Martin Luther's actions, and led to the Scottish Covenanters' movement, the precursor to Scottish Presbyterianism. This movement spread, and greatly influenced the formation of Puritanism among the Anglican Church in England. The Scottish covenanters were persecuted by the

Roman Catholic Church. This persecution by the Catholics drove some of the Protestant covenanter leadership out of Scotland, and into France and later, Switzerland.

France

Protestantism also spread into France, where the Protestants were nicknamed "Huguenots", and this touched off decades of warfare in France, after initial support by Henry of Navarre was lost due to the "Night of the Placards" affair. Many French Huguenots, however, still contributed to the Protestant movement, including many who emigrated to the English colonies. Though he was not personally interested in religious reform, Francis I (1515–47) initially maintained an attitude of tolerance, arising from his interest in the humanist movement. This changed in 1534 with the Affair of the Placards. In this act, Protestants denounced the mass in placards that appeared across France, even reaching the royal apartments. The issue of religious faith having been thrown into the arena of politics, Francis was prompted to view the movement as a threat to the kingdom's stability. This led to the first major phase of anti-Protestant persecution in France, in which the *Chambre Ardente* ("Burning Chamber") was established within the Parlement of Paris to deal with the rise in prosecutions for heresy. Several thousand French Protestants fled the country during this time, most notably John Calvin, who settled in Geneva.

Calvin continued to take an interest in the religious affairs of his native land and, from his base in Geneva, beyond the reach of the French king, regularly trained pastors to lead congregations in France. Despite heavy persecution by Henry II, the Reformed Church of France, largely Calvinist in direction, made steady progress across large sections of the nation, in the urban bourgeoisie and parts of the aristocracy, appealing to people alienated by the obduracy and the complacency of the Roman Catholic establishment. French Protestantism, though its appeal increased under persecution, came to acquire a distinctly political character, made all the more obvious by the noble conversions of the 1550s. This had the effect of creating the preconditions for a series of destructive and intermittent conflicts, known as the Wars of Religion. The civil wars were helped along by the sudden death of Henry II in 1559, which saw the beginning of a prolonged period of weakness for the French crown. Atrocity and outrage became the defining characteristic of the time, illustrated at its most intense in the St. Bartholomew's Day massacre of August 1572, when the Roman Catholic party annihilated between 30,000 and 100,000 Huguenots across France. The wars only concluded when Henry IV, himself a former Huguenot, issued the Edict of Nantes, promising official toleration of the Protestant minority, but under highly restricted conditions. Catholicism remained the official state religion, and the fortunes of French Protestants gradually declined over the next century, culminating in Louis XIV's Edict of Fontainebleau—which revoked the Edict of Nantes and made Roman Catholicism the sole legal religion of France. In response to the Edict of Fontainebleau, Frederick William I, Elector of Brandenburg declared the Edict of Potsdam, giving free passage to French Huguenot refugees, and tax-free status to them for ten years.

Netherlands

The Reformation in the Netherlands, unlike in many other countries, was not initiated by the rulers of the Seventeen Provinces, but instead by multiple popular movements, which in turn were bolstered by the arrival of Protestant refugees from other parts of the continent. While the Anabaptist movement enjoyed popularity in the region in the early decades of the Reformation, Calvinism, in the form of the Dutch Reformed Church, became the dominant Protestant faith in the country from the 1560s onward. Harsh persecution of Protestants by the Spanish government of Philip II contributed to a desire for independence in the provinces, which led to the Eighty Years' War and eventually, the separation of the largely Protestant Dutch Republic from the Catholic-dominated Southern Netherlands (present-day Belgium).

Hungary

Much of the population of the Kingdom of Hungary adopted Protestantism during the 16th century. After the 1526 Battle of Mohács the Hungarian people were disillusioned by the ability of the government to protect them and turned to the faith which would infuse them with the strength necessary to resist the invader. They found this in the teaching of the Protestant reformers such as Martin Luther. The spread of Protestantism in the country was aided by its large ethnic German minority, which could understand and translate the writings of Martin Luther. While Lutheranism gained a foothold among the German-and Slovak-speaking populations, Calvinism became widely accepted among ethnic Hungarians.

In the more independent northwest the rulers and priests, protected now by the Habsburg Monarchy which had taken the field to fight the Turks, defended the old Roman Catholic faith. They dragged the Protestants to prison and the stake wherever they could. Such strong measures only fanned the flames of protest, however.

Leaders of the Protestants included Matthias Biro Devai, Michael Sztarai, and Stephen Kis Szegedi. Protestants likely formed a majority of Hungary's population at the close of the 16th century, but Counter-Reformation efforts in the 17th century reconverted a majority of the kingdom to Roman Catholicism. A significant Protestant minority remained, most of it adhering to the Calvinist faith.

In 1558 the Transylvanian Diet of Turda declared free practice of both the Catholic and Lutheran religions, but prohibited Calvinism. Ten years later, in 1568, the Diet extended this freedom, declaring that "It is not allowed to anybody to intimidate anybody with captivity or expelling for his religion". Four religions were declared as accepted (recepta) religions, while Orthodox Christianity was "tolerated" (though the building of stone Orthodox churches was forbidden). Hungary entered the Thirty Years' War, Royal (Habsburg) Hungary joined the catholic side, until Transylvania joined the Protestant side. There were a series of other successful and unsuccessful anti-Habsburg/i.e. anti-Austrian/(requiring equal rights and freedom for all Christian religions) uprisings between 1604 and 1711, the uprisings were usually organized from Transylvania. The constrained Habsburg Counter-Reformation efforts in the 17th century reconverted the majority of the kingdom to Roman Catholicism.

Italy

Conclusion and legacy

The Reformation led to a series of religious wars that culminated in the Thirty Years' War, which devastated much of Germany, killing between 25 and 40% of its population. From 1618 to 1648 the Roman Catholic House of Habsburg and its allies fought against the Protestant princes of Germany, supported at various times by Denmark, Sweden and France. The Habsburgs, who ruled Spain, Austria, the Spanish Netherlands and much of Germany and Italy, were staunch defenders of the Roman Catholic Church. Some historians believe that the era of the Reformation came to a close when Catholic France allied itself, first in secret and later on the battlefields, with Protestant states against the Habsburg dynasty. For the first time since the days of Luther, political and national convictions again outweighed religious convictions in Europe.

The main tenets of the Peace of Westphalia, which ended the Thirty Years' War, were:

- All parties would now recognize the Peace of Augsburg of 1555, by which each prince would have the right to determine the religion of his own state, the options being Catholicism, Lutheranism, and now Calvinism (the principle of *cuius regio, eius religio*)
- Christians living in principalities where their denomination was *not* the established church were guaranteed the right to practice their faith in public during allotted hours and in private at their will.

The treaty also effectively ended the Pope's pan-European political power. Fully aware of the loss, Pope Innocent X declared the treaty "null, void, invalid, iniquitous, unjust, damnable, reprobate, inane, empty of meaning and effect for all times." European sovereigns, Roman Catholic and Protestant alike, ignored his verdict.

In *The Protestant Ethic and the Spirit of Capitalism*, Max Weber first suggested that cultural values could affect economic success, arguing that the Protestant Reformation led to values that drove people toward worldly achievements, a hard work ethic, and saving to accumulate wealth for investment. The new religions (in particular, Calvinism and other more austere Protestant sects) effectively forbade wastefully using hard earned money and identified the purchase of luxuries a sin.

RATIONALISM

In epistemology and in its modern sense, rationalism is "any view appealing to reason as a source of knowledge or justification" (Lacey 286). In more technical terms it is a method or a theory "in which the criterion of the truth is not sensory but intellectual and deductive" (Bourke 263). Different degrees of emphasis on this method or theory lead to a range of rationalist standpoints, from the moderate position "that reason has precedence over other ways of acquiring knowledge" to the more extreme position that reason is "the unique path to knowledge" (Audi 771). Given a pre-modern understanding of reason, "rationalism" is identical to philosophy, the Socratic life of inquiry, or the zetetic interpretation of authority (open to the underlying or essential cause of things as they appear to our sense of certainty). In recent decades, Leo Strauss sought to revive *Classical Political Rationalism* as a discipline that understands the task of reasoning, not as foundational, but as maieutic.

Since the Enlightenment, rationalism is usually associated with the introduction of mathematical methods into philosophy, as in Descartes, Leibniz, and Spinoza (Bourke 263). This is commonly called continental rationalism, because it was predominant in the continental schools of Europe, whereas in Britain empiricism dominated.

Rationalism is often contrasted with empiricism. Taken very broadly these views are not mutually exclusive, since a philosopher can be both rationalist and empiricist (Lacey 286–287). Taken to extremes the empiricist view holds that all ideas come to us through experience, either through the five external senses or through such inner sensations as pain and gratification, and thus that knowledge is essentially based on or derived from experience. At issue is the fundamental source of human knowledge, and the proper techniques for verifying what we think we know. Proponents of some varieties of rationalism argue that, starting with foundational basic principles, like the axioms of geometry, one could deductively derive the rest of all possible knowledge. The philosophers who held this view most clearly were Baruch Spinoza and Gottfried Leibniz, whose attempts to grapple with the epistemological and metaphysical problems raised by Descartes led to a development of the fundamental approach of rationalism. Both Spinoza and Leibniz asserted that, *in principle*, all knowledge, including scientific knowledge, could be gained through the use of reason alone, though they both observed that this was not possible *in practice* for human beings except in specific areas such as mathematics. On the other hand, Leibniz admitted that "we are all mere Empirics in three fourths of our actions". Rationalism is predicting and explaining behaviour based on logics.

Philosophical Usage

The distinction between rationalists and empiricists was drawn at a later period, and would not have been recognized by the philosophers involved. Also, the distinction was not as clear-cut as is sometimes suggested; for example, the three main rationalists were all committed to the importance of empirical science, and in many respects the empiricists were closer to Descartes in their methods and metaphysical theories than were Spinoza and Leibniz.

History

Socrates (ca 470–399B.C.E.)

Socrates firmly believed that, before humans can understand the world, they first need to understand themselves; the only way to accomplish that is with rational thought. To understand what this means, one must first appreciate the Greek understanding of the world. Man is composed of two parts, a body and a soul. The soul itself has two principal parts, an Irrational part, which is the emotions and desires, and a Rational part, which is our true self. In our everyday experience, the irrational soul is drawn down into the physical body by its desires and merged with it, so that our perception of the world is limited to that delivered by the physical senses. The rational soul is beyond our conscious knowledge, but sometimes communicates via images, dreams, and other means.

The task of the philosopher is to refine and eventually extract the irrational soul from its bondage, hence the need for moral development, and then to connect with the rational soul, and so become a complete person, manifesting the higher spiritual essence of the person whilst in the physical. True rationalism is therefore not simply an intellectual process, but a shift in perception and a shift in the qualitative nature of the person. The rational soul perceives the world in a spiritual manner-it sees the Platonic Forms-the essence of what things are. To know the world in this way requires that one first know oneself as a soul, hence the requirement to 'know thyself', i.e. to know who you truly are.

Socrates did not publish or write any of his thoughts, but he was constantly in discussion with others. He would usually start by asking a rhetorical (seemingly answerable) question, to which the other would give an answer. Socrates would then continue to ask questions until all conflicts were resolved, or until the other could do nothing else but admit to not knowing the answer (which was what most of his discussions ended with). Socrates did not claim to know the answers, but that did not take away the ability to critically and rationally approach problems. His goal was to show that, ultimately, our intellectual approach to the world is flawed, and we must transcend this to obtain true knowledge of what things are.

René Descartes (1596–1650)

Descartes thought that only knowledge of eternal truths – including the truths of mathematics, and the epistemological and metaphysical foundations of the sciences – could be attained by reason alone; other knowledge, the knowledge of physics, required experience of the world, aided by the scientific method. He also argued that although dreams appear as real as sense experience, these dreams cannot provide persons with knowledge. Also, since conscious sense experience can be the cause of illusions, then sense experience itself can be doubtable. As a result, Descartes deduced that a rational pursuit of truth should doubt every belief about reality. He elaborated these beliefs in such works as *Discourse on Method*, *Meditations on First Philosophy*, and *Principles of Philosophy*. Descartes developed a method to attain truths according to which nothing that cannot be recognised by the intellect (or reason) can be classified as knowledge. These truths are gained "without any sensory experience", according to Descartes. Truths that are attained by reason are broken down into elements that intuition can grasp, which, through a purely deductive process, will result in clear truths about reality.

Descartes therefore argued, as a result of his method, that reason alone determined knowledge, and that this could be done independently of the senses. For instance, his famous dictum, *cogito ergo sum*, is a conclusion reached a priori and not through an inference from experience. This was, for Descartes, an irrefutable principle upon which to ground all forms of other knowledge. Descartes posited a metaphysical dualism, distinguishing between the substances of the human body ("*res extensa*") and the mind or soul ("*res cogitans*"). This crucial distinction would be left unresolved and lead to what is known as the mind-body problem, since the two substances in the Cartesian system are independent of each other and irreducible.

Baruch Spinoza (1632–1677)

The philosophy of Baruch Spinoza is a systematic, logical, rational philosophy developed by him in the seventeenth century in Europe. It's a system of ideas built from basic building blocks with an internal consistency with which Spinoza tried to answer life's major questions and in which he proposed that "God exists only philosophically." He was heavily influenced by thinkers such as Descartes and Euclid and Thomas Hobbes as well as theologians in the Jewish philosophical tradition such as Maimonides, but his work was in many respects a departure from the Judeo-Christian tradition. Many of Spinoza's ideas continue to vex thinkers today and many of his principles, particularly regarding the emotions, have implications for modern approaches to psychology. Even top thinkers have found Spinoza's "geometrical method" difficult to comprehend.

Goethe admitted that he "could not really understand what Spinoza was on about most of the time." The *Ethics* contains unresolved obscurities and has a forbidding mathematical structure modeled on Euclid's geometry. But his philosophy attracted believers such as Albert Einstein. and much intellectual attention.

Gottfried Leibniz (1646–1716)

Leibniz was the last of the great Rationalists, who contributed heavily to other fields such as mathematics. His system however was not developed independently of these advances. Leibniz rejected Cartesian dualism, and denied the existence of a material world. In Leibniz's view there are infinitely many simple substances, which he called "monads" (possibly taking the term from the work of Anne Conway).

Leibniz developed his theory of monads in response to both Descartes and Spinoza. In rejecting this response he was forced to arrive at his own solution. Monads are the fundamental unit of reality, according to Leibniz, constituting both inanimate and animate things. These units of reality represent the universe, though they are not subject to the laws of causality or space (which he called "well-founded phenomena"). Leibniz, therefore, introduced his principle of pre-established harmony to account for apparent causality in the world.

Immanuel Kant (1724–1804)

Immanuel Kant started as a traditional rationalist, having studied the rationalists Leibniz and Wolff, but after studying David Hume's works, which "awoke [him] from [his] dogmatic slumbers", he developed a distinctive and very influential rationalism of his own, which attempted to synthesise the traditional rationalist and empiricist traditions.

Kant named his branch of epistemology Transcendental Idealism, and he first laid out these views in his famous work The Critique of Pure Reason. In it he argued that there were fundamental problems with both rationalist and empiricist dogma. To the rationalists he argued, broadly, that pure reason is flawed when it goes beyond its limits and claims to know those things that are necessarily beyond the realm of all possible experience: the existence of God, free will, and the immortality of the human soul. Kant referred to these objects as "The Thing in Itself" and goes on to argue that their status as objects beyond all possible experience by definition means we cannot know them. To the empiricist he argued that while it is correct that experience is fundamentally necessary for human knowledge, reason is necessary for processing that experience into coherent thought. He therefore concludes that both reason and experience are necessary for human knowledge.

LIBERALISM AND DEMOCRACY

Karl-Hermann Flach

Liberalism is the commitment to the greatest possible freedom of the individual and the preservation of human dignity in any given or changing social situation. Liberalism therefore does not mean freedom and dignity for a class but personal freedom and human dignity for the greatest number. Freedom and equality are not contradictory but complementary. The freedom of the individual is limited by the freedom of the other, the neighbour. Therefore, liberalism is not anarchism but a theory for a political system.

Liberals are aware that men and women are not in possession of ultimate truths. Liberals merely think they are in search of them. Liberals know that the road to insight is strewn with errors and today™s truth contains tomorrow™s error. Like others, liberal dialectics assume that a thesis is contrasted by an antithesis, both join to become a synthesis, thereby fanning a new thesis, against which a new antithesis must and will develop. But unlike contemporary types of dialectical materialism, liberals think dialectics will never come to an end. They believe there are neither definitive political solutions nor final states of society. The human and social contradictions will not be overcome but at best acquire a new quality. To this extent, liberalism is a political theory of relativity.

Therefore, no taboos exist for liberalism. For Liberals, any state of affairs is open for discussion and any opinion worthy of dispute. Liberalism therefore automatically desanctifies any subject which people with vested interests try to keep out of the general debate with spurious arguments.

Since Liberalism does not recognize any ultimate human truths and definitive political solutions, intellectual freedom and the protection of minorities are at the core of its platform. Any political and social progress starts with a deviation from established wisdom. In the eyes of Liberals, anyone who bans deviating ideas and persecutes the critical denial of the established wisdom as heresy hampers social and political progress. No one knows which of today™s minorities will be tom d that the human being is not omniscient and that not everything can be discovered and planned, it vehemently contradicts the notion that the end justifies the means. Experience tells Liberals that using objectionable means even for the most noble end gives these means a life of their own which will eventually wipe out, overgrow and make us forget the end. Thus, appropriateness of the means to any end is a basic demand by Liberals. It is at the centre of Liberal ethics.

Life promises freedom. Where there is no life, no freedom can develop. Where freedom is absent but life is present, there is still a chance for freedom. To this extent, Liberalism is opposed to war. War forces each party to increase the use of violence so strongly that the freedom of those defending freedom also risks being strangled. The same applies to violence as such. Violence affects the just and the unjust, the guilty and the innocent, those involved in action and those standing on the sidelines. Violence produces counterviolence and forces the parties to increase their violence constantly so that the means of violence will eventually far exceed its purpose.

On the other hand, there is a right of self-defence. It exists for countries and group of countries in the same way as for social groups and individuals. The liberal rejection of violence and the liberal right to defend freedom in self-defence are a contradiction. What is clear for the Liberal is that violence must be restricted to the right of self-defence. But self defence also harbours a risk of going too far and even legitimate defence is caught in the vicious spiral of violence. Liberals must live with this contradiction also. Liberalism therefore will always strive towards detente to reduce this contradiction in the relationship between states and in society.

Society requires constant change. Ossified structures of power and ownership work against freedom. Liberalism must therefore try to keep society open for change. It cannot deny or veil social conflicts but must always search for rules by which they should be fought out in a humane way. Liberalism can therefore never be static but must always be dynamic.

Any society revolves around power, interests, intrigues, ambition, influence and vanities; in any society, there is achievement and failure, error and weakness, elegance and ridiculousness. There has never been a human society without these human phenomena. Totalitarian structures of state and society differ from liberal and democratic ones not by banning these phenomena but by the simple fact that in the former, they must not be publicly discussed. Anyone who pretends that a society without weaknesses or conflict is a reality provides no information but veils the facts. Anyone who believes to have found a historical example of an ideal society without weakness or conflict has fallen victim to an idealistic error or distorts history. The perfect society as a goal was and remains a utopia. The ideal society as a pretended reality was and remains ideology. This is part of liberal convictions. Of course, ideology and utopia have a social and historical function. There must be utopias if there are to be changes to society. And there will be ideologies as long as there are (relatively) stable societies. Liberalism will not succumb to the charm of any utopia or to the seduction of any ideology. It recognizes the relative meaning of both, without their veils, as it were. And it eyes the way utopias are turned into ideologies with suspicion if the supporters of the utopia establish themselves and confront their models of thinking with reality.

There is a tension between Liberalism and democracy, but they are complementary. Democracy is a form of government and could be simply described as the theory of legitimate rule by the majority. Democracy may be totalitarian if the rule of the majority ruthlessly violates the rights of the minorities and diminishes their chances of becoming the majority. Liberalism is an understanding of the degree of government. Since Liberals know that in any society, power is a factor and cannot be eliminated, they do not try to abolish it but see their job as limiting, dividing up and controlling power and preserving the chance of replacing those in power. Liberalism and democracy happily coexist in many countries.

The intellectual strength of Liberalism is its organisational weakness. Its theory of relativity forces Liberals to constantly challenge their own positions. The Liberal ethics demanding a proportionality between ends and means cause Liberals to have intellectual scruples in the struggle for power and the use of power. The Liberal interpretation of tolerance automatically leads to an understanding of the position of opposed ideologues or utopians although they don™t need to have any hint of understanding for liberals. The liberal principle of detente also produces a constant weakness by comparison to political opponents who are not so fussy about using force if they are, e.g, conservatives believing they are legitimately defending law and order or left-wing utopians believing they are in sole possession of wisdom.

Liberals know that people are not equal, but because they do, they must be radically committed to equal opportunities so that everyone will find their place in society according to their talents, wishes, abilities and willingness to achieve-irrespective of social background, heritage and health. For a long time, the grand expression ixequal opportunityls remained empty words behind which extreme inequality was concealed.

However, the liberal perception of achievement and competition can only be justified if a level or at least near-level playing field exists in society. In the 19th and first half of the 20th century, liberals have failed to constantly strive for this. They tolerated the cementing of social conditions which turned the theoretical and legal notion of freedom into a weapon in the hands of a limited class to ward off the claims of broad sections of society.

As early as before the First World War, Friedrich Naumann fittingly condemned the lack of any social component in Liberalism.

7

Fields of Social Work

LABOUR WELFARE

Welfare includes anything that is done for the comfort and improvement of employees and is provided over and above the wages. Welfare helps in keeping the morale and motivation of the employees high so as to retain the employees for longer duration. The welfare measures need not be in monetary terms only but in any kind/forms.

Employee welfare includes monitoring of working conditions, creation of industrial harmony through infrastructure for health, industrial relations and insurance against disease, accident and unemployment for the workers and their families.Labor welfare entails all those activities of employer, which are directed towards providing the employees with certain facilities and services in addition to wages or salaries.

Labour welfare has the following objectives:

1. To provide better life and health to the workers
2. To make the workers happy and satisfied
3. To relieve workers from industrial fatigue and to improve intellectual, cultural and material conditions of living of the workers.

The basic features of labour welfare measures are as follows:

1. Labour welfare includes various facilities, services and amenities provided to workers for improving their health, efficiency, economic betterment and social status.

2. Welfare measures are in addition to regular wages and other economic benefits available to workers due to legal provisions and collective bargaining
3. Labour welfare schemes are flexible and ever-changing. New welfare measures are added to the existing ones from time to time.
4. Welfare measures may be introduced by the employers, government, employees or by any social or charitable agency.
5. The purpose of labour welfare is to bring about the development of the whole personality of the workers to make a better workforce. The very logic behind providing welfare schemes is to create efficient, healthy, loyal and satisfied labour force for the organization. The purpose of providing such facilities is to make their work life better and also to raise their standard of living.

The important benefits of welfare measures can be summarized as follows: They provide better physical and mental health to workers and thus promote a healthy work environment· Facilities like housing schemes, medical benefits, and education and recreation facilities for workers' families help in raising their standards of living. This makes workers to pay more attention towards work and thus increases their productivity.· Employers get stable labour force by providing welfare facilities. Workers take active interest in their jobs and work with a feeling of involvement and participation.·

Employee welfare measures increase the productivity of organization and promote healthy industrial relations thereby maintaining industrial peace.·The social evils prevalent among the labors such as substance abuse, etc. are reduced to a greater extent by the welfare policies. Organizations provide welfare facilities to their employees to keep their motivation levels high. The employee welfare schemes can be classified into two categories viz. statutory and non-statutory welfare schemes. The statutory schemes are those schemes that are compulsory to provide by an organization as compliance to the laws governing employee health and safety. These include provisions provided in industrial acts like Factories Act 1948,

Dock Workers Act (safety, health and welfare) 1986, Mines Act 1962. The non statutory schemes differ from organization to organization and from industry to industry.

Statutory Welfare Schemes

The statutory welfare schemes include the following provisions:

1. Drinking Water: At all the working places safe hygienic drinking water should be provided.
2. Facilities for sitting: In every organization, especially factories, suitable seating arrangements are to be provided.
3. First aid appliances: First aid appliances are to be provided and should be readily assessable so that in case of any minor accident initial medication can be provided to the needed employee.
4. Latrines and Urinals: A sufficient number of latrines and urinals are to be provided in the office and factory premises and are also to be maintained in a neat and clean condition.
5. Canteen facilities: Cafeteria or canteens are to be provided by the employer so as to provide hygienic and nutritious food to the employees.
6. Spittoons: In every work place, such as ware houses, store places, in the dock area and office premises spittoons are to be provided in convenient places and same are to be maintained in a hygienic condition.
7. Lighting: Proper and sufficient lights are to be provided for employees so that they can work safely during the night shifts.
8. Washing places: Adequate washing places such as bathrooms, wash basins with tap and tap on the stand pipe are provided in the port area in the vicinity of the work places.
9. Changing rooms: Adequate changing rooms are to be provided for workers to change their cloth in the factory area and office premises. Adequate lockers are also provided to the workers to keep their clothes and belongings.

10. Rest rooms: Adequate numbers of restrooms are provided to the workers with provisions of water supply, wash basins, toilets, bathrooms, etc.

Non Statutory Schemes

Many non statutory welfare schemes may include the following schemes:

1. Personal Health Care (Regular medical check-ups): Some of the companies provide the facility for extensive health check-up
2. Flexi-time: The main objective of the flextime policy is to provide opportunity to employees to work with flexible working schedules. Flexible work schedules are initiated by employees and approved by management to meet business commitments while supporting employee personal life needs
3. Employee Assistance Programs: Various assistant programs are arranged like external counselling service so that employees or members of their immediate family can get counselling on various matters.
4. Harassment Policy: To protect an employee from harassments of any kind, guidelines are provided for proper action and also for protecting the aggrieved employee.
5. Maternity & Adoption Leave – Employees can avail maternity or adoption leaves. Paternity leave policies have also been introduced by various companies.
6. Medi-claim Insurance Scheme: This insurance scheme provides adequate insurance coverage of employees for expenses related to hospitalization due to illness, disease or injury or pregnancy.
7. Employee Referral Scheme: In several companies employee referral scheme is implemented to encourage employees to refer friends and relatives for employment in the organization

SOCIAL WORK, CORRECTIONS, AND THE STRENGTHS APPROACH

The theoretical framework for this paper is the strengths/ empowerment perspective, the approach which most closely parallels the rehabilitation model of correction. Both authors have worked in various capacities in the criminal justice system; the first author published a monograph on women in prison and later counseled offenders with chemical dependency problems; the second author worked as a probation officer for seven years in Oregon and Pennsylvania. Our purpose in writing this article is to present the case for the strengths approach in corrections, an approach which has been a recurrent theme in social work history and which is receiving increasing attention today.

Central to the profession of social work is a concern with social justice. According to the CASW Code of Ethics (1991 Preamble), "social workers are dedicated to the welfare and self realization of human beings... and to the achievement of social justice for all." And to the U.S. NASW Code of Ethics (1996:V1:6) similarly, "the social worker should advocate changes in policy and legislation...to promote social justice." The values of contemporary society, however, are sometimes clearly at odds with the ideals and principles of the profession. A politically popular and increasingly widespread reaction on both sides of the Canadian/U.S. border has been a "lock 'em up; throw away the key" mentality. Punishment comes first and treatment last under the modern political agenda, an agenda at sharp variance with the humanitarian and egalitarian ideals, which Robert Mullaly (1993) delineates as the cornerstone of social work's ideal society.

Social work has been promoting social justice for some time, all the way back to the settlement houses and children's aid societies. And until the mid-1920s, a substantial amount of social work effort, as Jerome Miller (1995) informs us, was directed at institutional wards of state — individuals confined to prisons, reform schools and the like. And long before that, the first days in the late 1800s in England, the charities and corrections movement regulated the poor by depriving the "undeserving" of aid. The two words, charity and corrections, in fact, were once used almost interchangeably (van Wormer, 1997). In later years, the mantle of professionalism, however, geared them away from authoritarian thinking and authoritarian institutions into work with troubled individuals in a variety of less coercive settings, namely, community mental health centres and child welfare. In the U.K. and Canada, and to a lesser extent in the U.S., social workers are becoming increasingly involved in working with offenders. Given the tremendous upsurge in drug related prosecutions, a heightened focus on substance abuse treatment is only logical. Treatment of sexual offenders, battering men, and their victims are other areas in need of enhanced social work services. Mental health counselling should be a high priority as well. An underlying assumption of this paper is that social workers, with their strengths, ethnic-centered awareness, have a major contribution to make to the field of criminal justice. Social workers have a contribution to make in terms of one-on-one counselling and in shaping policy.

The Contemporary Scene

The globalization and privatization of society are reflected in the homogenization of news stories: The aftermath of shootings in a schoolyard which would once have been merely regional news is beamed onto TV screens across the world. Meanwhile, newspaper headlines from Dallas to Winnipeg report on the urgency to crack down on crime, crime which according to the federal sources in both the U.S. and Canada, is actually on the decrease. In Canada, according to a speech by the solicitor general, crime rates are down for the sixth year in a row (Scott, 1998). On May 13, 1998, banner headlines in the Winnipeg Free Press proclaimed, "War on Youth Crime." The Liberal Party proposes lowering the age limit to 14 from 16 for serving adult sentences and publishing the names of youths convicted of crimes among other harsh proposals (Samyn, 1998). Still, according to Turpin (1997) writing in Corrections Today, in the most recent Canadian

election, crime was not a major campaign issue. This was in sharp contrast to elections in Britain and the U.S., however, where even the left wing parties came out on the offensive, calling for more police, tougher prosecutions and more law and order in general. Reflecting an Americanization of penal approaches, Britain recently has appointed its first drug czar. Although Turpin correctly perceives Canada as much more subdued regarding criminality than the U.S. or Britain, it seems likely that there is a trend toward less compassion here too. The hype in international mass media, the impact of the global economy, the appeal of right wing zealotry to people who feel economically powerless, and contagion from events south of the 48th and 49th border—all bode ill for progressive criminal justice policies. Ultimately, the current set of global economic and political forces that are driving countries to reduce their federal budget deficit combined with increased health care expenditures will lead to similar solutions. A study of U.S. and Canadian newspaper and Internet services reveals the following parallel political developments with special relevance to women:

- Budget cuts to women's shelters; reduction in welfare benefits that would enhance battered women's escape from dangerous situations;
- A social climate in which the welfare state is seen as the problem rather than the solution that is especially hard on woman who as caregivers are more dependent than men on aid by the state;
- Gender-blind policies that often work against women as mothers are pushed into a low-paying labour market;
- As more men are getting custody of their children, women increasingly are required to pay child support; harsh punishments are meted out for women who break the law and keep their children after visitation;
- Rapidly increasing incarceration rates for women especially in connection with the international war on drugs; the U.S. saw the execution of two women in 1998;- Impact of racism and classism reflected in high percentage of convicted women who are aboriginal or of African or Hispanic descent;
- Recent scandals in women's prisons involving extreme brutality, especially in Georgia in the U.S. and in the Federal Prison for Women in Kingston, Ontario.

On the bright side, in Canada, as we shall see, the correctional system is being redesigned and decentralized for federally sentenced women; a wealth of innovative proposals has emerged following a spate of highly publicized reports of female inmate mistreatment, especially at the hands of male guards. In Canada, furthermore, there is a strong move toward the restoring of balance between offender and victim. This concept, which has become known as *restorative justice*, has been widely practiced in work with Native offenders and journals of all ethnic backgrounds.

A society's treatment of those who break its laws is widely regarded as a barometer of its social climate. Violent societies tend to mete out severe and often violent punishments as well as to provide conditions of oppressions ripe for the criminalization of citizens in the first place. Conditions of oppression are the breeding grounds of resentment and hatred associated with crime (Gilligan, 1986). In moralistic societies such as the U.S., a nation which has never been able to cast off the shackles of its Puritan heritage, and which has almost prided itself on demeaning work environments, dire poverty in the midst of plenty, a steady diet of horrible violence in the mass media, and high availability of guns, the climate is conducive to violent crime as well as to harsh punishment. Even when the crime rate is not particularly high in a given area, moreover, mass media highlighting of horrifying events from far away serves to incite fear in the general public and perpetuate cries for revenge. Kinder and gentler societies such as Sweden and Norway, in contrast, have much lower crime rates and much more humane treatment of criminals.

This is the law and order setting, then, in which the practice of social work makes its entrance. Social work, as we are all aware, is the profession dedicated to maximizing the dignity and worth of individuals and of reinforcing their strengths and resources. It is immediately obvious that these ideals of empowerment and empathy may create some conflicts for the worker in a system constrained by punitive legislation. And yet, for women under the jurisdiction of the courts, in circumstances of extreme disempowerment, the need for an empathic connection, an affirming voice, is paramount.

The Strengths Perspective

At the heart of the strengths perspective is a belief in the basic goodness of humankind, a faith that individuals, however downtrodden or debilitated, can discover strengths in themselves that they never knew existed. The strengths or empowerment approach is a crucial part of effective therapy and increasingly articulated in the social work literature (Mullaly, 1993). No matter how little or how much may be expressed at one time, as Weick, Rapp, Sullivan, and Kisthardt (1989) explain, people often have a potential that is not commonly realized. A belief in human potential is tied to the notion that people have untapped, undetermined reservoirs of mental, physical, emotional, social and spiritual abilities which can be mobilized in times of need. This is where professional helping comes into play — in tapping into the possibilities, tapping into not what is but what can be.

Deficit, disease, and dysfunction metaphors permeate treatment at every stage of the process, from intake to termination (Cowger, 1994). In the criminal justice system, clients often find their very selfhood defined by their crimes. For such persons, whose views of therapy and of all authority figures are apt to be decidedly negative, a positive approach is essential to establish the one crucial ingredient of effective treatment — trust. Sometimes one encounter or one supportive relationship — whether with a teacher, social worker, or priest — can offer a turning point in a life of crime.

The most poignant example of a reversal of a life of crime, of a seemingly miraculous turnabout, was revealed to the world in the case of 35 year old Karla Faye Tucker, the first woman put to death in Texas since the Civil War. It is not her execution, however, but the loss of what could have been, that makes her case tragic. Here was a drug-addicted axe-murderer, turned born-again Christian, who helped fellow inmates and moved the hearts of compassionate people all over the world. " I'll be face to face with Jesus now," she said as she went to her untimely death.

Another murderer, Jean Harris, a high school principal at an exclusive girls' school, also committed murder in a drug-affected state, and she also found repentance and even a humility of sorts in prison. During her term at Bedford Hills Correctional Facility in New York state, Harris was credited with setting up a thriving model Children's Centre operated by prisoners

(Faith, 1993). During Harris's confinement and personal suffering, her attitude changed from bitterness and denial to love for her fellow human beings.

Let us briefly consider the relevance of the strengths approach for working with female offenders. These two examples — one of a woman born into the most miserable of circumstances, the other, a socialite — illuminate a theme we see expanded upon in this paper, the theme of personal empowerment. One of the major tasks of the professional helper is to facilitate such change. Within the justice context, the challenge consists of promoting personal power in people whose lives have become circumscribed to a varying degrees and whose very existence has been devalued and even criminalized.

Of special relevance to criminal behaviour, and without which change is unlikely, is the taking of personal responsibility for one's actions and for one's life. The treatment relationship can serve as a powerful tool for helping the client change cognitive misconceptions that result in self destructive thoughts and behaviour. Even in a life most crushed by circumstances of time and place, there nevertheless exists the potential for actions other than those (for example, heavy drinking, violent outbursts, etc.) that have become problematic. This belief in the human potential is at the core of the therapeutic relationship.

Brief Literature Review

We are dealing here with the literatures of two separate enterprises — criminal justice and mental health counselling. Whereas the criminal justice emphasis is largely on the state enterprise and legal prerogatives, social work, in its mental health component, has as its focal point, the individual within the system. And yet the two literatures share a commonality : Both are applied as opposed to strictly academic fields; both are closely bound up with the social and political forces of the day. Prison reform, innovative rehabilitation programs, and generous social services tend to go together. Preparation for war, mandatory sentencing laws, and spending cutbacks tend to go together also. The way criminals are treated in a society, in short, reflects the ethos of the culture.

CRIMINAL JUSTICE LITERATURE AND REHABILITATIVE GOALS

To Theodore Zeldin, (1994) the most insidious impediment to compassion is a cynical or despairing view of humanity. This phenomenon, as Zeldin further states, can be illustrated by the experience of the U.S.: Disillusioned by mass media sensationalism in crime reporting, high criminal recidivism rates, debates over treatment effectiveness, and general political conservatism, legislators have turned to a punitive, severe sentencing approach that is immensely popular with the general public. In Canada, likewise, a public outcry against the leniency of the courts has tempered expansion of the kind of therapeutic programming that once was very much in vogue (Evans, 1995). Most of the vast expenditures in the U.S. criminal justice system, accordingly, are for law enforcement, punishment and custody, not for prevention or treatment. The predominant treatment modality utilized in correctional treatment programming today is the innocuously sounding Cognitive Skills Program. Developed in Canada, the Correctional Program Assessment Inventory is currently in its sixth edition. What Gendreau and Ross (1980) heralded as the cognitive revolution in corrections was inspired by Yochelson and Samenow's (1976) voluminous writings and popular workshops on the criminal personality. Based on their work exclusively with male antisocial offenders at St. Elizabeth's Hospital for the criminally insane in Washington, D.C., the "revolutionary" framework was designed to tear down criminals' defences, the tendency, for example, of rapists and robbers to blame their victims for the crimes inflicted upon them. Van Voorhis, Baswell, and Lester (1997) praise Yochelson and Samenow's work as especially useful to counsellors and custodial staff in correcting inmates' errors in thinking. Institutional staff are taught the following correctional techniques:

- Accept no excuses for irresponsible attitudes or behaviours.
- Point out ways in which the offender may be refusing to accept responsibility.
- Call attention to, and do not accept "power thrusts."

- Teach offenders that trust must be earned, and call attention to other instances when the offender is betraying the trust of others.

These concepts are used with incarcerated DWI (driving while intoxicated) offenders in Iowa and also at the women's prison in Mitchellville, Iowa. In sharp contrast to the strengths perspective, this approach is exclusively negative. And yet the focus on cognitive errors is one which can easily be adapted (but from a positive rather than a negative perspective) to help women believe in themselves and in their potential.

One goal of what Bayse (1996) terms the moral-cognitive approach serves to encourage male inmates' awareness of how they described their victims so as to arouse feelings of guilt and self-disgust. Perhaps this focus may be warranted with the type of person for whom they were designed, the diagnosable psychopath or man without a conscious, no called the person with antisocial personality. Citing Yochelson and Samenow's work, Bayse (1996) further asserts that narcissism or self-centeredness is the central theme of the criminal's psychological makeup. The criminal views life, friendships, and even love with the thought of, "What's in it for me?" Helping victimizers to empathize with their victims, to stop devaluing them, is instrumental in helping them mature ethically and to quit using people.

Many men in trouble with the law, however, are non-violent offenders, and even many of the violent offenders are putting on an act of bravado for survival within prison walls. (Psychological testing, such as the Minnesota Multiphasic Personality Inventory [MMPI], can fairly effectively differentiate among various types of criminal mentalities.) The overwhelming majority of women caught in the throes of the criminal justice system have been convicted of drug offenses or crimes of passion. Still others have been merely "in the wrong place at the wrong time" or are taking the rap for somebody else. Some have been convicted more because of poor legal defence than their own criminal behaviour. Many of female offenders' problems most likely stem from addictive tendencies and/or relationship issues. They are in trouble with the law because essentially a public health problem has been criminalized. The narrow, one-size-fits-all approach can be downright detrimental to persons who do not fit the criminal blaming mold.

Rarely is the strengths or empowerment perspective articulated as such in the criminal justice literature. A computer search of the criminal justice abstracts index (as of February 1998) reveals no listing for articles with the heading strengths approach or strengths perspective. A search through the criminal justice journals themselves, however, revealed a notable exception, a strengths-based practice article for work with adolescents (Clark, 1998). Writing in Federal Probation, Clark points us in the direction of a focus on solutions rather than problems, and a focus on youth capabilities rather than liabilities. Elsewhere, the empowerment concept, however, is used as a descriptive term for progressive work with juveniles, female victims, and occasionally female offenders according to the computer index. The gender difference in the use of an empowerment approach is striking.

Despite the absence of a comprehensive strengths formulation, several works on correctional counselling do infuse principles of a positive, client-oriented treatment philosophy throughout the chapters. As for example, Paul Haun's (1998), Emerging Criminal Justice: Three Pillars for a Proactive Justice System. Calling for reinforced community corrections and punishments for crimes that allow for non-restrictive environments, Haun proposes a restorative approach to criminal justice, one built on the concepts of community healing, social support, and innovative community based programming.

The American Correctional Association (ACA), a professional organization which advocates for the professional interests of workers in jails, prisons, and the community maintains a focus on rehabilitation and treatment as proper correctional goals. During the annual Congress of Correction, The ACA (1997) adopted the following policies for correctional professionals and agencies recommending substance abuse treatment and parent training programs to break the cross-generational "cycle of violence."

Paradoxically, the ACA also passed a resolution in support of more funding for jails and prisons. One would think that a moratorium in a new prison construction would be more to the point. On the other hand, continuing expansion of the prison industry guarantees unprecedented job opportunities for correctional personnel, so this perhaps explains the seeming inconsistency in professional policies. The ACA opposition to legislation barring color television or college courses or weightlifting options, in part, is an opposition to the loss of discretion by correctional authorities to exercise their best professional judgement to make rules for their facilities (Alexander, 1996).

The Correctional Service of Canada, similarly, seeks to maintain a balance between the stress on control of offenders and an awareness of the importance of assisting offenders to become law-abiding citizens. Within the custodial facilities, accordingly, a wide variety of programs and services are provided, including inmate employment and vocational training programs. Consistent with the North American stress on individual responsibility, inmates must seek out their own rehabilitative programs; the responsibility for participation has shifted away from the providers to the offenders for maximum effectiveness.

A major criticism of the Canadian system of justice is the overcrowding of facilities related to the ever increasing portion of the population that is incarcerated. (Canada ranks third in the world in the number of adults incarcerated although a long way behind Russia and the U.S., each of which has almost three times the Canadian percentage. Canada's rate of locking up children is excessively high as well [Cayley, 1999]).

Descriptive studies of recent programming in the Canadian correctional system are provided by Kerr (1998) and Hannah-Moffat (1999). In Canada, as Kerr reveals, women's correctional programs are informed by five basic principles: empowerment; meaningful and responsible choices; respect and dignity; a supportive environment; and shared responsibility. The system, notes Kerr, is moving away from the old punishment paradigm into a healing paradigm. This programming, as we learn from Hannah-Moffat, can be traced to the reform strategies of the 1990s which culminated in a new woman-centered model of punishment. The Canadian concern with addressing the uniqueness of women's needs marks a sharp contrast to the U.S. feminist focus on equality — equalization of male/female prison opportunities, especially in the educational/vocational realm (van Wormer and Bartollas, in press).

As rates of imprisonment have soared in Canada, criticism of the situation has increased coupled with a search for new directions (Scott, 1998). A vision of justice as peacemaking rather than punishment is an encouraging development. Emanating from Mennonite church conflict resolution teachings and Aboriginal practices, this new but not new vision of justice has spread into the mainstream. The Correctional Service of Canada, in partnership with First Nation communities, has established federal healing facilities for Aboriginal offenders (Scott, 1998). The challenge, according to Scott, is to explore restorative justice options in all communities. Typically, the procedure involves the convening of family group conferences moderated by a state official to reach agreements on restitution when a wrong has been committed; the emphasis is on restoration and concensus rather than conflict. The reoffense rate for young offenders participating in this formality has been shown to be far below that of traditional approaches (Cayley, 1999).

Literature from the Helping Professions

Within the social work practice literature, a focus on client strengths has received increasing attention in recent years. The strengths perspective, as Kirst-Ashman and Hull (1997) note, assumes that power resides in people and that we should do our best to promote power by refusing to label clients, avoiding paternalistic treatment, and trusting clients to make appropriate decisions. Two popular textbooks, for example, Generalist Social Work Practice: Empowering Approach and The Empowerment Approach to Social Work Practice (Lee, 1994) incorporate the principle of strengths into every phase of the helping process. Although the literature consistently articulates the importance of a stress on clients' strengths and competencies, however, we must all be cognizant of the reality of standard clinical practice built on a treatment problem/ deficit orientation, a reality shaped by agency accountability and the dictates of managed care. Third party payment schemes mandate a diagnosis based on relatively serious disturbances in a person's functioning and short-term therapy to correct the presenting problem. Furthermore, the legal and political mandates of many agencies, the elements of social control embodied in both the institution and ethos of the agency, may strike a further blow to the possibility of partnership and collaboration between client and helper (Saleebey, 1997).

The strengths perspective has been applied to a wide variety of client situations: work with the mentally ill, child welfare clients, homeless women in emergency rooms, the elderly, and African American families. The concept of strength is also part and parcel of the growing literature on empowerment, feminist therapy, narrative therapy, client/person centered approach, and the ethnic-sensitive model. In his comprehensive overview of social work theory, Francis Turner (1996) perceives two common threads unifying contemporary theory. These are the person-in-the-situation conceptualization and a holistic understanding of clients in terms of their strengths and available resources.

In their article, "Empowering Female Offenders: Removing Barriers to Community Based Practice," Wilson and Anderson (1997) provide a prime illustration of strengths-based approach to correctional treatment. A key component of their practice model is the placement of competence and coping within a sociopolitical context. Empowerment practice with female inmates entails intervention directed at the economic, educational, social, and political structures of society in addition to strengths-focused individual and group therapy with women.

Effectiveness Studies

The Cognitive Skills Program, developed in Canada, has been held up as an exemplary, effective, and properly evaluated program. A critical examination of the program and its evaluation, however, reveals serious flaws, according to Matthews and Pitts. The major failing of the evaluation is that it tells us very little about what works and what doesn't. Scott, in his position as solicitor general, declares that the Correctional Service of Canada is committed to a research-based approach.

While recidivism rates for inmates in cognitive skill and sex offender programs have been reduced, according to Scott, we also know that programs offered in the community are more effective than programs behind bars.

Research on the effectiveness of female inmate programs are scarce. Research based on the strengths model in work with female offenders is even more scarce. Impressive results are being reported from New Zealand in correctional workers' use of family group conferences to address youth crimes; such conferences which resolve conflict through restorative justice avoid the negatives that accompany traditional sentencing practices. Costs have fallen dramatically and the reoffending rate significantly reduced (Cayley, 1999).

In his review of all the research to date on the strengths model of case management, Rapp (1998) concluded that although research is limited to two experimental (involving a control group), one quasi-experimental, and three non-experimental studies, results have been consistently positive. The focus of the studies was persons with severe mental disorders, and the success rate was measured in terms of a reduction in the need for hospitalization and an unanticipated generalization of success in other areas such as sociability and community involvement. These positive results, although limited in scope, augur well for clients who are involved in a close treatment relationship for emotional problems, a relationship characterized, as Rapp terms it, by trust, friendliness, reciprocity, and purpose.

In a small scale program evaluation of therapeutic services at the Canadian Prison for Women, Kathleen Kendall (1993) confirmed the findings of previous reports which identified mental health and substance abuse services as critical programming areas for incarcerated women. The prison where the program evaluation was conducted had suffered the loss of seven inmates to suicide in a five year period; six of the victims were aboriginal. The program evaluation involved qualitative interviews with the 40 inmates and 20 staff members.

Because the perception among staff was that grueling therapy sessions with inmates had pushed them into dealing with disturbing aspects of the past, and over the brink into suicide, inmate perceptions were very important. Prisoners reported overwhelming support for the counsellors at the prison. Kendall attributes the warm response to the feminist therapy approach and trauma expertise of the therapists. Identified as most helpful to the inmates were: assistance in taking control over their own lives, the opportunity to value and be valued by others, and the existence of mutually respectful relationships.

The feminist approach provided at the Canadian federal prison for women parallels the empowerment approach advocated in this article. Kendall describes the framework as consisting of the following components:

- A recognition of the close connection between women's marginalized status (e.g. poverty, abuse, sexism, racism) and their criminal activity;
- Stress on women's ability to resist violence in its various form and to find creative ways of coping;
- The belief that as women develop a deeper awareness of their own strengths they will take greater control over their own lives;
- An awareness of the paradox that prisons generally remove whatever autonomy women have left, yet expect mature behaviour from them, an experience reminiscent of earlier abusive experiences.

Kendall summarizes her findings by noting that although the therapeutic services provided by the prison were helpful, the creation of real choices for women lies in developing genuine alternatives to incarceration. Since her report was completed, the federal prison for women is being decentralized into regional centres for maximum community involvement. Further research is needed into the long term effectiveness of a strengths/ empowerment approach with adult female offenders.

SOCIAL WORKER-CORRECTIONS

Purpose of Classification Specification

This classification specification is the basic authority under Wis. Admin. Code ER 2.04 for making classification decisions relative to present and future professional positions which provide professional social work and case management services to a specific client population within the Department of Corrections. Positions may serve a very specific client population within an adult or juvenile correctional facility while others provide service to a broad range of inmates throughout the facility. This classification specification will not specifically identify every eventuality or combination of duties and responsibilities of positions that currently exist, or those that result from changing program emphasis in the future. Rather, it is designed to serve as a framework for classification decision-making in this occupational area.

Classification decisions must be based on the "best fit" of the duties within the existing classification structure. The "best fit" is determined by the majority (i.e., more than 50%) of the work assigned to and performed by the position when compared to the class concepts and definition of this specification or through other methods of position analysis. Position analysis defines the nature and character of the work through the use of any or all of the following: definition statements; listing of areas of specialization; representative examples of work performed; allocation patterns of representative positions; job evaluation guide charts, standards or factors; statements of inclusion and exclusion; licensure or certification requirements; and other such information necessary to facilitate the assignment of positions to the appropriate classification.

Inclusions

This classification encompasses professional social work positions located exclusively within the Department of Corrections. Wis. Stats. 457.01 defines "Social work" as "applying psychosocial, psychotherapeutic or counselling principles, methods or procedures in the assessment, evaluation, psychosocial or psychotherapeutic diagnosis, prevention, treatment or resolution of a social, psychological, personal, emotional or mental disorder of an individual, couple, family, group of individuals or community, including the enhancement or restoration of, or the creation of societal conditions favourable to the enhancement or restoration of, the capacity of an individual, couple, family, group of individuals or community for social functioning or the delivery of services to a group of individuals or a community to assist the group or community in providing or improving the provision of social or health services to others." Positions allocated to this series provide professional social work and case management services to a specific client population. Social work services include the following functions (1) evaluating and assessing difficulties in psychosocial functioning of a group or another individual; (2) developing plans or policies to alleviate those difficulties, and either carrying out the plan or referring individuals to other qualified resources for assistance; and (3) intervention planning, which may include psychosocial evaluation and counselling of individuals, families and groups; advocacy; referral to community resources, and facilitation of organizational change to meet social needs. Employes occupying positions in this classification perform any combination of these functions.

Exclusions

Excluded from this classification are the following types of positions:

1. Positions that meet the statutory definition of supervisor or management as defined in Wis. Stats. 111.81(19) and (13) as administered and interpreted by the Wisconsin Employment Relations Commission.
2. Positions that are engaged in the direct provision of probation and parole activities a majority of the time and are more appropriately classified as Probation and Parole Agent.
3. Positions that are responsible for development, oversight, and monitoring of a specific treatment or treatment related program within an institution a majority of the time and are more appropriately classified as Treatment Specialist.
4. Positions that implement treatment plans for AODA clients within an institution a majority of the time but do not have primary responsibility for development of the treatment plan and are more appropriately classified as Substance Abuse Counselor or Client Services Assistant.

5. Social Worker positions in any state agency other than the Department of Corrections.
6. All other positions that are more appropriately identified by other classification specifications.

Entrance Classification

Employees enter positions within this classification series by competitive examination.

DEFINITIONS

Positions in this classification series provide responsible, independent social work services within a correctional institution for juveniles or adults. Social work services include, but are not limited to, each of the following components: (1) evaluation and assessment of difficulties in psychosocial functioning of a group or another individual; (2) developing plans or policies to alleviate those difficulties, and either carrying out the plan or referring individuals to other qualified resources for assistance; and (3) intervention planning, which may include psychosocial evaluation and counselling of individuals, families and groups; advocacy; referral to community resources, and facilitation of organizational change to meet social needs.

Positions in this classification series carry total caseload responsibility for all types of clients including multi-disciplinary and inter-service complexities. Positions may specialize in a particular type of caseload or may serve a broad range of client types. Duties include obtaining information from clients, members of their families and others to identify social, economic, emotional, health or physical problems and to determine eligibility and the need for casework or other services. Employes may provide counselling services, therapeutic intervention, and treatment services to clients and members of their families to aid them in achieving a more satisfactory adjustment of their specific problems or situation. Social Workers work in close cooperation with other social agencies, hospitals, clinics, courts and community resources in planning to meet the needs of clients, and assist the clients in utilizing these resources. Employees may perform in an advisory capacity to other professional staff in specialized areas through participation in conferences and meetings for purposes of assessment, diagnosis and plan of treatment.

Representative Positions : Department of Corrections, Division of Adult Institutions: Under the general supervision of the institution social services director, treatment director, unit manager, social services supervisor, or correctional centre superintendent, assesses client/inmate problems and capacities; formulates a case plan; monitors clients/inmate's progress; provides counselling and individual and group therapy; and develops and refers clients to appropriate institution and community resources upon transfer or release. Coordinates multidisciplinary treatment efforts with other institution staff, parole agents, clients/inmates and community resources. Make recommendations relative to inmate security classification. May provide services to a diverse client population or a specialized population such as that at the Drug Abuse Correctional Centre or other specialized treatment units (e.g. sex offender) throughout the correctional system.

Department of Corrections, Division of Juvenile Corrections: Within one of the juvenile correctional facilities and under the general supervision of an institution unit supervisor or assistant unit supervisor or the social services director, identifies and assesses the nature and causes of client's problems and capacities; formulates service delivery plan to aid client; monitors and implements the case plan; provides counselling and guidance and develops and refers client to appropriate institution and community resources. Coordinates treatment efforts with other institution staff, aftercare agents, family, and/or community resources; and represents the institution in Office of Juvenile Offender Review proceedings.

Qualifications

The qualifications required for these positions will be determined at the time of recruitment. Such determinations will be made based on an analysis of the goals and worker activities performed and by an identification of the education, training, work, or other life experience which would provide reasonable assurance that the knowledge and skills required upon appointment have been acquired. Must be certified or eligible to become certified at the appropriate level of "social worker" by the Examining Board of Social Workers, Marriage and Family Therapists and Professional Counsellors within the Department of Regulation and Licensing. Select positions may require this certification plus one year of supervised social work experience in a long term care setting in order for the facility to meet federal certification requirements as a long term care facility.

PSYCHIATRIC SOCIAL WORK

History – Scope – Changing perspective of Psychiatric Social Work – Changing trends in Mental Health Care – Indian view of Mental Health and wellbeing.

History

- Mental health considered as illness because of demons and sins
- Barbaric treatment during medieval period in the name of cleansing and propitiation (pacify)
- Common adopted treatments were blood letting, starvation, blistering, purging (removal), whippings.
- There was overcrowding in insane asylums, criminal houses, jails and prisons.
- Pioneers in mental health care – Dorothea lynde dix, Rank, Meyer, Sullivan
- First social worker in mental health is considered as handmaidens to psychiatry
- First social worker in mental health field was in Massachusetts Neurological Department – then Manhattan state hospital NY – Boston psychopathic hospital.
- The surgeon general asked American Red Cross to establish SW federation in hospitals after World War I
- Child Guidance Movement supported SW'ers
- II world war emphasized need of SW for war veterans.
- Mental health act insisted the importance of social worker in psychiatric field.

- American Association of Psychiatric Social Workers – AAPSW (now merged into NASW – National Association for Social Workers) was formed – released journals and newsletters.
- Now – a – days PSW recognised worldwide.

Dates and important events in the history of Psychiatric social work:

- Began in hospital setting in 1905 – nurse Garnet I. Pelton appointed by physician Richard Cabot at Massachusetts General Hospital in Internal Medicine Clinic
- 1907 – SW'ers placed in Neurology clinic of MGH – said to be the beginning of psychiatric Social work
- No distinction between MSW and PSW
- Ida Cannon succeeded Garnet I. Pelton – said – practice from Dr's office to home visits – diagnosis and treatment.
- Speech by Cabot – 'Hospital and Dispensary SW' @ international conference of SW Paris 1928 – agreed that primary function of SW'er is to teach Dr's and nurses about the social & psychological aspects of disease
- Period of Conflict – cannon spoke about – the direct treatment role of SW inhealth care, ie, removing obstacles in patients surroundings for successful treatment Cabot spoke about – SW'er a bridge, ie, liaison between hospital and patients.

SOCIAL PSYCHIATRY

Social psychiatry is a branch of psychiatry that focuses on the "interpersonal" and cultural context of mental disorder and mental wellbeing. It involves a sometimes disparate set of theories and approaches, with work stretching from epidemiological survey research on the one hand, to an indistinct boundary with individual or group psychotherapy on the other. Social psychiatry combines a medical training and perspective with fields such as social anthropology, social psychology, cultural psychiatry, sociology and other disciplines relating to mental distress and disorder. Social psychiatry has been particularly associated with the development of therapeutic communities, and to highlighting the effect of socioeconomic factors on mental illness. Social psychiatry can be contrasted with biopsychiatry, with the latter focused on genetics, brain neurochemistry and medication. Social psychiatry was the dominant form of psychiatry for periods of the 20th century but is currently less visible than biopsychiatry.

History

The events of the first half of the 20th century brought the issue of the relationship between the individual and the community to the fore. Psychiatrists who showed a willingness to confront these issues at home, after the war, called themselves social psychiatrists. Psychoanalytic psychotherapy and all its offshoots were grounded in an approach to the patient that focused almost exclusively on the individual—the relational aspects of therapy were implicit in the relationship between therapist and patient, but the main source of problem and motivation for change was seen as being intrapsychic (within the individual).

The social and political contexts were largely disregarded. Sarason observed in 1981, that "it is as though society does not exist for the psychologist. Society is a vague, amorphous background that can be disregarded in one's efforts to fathom the laws of behaviour" (Sarason 1981).

Early landmarks in social psychiatry included: Karen Horney, MD, who wrote about personality as it interacts with other people (1937); Erik Erikson, who discussed the influence of society on development (1950); Harry Stack Sullivan's (1953) integration of sociological and psychodynamic concepts, and his work on the role of early interpersonal interactions in the development of the self; Cornell University's Midtown Manhattan Study, which looked at the prevalence of mental illness in Manhattan; August Hollingshead, PhD, and Frederick Redlich, MD, looked at the influence of social class on psychiatric conditions (1958); Alexander H. Leighton, MD, looked at the relationship between social disintegration and mental illness (1959); Burrow was an early pioneer of the social causes of mental disorder and suggested "Sociatry" as the name for this new discipline.

Over the years many sociologists have contributed theories and research which has enlightened psychiatry in this area (e.g. Avison and Robin's); The relationship between social factors and mental illness was demonstrated by the early work of Hollingshead and Readlich in Chicago in the 1930s, who found a high concentration of individuals diagnosed with schizophrenia in deprived areas of the city has been replicated numerous times throughout the world, although controversy still exists as to the extent of drift of vulnerable individuals to these areas or of a higher incidence of the disorder in the socially disadvantaged; the Midtown Manhattan Study conducted in the 1950s by Cornell University hinted at widespread psychopathology among the general population of New York City; the Three Hospitals Study was a very influential work that has been replicated, that demonstrated forcefully that the poverty of the environment in poor mental hospitals lead to greater handicaps in the patients.

Social psychiatry was instrumental in the development of therapeutic communities. Under the influence of Maxwell Jones, Main, Wilmer and others, combined with the publications of critiques of the existing mental health system and the sociopolitical influences that permeated the psychiatric world, the concept of the therapeutic community and its attenuated form—the therapeutic milieu—caught on and dominated the field of inpatient psychiatry throughout the 1960s. The aim of therapeutic communities was a more democratic, user-led form of therapeutic environment, avoiding the authoritarian and demeaning practices of many psychiatric establishments of the time. The central philosophy is that clients are active participants in their own and each other's mental health treatment and tnat responsibility for the daily running of the community is shared among the clients and the staff. "TCs" have often eschewed or limited medication in favour of psychoanalytically-derived group-based insight therapies.

Current Work

Social psychiatry has been important in developing the concept of major "life events" as precipitants of mental ill health, including for example bereavement, promotion, moving house, having a child. Originally inpatient centres, many therapeutic communities now operate as day centres, often focused on borderline personality disorder and run by psychotherapists or art therapists rather than psychiatrists.

Social psychiatrists help test the cross-cultural use of psychiatric diagnoses and assessments of need or disadvantage, showing particular links between mental illness and unemployment, overcrowding and single parent families. Social psychiatrists also work to link concepts such as self-esteem and self-efficacy to mental health, and in turn to socioeconomic factors.

Social psychiatrists work on social firms in regard to people with mental health problems. These are regular businesses in the market that employ a significant number of people with disabilities, who are paid regular wages and work on the basis of regular work contracts. There are approximately 2,000 social firms in Europe and a large percentage of people with disabilities who work in social firms have a psychiatric disability. Some are specifically for people with psychiatric disabilities. Social psychiatrists often focus on rehabilitation in a social context, rather than "treatment" per se. A related approach is community psychiatry.

Facilitating the social inclusion of people with mental health problems is a major focus of modern social psychiatry.

MEDICAL SOCIAL WORK

Medical social work is a sub-discipline of social work, also known as Hospital social work. Medical social workers typically work in a hospital, skilled nursing facility or hospice, have a graduate degree in the field, and work with patients and their families in need of psychosocial help. Medical social workers assess the psychosocial functioning of patients and families and intervene as necessary. Interventions may include connecting patients and families to necessary resources and supports in the community; providing psychotherapy, supportive counselling, or grief counselling; or helping a patient to expand and strengthen their network of social supports. Medical social workers typically work on an interdisciplinary team with professionals of other disciplines.

Britain and Ireland

Medical social workers in Britain and Ireland were previously known as Almoners, or Hospital Almoners. In Ireland, the origins of medical social workers go back to Dr. Ella Webb, who in 1918 established a dispensary for sick children in the Adelaide Hospital in Dublin, and to Winifred Alcock who trained as an Almoner and worked with Dr. Webb in her dispensary. In 1945 the Institute of Almoners in Britain was formed, which in 1964 was renamed as the Institute of Medical Social Workers. The Institute of Medical Social Workers was one of the founder organizations of the British Association of Social Workers which was formed in 1970. In Britain, Medical Social Workers were transferred from the NHS into local authority Social Services Departments in 1974, and generally became known as Hospital Social Workers.

United States

The Massachusetts General Hospital was the first American hospital to have professional social workers on site in the early 1900s. The position was created by Richard Clarke Cabot to help patients to deal with areas of their life that made treatment difficult. This was important from an epidemiological point of view, as it made it easier to control and prevent outbreaks of syphilis and tuberculosis.

THE MEDICAL SOCIAL WORKER PROFESSION

Role and Required Skills

The medical social worker has a critical role in the area of discharge planning. It is the medical social worker's responsibility to ensure that the services the patient requires are in place in order to facilitate a timely discharge and prevent delays in discharge that can cost the hospital thousands of dollars per day. For example, the medical doctor may inform the medical social worker that a patient will soon be cleared for discharge (a term that means that the patient no longer requires hospitalization) and will need home care services. It is the medical social worker's job to then arrange for the home care service to be in place so that the patient can be discharged. If the medical social worker fails to arrange for the home care service, the patient may not leave the hospital resulting in a delay in discharge. In such situations, the treating physician is ultimately held responsible for the delay. Nevertheless, the medical social worker often bears the brunt of the blame for the delay in discharge and his or her failure to perform often attracts the attention of management.

Another skill required of the medical social worker is the ability to work cooperatively with other health care staff as part of a multidisciplinary treatment team. They need to have good analytical and assessment skills, an ability to communicate clearly with both patients and staff, and an ability to quickly engage the patient in a therapeutic relationship. The Medical Social Worker will inevitably have to be able to process almost a never-ending flow of paperwork, whilst retaining a willingness to advocate for the patient, especially in situations where the medical social worker has identified a problem that may compromise the discharge and put the patient at risk in the community.

For example, the medical doctor reports that a medically frail elderly patient is medically cleared for discharge and plans to discharge the patient home with home care services. However, after assessing the patient's psychosocial needs, the medical social worker determines that the patient does not have the requisite ability to direct a home care worker and recommends that the discharge be deferred pending further assessment of this problem. In such a case, it is the medical social worker's ethical duty to inform the medical doctor that the discharge may place the patient at risk and advocate for another, more appropriate discharge even if it means that the patient's discharge has to be postponed. It is precisely in such cases that the medical social worker proves his or her worth-by placing the needs of the patient above all other considerations.

Challenges

As medical social workers often have large case-loads and have to meet tight deadlines to arrange for necessary services, medical social work is on the whole a very demanding job. Medical social workers often confront highly complex cases involving patients with multiple psycho-social issues, all of which require intervention and result in delays in discharge. For instance, in a major urban acute care medical centre, it is not uncommon for the medical social worker to assess patients who experience one or many of the following social problems: homelessness, multiple chronic medical and psychiatric conditions, lack of stable employment, previous incarceration, and substance abuse problems. Any of these, separately and together, can impede timely discharge. Sometimes situations as mundane as the patient needing money for transport or clothing can lead to delays in discharge, especially if these needs are not identified early. This is why a complete and timely assessment of the patient's psychosocial needs is critical.

RURAL SOCIAL WORK PRACTICE

Managing dual relationships in social work practice can present many challenges to professional boundaries. These challenges are heightened in small communities and rural areas, where dual and multiple relationships are a consequence of dense networks. A dual relationship can be defined as a set of multiple relationships in which one is professional, and the other(s) are of a social, financial, or professional nature. Dual relationships may create boundary issues for the practitioner. Reamer (2001) describes boundary issues as circumstances in which human service professionals encounter actual or potential conflicts between their professional duties, and their social, sexual, religious, or business relationships".

A direct service issue that arises within rural social work practice from the increased likelihood of encountering dual relationships is the maintenance of client confidentiality and privacy. This article will explore this particular practice issue and provide guidelines on how to protect privacy and confidentiality from clinical, organizational, and community perspectives.

There is limited scholarship available that examines dual relationships in rural practice (Miller, 1998). There is an even smaller amount that examines confidentiality and privacy issues in rural areas. Green and Mason (2002) published one of the most extensive articles on this issue. They report on a research project that examined the experiences of social work and welfare practitioners practicing in rural areas in regard to personal and professional role boundaries. Three issues that emerged from the study concerning confidentiality were guarding privileged knowledge, the use of client-related knowledge gained informally, and rural service delivery considerations that protect client privacy and confidentiality. The authors point out that absolute confidentiality is difficult to obtain in rural areas. Ethical conflicts are often created between a practitioners duty to the client and a duty to others. The argument is made that confidentiality should be a guarantee against disclosures except in clearly defined circumstances such as situations in which there is suspected child abuse, when the client is suicidal, or when there is a threat to another person. Confidentiality is particularly challenged since rural social work practice involves working with communities, groups, teams, and other agencies. The authors also point out that clients may choose not to obtain services, because of their concerns about how confidential information is handled.

Barbopoulos & Clark (2003) acknowledge that privacy and confidentiality present particular challenges to practitioners providing direct services to rural clients. Client privacy is difficult to maintain, as people know one another and are more likely to be seen in the location in which services are provided. Rural communities also allow opportunities for nonprofessional interactions with clients, friends of clients, or relatives of clients.

In a survey of college therapists, Sharkin and Birky (1992) found that 95% of their sample had accidental meetings with clients. Nonprofessional interactions in rural settings run the gamut from minor accidental meetings to substantial overlapping relationships. In another study, Schank and Skovholt (1997) surveyed members of the Minnesota Psychological Association practicing in rural areas and found that all respondents reported overlapping relationships. These overlapping relationships included ones with multiple family members for 75% of the participants, and situations in which different clients had relationships with each other for 56% of the participants. Respondents reported that boundary setting was particularly important to the protection of client confidentiality. The authors assert that clear expectations and boundaries strengthen the therapeutic relationship and urge practitioners to obtain informed consent, protect confidentiality, and explain the limits of confidentiality discussing any overlapping relationships as essential to ensure sound professional practice in small communities.

Theoretical Framework

A social workers obligation to maintain confidences is linked to the deontological conception of morality. According to this theory, actions or rules are right if they comply with a principle or principles of obligation. Deontology maintains that actions are morally wrong because an action is classified as a moral violation. Deontologists believe that relationships carry with them certain obligations, such as obligations social workers have with their clients. These obligations include confidentiality and respect for privacy (Beauchamp, 1991; Frankena, 1973). The *NASW Code of Ethics* would be considered a set of rules that every social worker must abide in to prevent immoral behaviour. Within this code, privacy and confidentiality is considered an ethical standard to be upheld by practicing social workers. Parameters are set related to the management of confidentiality within the boundaries of professional relationships. Other relevant Codes of Ethics, such as those developed by the Clinical Social Work Federation, the Canadian Association of Social Workers, and the American Psychological Association, also include confidentiality as an important ethical standard.

In addition to obligation duties, social workers as individuals can turn to virtue ethics for guidance. Theories of virtue depend on an assessment of moral traits that establish an individual's moral character. A moral virtue is a character trait that is morally valued. Aristotle, a virtue ethicist, maintained that the virtue of people consists of how well they do their work and their ability to function successfully. A virtue is a disposition, habit, quality, or trait of a person. He believed that there is an innate capacity for virtuous behaviour which is developed through proper training and experience. Confidentialness and respectfulness for privacy are considered virtue standards. Applying this theory to the social work profession, social workers as individuals should aspire to cultivate confidentialness and respectfulness for privacy as character traits. To this end, guidelines are provided herein for clinical, organizational, and community practice to assist in the development of confidentialness and respectfulness for privacy for practitioners who work in rural environments.

Clinical Considerations and Guidelines

Dual relationships are inherent in rural social work practice and create challenges to maintaining client confidentiality. Confidentiality can be described as the regulation, both legal and ethical, that protect the clients rights of privacy. Privacy refers to the degree of control a client has over what happens to information about him/her held by the worker. Although boundary violations (where the worker is manipulative, exploitive, coercive, or deceptive to the client) may occur in rural areas, boundary crossings may emerge more frequently. Boundary crossings refer to the mix of professional and personal relationships in which the anonymity of clients and workers can be unavoidably compromised (Healy, 2003).

Rural areas include strong community ties with ample opportunity for chance encounters and boundary crossings with clients (Healy, 2003). Essentially, rural social workers are never off-duty within their communities since they often live and work in the same town, causing professional and personal relationships to blend. To be a member of a rural community means that close knit bonds exist and there is the expectation to engage in cultural mores and community events. To be seen in the community and to support activities builds trust and support for the professional role. Information received in informal settings or outside the realm of professional relationships presents challenges to the practitioner. For instance, clients and social workers may encounter each other in the grocery store, place of worship, or little league baseball game. Clients may regard these times as opportunities to ask for further assistance. Boundary crossings are not always harmful (Reamer, 2003); however, it is important for the practitioner to develop skills in assessing the potential harm or benefit in boundary crossings that may present themselves in clinical practice and to discuss these situations with the client.

The rural social worker is responsible for maintaining appropriate boundaries regarding confidentiality and the protection of client-related information. Although the National Association of Social Workers and state licensing boards set standards and parameters in regard to confidentiality and privacy matters, no guidelines or practice tools are offered to address these standards, particularly within rural areas.

The professional literature offers some guidance. Kagle and Giebelhausen (1994) advocate the avoidance of dual relationships whenever possible, and suggest rural practitioners work and live in different geographical regions. Other authors note that these solutions are often not possible in rural areas, and leave the practitioner with no direction on how to manage dual relationships in an ethical manner (Green & Mason, 2002; Healy, 2003; Evans & Harris, 2004).

Guidelines for Protecting Client Confidentiality

The authors present a set of guidelines that attempt to balance the protection of privacy while acknowledging that chance encounters occur in rural areas. The following practice guidelines account for the complex nature of dual or multiple relationships and the opportunities for boundary crossings in rural areas.

1. Always use informed consent procedures in professional relationships. A discussion of policy and ethical considerations, particularly confidentiality rules, is an important component to the client-worker relationship in rural areas. While addressing informed consent, discussions need to deal with the types of boundary crossings and their possible risks to client confidentiality.
2. Include a discussion of dual relationships and potential for boundary crossings during the assessment process. In the completion of psychosocial assessments, include a discussion of relationships and activities that the client is engaged in that may present the potential for boundary crossings between the client and the worker. The use of genograms and eco-maps will help in this

process. For instance, during the assessment process, a client genogram may uncover mutual relationships between the client and the worker, whereas a client eco-map may identify mutual social systems. When a potential conflict is discovered, the client and worker should engage in a mutual discussion about how potential encounters should be handled. This technique allows clients to take control of their privacy and reinforces their empowerment. In addition, this type of discussion strengthens the client-worker relationship as they work together to develop a plan of action that protects confidentiality.

3. Develop a plan of action regarding how boundary crossings will be handled. The development of a plan of action regarding boundary crossings prior to their occurrence enhances a clients ability to maintain control of his/her privacy. For instance, upon completing an eco-map, a worker may note that the client shares the same place of worship. A discussion of this association with the client will help each to prepare for chance encounters. Each discussion of mutual associations during the assessment process should include the development of a plan for how to address them. A plan of action should include points of choice making for clients, such as whether and how the client and worker should acknowledge each other in public places.
4. Conduct periodic evaluations on how boundary crossings are being handled. Exploring boundary crossings and their impact on client confidentiality needs to occur throughout the helping process. This evaluation should include a review of the plan of action, and a discussion of information, relationships, and mutual social systems not identified during the assessment phase. Also, any unplanned encounters should continue to be a point of discussion between the worker and client in regard to their impact on confidentiality and the helping relationship.

These guidelines are offered as suggestions for how social workers can manage client confidentiality, potential boundary crossings, and dual relationships in the delivery of services in rural areas. These guidelines are particularly suited for the practitioner working within a clinical practice.

However, agency attention to the issues of dual relationships, confidentiality, and privacy rights cannot be confined to micro and meso level practice issues. There are challenges at the macro level that involve the management of privacy and confidentiality within agencies and communities located in rural areas.

Macro Considerations and Guidelines

If little is known about how rural social workers in direct practice address dual relationships and confidentiality issues, even less is known about how these issues impact macro practice in rural areas. Organizations have multiple relationships with other organizations in the community and internally with their clients, and members of the board, staff, and volunteers. Social workers, in leadership positions in their organizations and within the community as a whole, have a number of responsibilities to manage dual relationships and protect client confidentiality.

ORGANIZATIONAL POLICIES ON CONFIDENTIALITY

All organizations should have policies on confidentiality, which are shared with clients and staff. It is recommended that confidentiality policies include criteria for release of information about clients, the limitations of confidentiality, information about applicable state statutes and funder regulations, how to handle subpoenaed information, guidelines for what is included and excluded in permanent client files, and who has access to client files. Policies that address the protection of client information stored in computer files are also necessary to safeguard this material. Additionally, guidelines need to be developed on how staff use and manage e-mail communication that may include client information.

Clients should be informed in writing about the organizations confidentiality policies, as well as their limitations, especially with regard to disclosures of abuse of children, older adults, and persons with disabilities. Additionally, it is suggested that social work administrators include information about state laws that address whether certain professionals or persons working in specific types of agencies have privileged communication, and the limits of that privileged communication. One tool that can be used to inform clients of these policies is the development of a flyer that addresses boundary issues, confidentiality policies, and client rights. This tool may be used within the helping relationship between client and worker, and may serve to enhance the client-worker relationship through providing an opportunity for talking openly and genuinely about client confidentiality and privacy rights.

Agency policies should also address the termination of employees, board members, or volunteers who violate organizational policy on client confidentiality. It is helpful to present policies on confidentiality and organizational expectations related to these policies at the time of hire or appointment.

Also, the employer needs to inform personnel of client confidentiality policies, and the consequences for violating such policies. All employees and volunteers, including board members of human service agencies, should receive training on this information. It is suggested that employees, volunteers, and board members sign a statement indicating they have been informed, understand, and agree to abide by the policies they received information on during the training. It is recommended that instruction on agency policies occur periodically to reinforce personnels knowledge and awareness of them.

Use of Consultants

Another area that may involve potential breaches of confidentiality by persons serving dual roles within the organization is the use of consultants (Yankey, 1998). Agencies should avoid hiring as a consultant someone who already has a relationship with the organization, whether they are board members, volunteers, or clients. As an administrative decision, it may be best to use out of town consultants. In consultation practice, the use of distance as a boundary may be more easily arranged than in direct community practice, and it is consistent with Kagle and Giebelhausens (1994) recommendation for rural practice management. Nevertheless, all consultants should be asked to sign a confidentiality pledge form. A professional social worker who functions as a consultant in the community should not accept an appointment with organizations where protection of confidentiality cannot be established. The status of former client of the agency on the part of the consultant or close personal relationship with former clients of an agency should rule out a consultation relationship with that agency.

Finally, more information is needed about how rural organizations handle dual relationships and confidentiality. Do models exist that create a balance between managing an agency and maintaining relationships in rural areas while protecting client confidentiality and respecting boundaries? How do rural agencies handle the protection of confidentiality between board members, staff, and clients in rural-based organizations? Are there ways in which organizations have organized their physical space (private waiting rooms, separate areas for entrance and exit) to ensure client confidentiality? More emphasis on these issues within the professional literature will help to strengthen rural social work practice.

WELFARE STATE

A welfare state is a concept of government where the state plays the primary role in the protection and promotion of the economic and social well-being of its citizens. It is based on the principles of equality of opportunity, equitable distribution of wealth, and public responsibility for those unable to avail themselves of the minimal provisions for a good life. The general term may cover a variety of forms of economic and social organization. There are two main interpretations of the idea of a welfare state:

- A model in which the state assumes primary responsibility for the welfare of its citizens. This responsibility in theory ought to be comprehensive, because all aspects of welfare are considered and universally applied to citizens as a "right".
- Welfare state can also mean the creation of a "social safety net" of minimum standards of varying forms of welfare.

There is some confusion between a "welfare state" and a "welfare society," and debate about how each term should be defined. In many countries, especially in the United States, some degree of welfare is not actually provided by the state, but directly to welfare recipients from a combination of independent volunteers, corporations (both non-profit charitable corporations as well as for-profit corporations), and government services. This phenomenon has been termed a "welfare society," and the term "welfare system" has been used to describe the range of welfare state and welfare society mixes that are found. The welfare state involves a direct transfer of funds from the public sector to welfare recipients, but indirectly, the private sector is often contributing those funds via redistributionist taxation; the welfare state has been referred to as a type of "mixed economy".

Etymology

English term "welfare state" is believed by Asa Briggs to have been coined by Archbishop William Temple during the Second World War, contrasting wartime Britain with the "warfare state" of Nazi Germany. Friedrich Hayek contends that the term derived from the older German word *Wohlfahrtsstaat*, which itself was used by nineteenth century historians to describe a variant of the ideal of *Polizeistaat* ("police state"). It was fully developed by the German academic *Sozialpolitiker*—"Social Politics"—from 1870 and first implemented through Bismarck's "state socialism". Bismarck's policies have also been seen as the creation of a welfare state.

In German, a roughly equivalent term (*Sozialstaat*, "social state") had been in use since 1870. There had been earlier attempts to use the same phrase in English, for example in Munroe Smith's text "Four German Jurists", but the term did not enter common use until William Temple popularized it. The Italian term "Social state" (*Stato sociale*) has the same origin. The term "Wohlfahrtsstaat", which is a direct translation from English, is used to describe Sweden. The Swedish welfare state is called Folkhemmet (literally; the folk home) and goes back to the 1936 compromise between the Union and big Corporate companies. It is a Mixed economy, built on strong unions and a strong system of Social security and universal health care.

In French, the synonymous term "providence state" was originally coined as a sarcastic pejorative remark used by opponents of welfare state policies during the Second Empire (1854–1870). In Spanish and many other languages, an analogous term is used: *estado del bienestar*; translated literally: "state of well-being".

In Portuguese, a similar phrase exists: *Estado de Providência*; which means "Providing State", as in the State should provide citizens their demands in order to achieve people's well-being. In Brazil it is referred to as *Estado de Bem-Estar Social*, translated as social well-being state.

History of Welfare States

The existence of military pensions can be traced back at least to the Roman Empire. The Mauryan Empire was the first welfare state that became of the form when Emperor Ashoka introduced reforms after the Kalinga war. The modern welfare state developed during the late 19th and 20th century in response to Karl Marx's theory of the inherent instability of capitalism in an attempt to protect the capitalist system from a socialist revolution. The first practical implementation of the welfare state was instituted by German Chancellor Otto von Bismarck as a direct attempt to stave off socialism. These welfare programs differed from previous schemes of poverty relief due to their relatively universal coverage. The development of social insurance in Germany under Bismarck was particularly influential. Some schemes, like those in Scandinavia, were based largely in the development of autonomous, mutualist provision of benefits. Others were founded on state provision. The term was not, however, applied to all states offering social protection. The sociologist T.H. Marshall identified the welfare state as a distinctive combination of democracy, welfare and capitalism. Examples of early welfare states in the modern world are Germany, all of the Nordic Countries, the Netherlands, Uruguay and New Zealand and the United Kingdom in the 1930s. Changed attitudes in reaction to the Great Depression were instrumental in the move to the welfare state in many countries, a harbinger of new times where "cradle-to-grave" services became a reality after the poverty of the Depression. During the Great Depression, it was seen as an alternative "middle way" between communism and capitalism. In the period following the Second World War, many countries in Europe moved from partial or selective provision of social services to relatively comprehensive coverage of the population. The activities of present-day welfare states extend to the provision of both cash welfare benefits (such as old-age pensions or unemployment benefits) and in-kind welfare services (such as health or childcare services). Through these provisions, welfare states can affect the distribution of wellbeing and personal autonomy among their citizens, as well as influencing how their citizens consume and how they spend their time.

After the discovery and inflow of the oil revenue, Saudi Arabia, Brunei, Kuwait, Qatar, Bahrain, Oman, and the United Arab Emirates all became welfare states for their respective citizens if not for guest labourers. In the United Kingdom, the beginning of the modern welfare state was in 1911 when David Lloyd George suggested everyone in work should pay national insurance contribution for unemployment and health benefits from work.

In 1942, the Social Insurance and Allied Services was created by Sir William Beveridge in order to aid those who were in need of help, or in poverty. Beveridge worked as a volunteer for the poor, and set up national insurance. He stated that 'All people of working age should pay a weekly national insurance contribution. In return, benefits would be paid to people who were sick, unemployed, retired or widowed.' The basic assumptions of the report were the National Health Service, which provided free health care to the UK. The Universal Child Benefit was a scheme to give benefits to parents, encouraging people to have children by enabling them to feed and support a family. One theme of the report was the relative cheapness of universal benefits. Beveridge quoted miner's pension schemes as some of the most efficient available, and argued that a state scheme would be cheaper to run than individual friendly societies and private insurance schemes, as well as being cheaper than means-tested government-run schemes for the poor. The cheapness of what was to be called National Insurance was an argument alongside fairness, and justified a scheme in which the rich paid-in and the state paid-out to the rich, just as for the poor. In the original scheme, only some benefits called National Assistance were to be paid regardless of contribution. Universal benefits paid to rich and poor such as child benefit were particularly beneficial after the second world war when the population of the United Kingdom declined. Universal Child Benefit may have helped drive the Baby boom. The impact of the report was huge and 600,000 copies were made.

Beveridge recommended to the government that they should find ways of tackling the five giants, being Want, Disease, Ignorance, Squalor and Idleness. He argued to cure these problems, the government should provide adequate income to people, adequate health care, adequate education, adequate housing and adequate employment. Before 1939, most health care had to be paid for through non government organisations, this was done through a vast network of friendly societies, trade unions and other insurance companies which counted the vast majority of the UK working population as members. These friendly societies provided insurance for sickness, unemployment and invalidity, therefore providing people with an income when they were unable to work. But because of the 1942 Beveridge Report, in 5 July 1948, the National Insurance Act, National Assistance Act and National Health Service Act came into force, thus this is the day that the modern UK welfare state was founded. Institutions run by local councils to provide health services for the uninsured poor-part of the poor law tradition of workhouses-were merged into the new national system.

Welfare systems were developing intensively since the end of the World War II. At the end of century due to their restructuring part of their responsibilities started to be channeled through non-governmental organizations which became important providers of social services.

Three Forms of the Welfare State

According to Esping-Andersen (1990), there are three ways of organizing a welfare state instead of only two. Rothstein argues that the first model the state is primarily concerned with directing the resources to "the people most in need". This requires a tight bureaucratic control over the people concerned. According to the second model the state distributes welfare with as little bureaucratic interference as possible, to all people who fulfill easily established criteria (e.g. having children, receiving medical treatment, etc.). This requires high taxing. This model was constructed by the Scandinavian ministers Karl Kristian Steincke and Gustav Möller in the 30s and is dominant in Scandinavia. The third model is similar to the one found in Britain (Beveridge model) and is based more on citizenship and a certain level of welfare 'as a right', which may then be modified according to needs.

Esping-Andersen argues, based on comparative histories of actual welfare states, that they fall into three types of policies: liberalist (heavily means tested, limited services), corporatist (pre-market conservative welfare state in origin, social insurance schemes), and social democratic (universalistic "Beveridge" style social rights based on citizenship instead of working life).

STATE ACTION, SOCIAL WELFARE RIGHTS, AND THE JUDICIAL ROLE

Consider the following cases: (1) A man employed by a private college informs his employer (in response to an inquiry) that he is a gay. The employer fires him. The former employee sues the college, claiming that the college's action violates the nation's constitutional requirement that everyone be treated equally. (2) A hearing-impaired person seeks medical care from a hospital, which indicates its willingness to provide the care on the condition that the patient provide, and pay for, a sign-language interpreter to assist in the delivery of the medical care. The patient sues the hospital, claiming that its refusal to provide service violate the constitutional norm of equality. (3) A group of farm laborers organizes itself and approaches the workers' employer, seeking to bargain collectively over wages, hours, and conditions of labour. The employer refuses to bargain. The union sues the employer, claiming that the refusal to bargain violates the workers' constitutionally protected right of association.

In each of these cases the plaintiffs seek to invoke constitutional norms against a non-governmental actor. Constitutional systems address their ability to do so through the doctrines of state action or horizontal effect: The plaintiff loses if the defendant is not a "state actor," or if the constitutional system does not give constitutional guarantees direct horizontal effect.

Another way of describing the cases is this: In each the defendant has acted in a manner authorized by background rules of property and contract, rules which have not been modified by legislation applicable to the action the defendant took. The college relies on the employment-at-will doctrine; the hospital and the farm owner rely on the rule of contract law that no one is required to make a contract on terms other than those to which he or she agrees. The plaintiff's claim is therefore that the nation's constitution necessarily alters those background rules. The state action/horizontal effect doctrine identifies the circumstances under which such claims are legally valid.

The Canadian Supreme Court's initial foray into the state-action field involved the following facts: An employer locked out workers associated with a labour union. The employer operated a delivery business primarily in Ontario. It subcontracted for delivery services in British Columbia with another delivery business. The union wanted to picket the British Columbia business, and sought a declaration from the relevant labour board that the British Columbia business was an "ally" of the Ontario one. Such a declaration would have insulated the union from liability in tort for picketing at the British Columbia business. The labour board refused to make the requested declaration. The British Columbia business then obtained an injunction from a trial court against picketing, a remedy traditionally available to prevent the tort of inducing breach of contract. The union challenged the injunction as a violation of the right to freedom of expression guaranteed by the Charter of Rights.

The Canadian Supreme Court held that the Charter did not "apply to private litigation divorced completely from any connection with the Government." It relied on a combination of textual and functional reasons. Section 32 of the Charter states that the Charter applies "to the Parliament and government of Canada" and "to the legislature and government of each province" in respect of "all matters within" their respective authority. The natural reading of this provision, according to the Supreme Court, is that "government" refers to the executive branch, not to the government "in its generic sense – meaning the whole of the governmental apparatus of the state" including the judiciary; if the latter were the meaning, the specific mention of "Parliament" and "the legislature" would be unnecessary. Functionally, "the Charter, like most written constitutions, was set up to regulate the relationship between the individual and the Government."

So far, so good: The Charter does not apply to background rules of property and contract. That the tort of inducing a breach of contract might be in some tension with norms dealing with the right of association does not authorize the courts to find the tort, or an injunction aimed at preventing the tort, unconstitutional. Similarly, that the employment-at-will doctrine is in some tension with constitutional nondiscrimination norms does not authorize the courts to find a discriminatory firing to be a breach of contract. All three plaintiffs described at the outset should lose, because they were arguing that the Charter directly shaped the background rules of contract and property.

Now, consider some additional facts. In the gay rights case, the province in which the college was located had a human rights act that prohibited discrimination on the basis of race, religious beliefs, sex, marital status, age, ancestry, and place of origin. The act did not include sexual orientation as a protected category. In the medical care case, the government reimburses hospitals and other care providers for the costs of medically required services. The administrators of the reimbursement system decided, before the litigation arose, that sign-language interpretation was not a medically required service, and therefore decided not to reimburse hospitals and care providers for that service. In the farm workers' case, the applicable labour relations act initially had excluded farm laborers, then was amended to include farm laborers, thereby imposing an obligation on employers to bargain collectively with farm workers' unions. Later, the statute was again amended, this time to exclude farm laborers.

Do these facts change the state action/horizontal effect analysis? It is hard to see how they should if the Charter in fact does not apply to background rules of contract and The Canadian Supreme Court expressly acknowledged that its holding on direct horizontal effect did not rule out the possibility that the Charter would have indirect horizontal effect by influencing the courts' development of the contours of the background rules in light of Charter norms. See id. at 603 (answering "in the affirmative" to "the question whether the judiciary ought to apply and develop the principles of the common law in a manner consistent with the fundamental values enshrined in the Constitution.").

property. The human rights act affects some, indeed many, of the college's background rights of property and contract – but not its right to make employment decisions on grounds not covered by the act. The medical reimbursement system shifts the cost of providing medically required care from the patient or the hospital to taxpayers generally, but it does not shift the cost of other services – newspaper delivery, for example, or services not found to be medically required – to the taxpayers. The hospital remains free to provide those services only to patients who are willing (and able) to pay for them. By repealing the inclusion of farm workers in the labour relations act, the legislature restored the status quo ante, in which employers had the ordinary common-law right to deal with employees on whatever terms the employer chose.

Yet, in all three cases the Canadian Supreme Court held that the Charter had been violated, or so I believe to be the best reading of the cases. The litigation structure of the cases the Court considered obscures the true holdings. In each real case the plaintiffs did not sue the employer or the hospital. Rather, they sued public officials, seeking declarations that the statutes excluding them from coverage violated the Charter. Yet, in agreeing with those claims, the Canadian Supreme Court effectively held that the Charter modified background rules of contract and property. The only thing the actual litigation structure did, compared to the one I described at the outset, was to allow the Court to put aside questions of remedy and retroactivity. government officials "who possess the power, by virtue of the state rules at issue, to put 'private' actors in a position to inflict injury'").

The state action/horizontal effect question is equivalent to asking whether, or under what circumstances, constitutional norms alter background rules of contract, tort, and property. The question arises because in many modern circumstances market outcomes – that is, those that result when people exercise the rights (and invoke the immunities) they have under the background rules of contract, tort, and property – seem to many as inconsistent with constitutional norms regarding the level and, particularly, the distribution of important goods.

In my hypothetical litigation structure, the gay former employee sues for breach of contract, seeking damages or reinstatement; the employer defends, pointing out that no statute alters its background property and contract rights; the plaintiff points to the human right act, saying that the Charter requires that the act include sexual orientation as a protected category, and that the employer's defence is overcome by the constitutionally obligatory human rights act. At that point the employer might contend that it is unfair to impose liability (particularly monetary liability) for violating a norm articulated by the courts only in the litigation itself. Cf. Lugar v. Edmondson Oil. Col. 457 U.S. 922, — (1982) (Powell, J., dissenting) (arguing that holding "a private citizen who did no more than commence a legal action of a kind traditionally initiated by private parties" is "plainly unjust to the respondent.").

State Action and the Activist State

Two public law doctrines responded to concerns about the level and distribution of goods. Legislatures could modify background rules of contract, property, and tort by exercising a police power. That power was narrowly defined, like the sub-rules in private law, and for similar reasons. The scope of the police power in classical legal theory can best be understood, I believe, as resulting from essentially prophylactic considerations: Courts agreed that legislatures might properly be concerned that courts in common-law litigation could not accurately identify all the occasions on which fraud, coercion, and the like actually occurred, and so allowed legislatures to exercise a police power targeted at fraud, coercion, and the like, but hitting somewhat more broadly than the courts themselves would.

In addition, courts developed a constitutional doctrine directly limiting legislative distribution of goods. Classical legal theory condemned as class legislation laws that intentionally, not incidentally, deprived people of the share of goods they could obtain on the market or, derivatively, through securing legislation within the scope of the police power. The U.S. Supreme Court's decision in Romer v. Evans can be understood as an application of classical legal theory to gay rights. The case's precise meaning is notoriously unclear, but at least one reasonable reading of the decision is that it holds a state-wide ban on legislation treating sexual orientation as a protected category unconstitutional because the ban was motivated by a simple desire to inflict harm. With classical legal theory's treatment of concerns about the level and distribution of important goods in hand, we can return to the Canadian cases. The activist state is defined by its concern about the level and distribution of important goods, so it is hardly surprising that the state action/horizontal effect question receives different answers in such states from those it received in the classical liberal state. In private law, a critique of formalism accompanied the rise of the activist state. That critique undermined the narrow definitions of the "exceptional" doctrines of fraud, coercion, and the like. A stylized account of the development is this: Courts began with the narrow definition of coercion, sharply distinguishing it from freedom. But, in some cases, the plaintiff's freedom seemed significantly constrained, although not as severely constrained as it had been in the cases initially defining coercion. The courts treated these new cases as involving coercion as well. At some point, it became clear that coercion, as the courts had defined it, was not a category sharply distinguished from freedom but simply a particular location on a continuum of varying degrees of freedom. The critique of formalism was that drawing a line anywhere along this continuum was an arbitrary choice, not guided by any defensible liberal theory of freedom and coercion. Once the ideas of fraud, coercion, and nuisance expanded in the activist state, the way was open for private law to accommodate concerns for the level and distribution of important goods by correcting market-based outcomes through the use of expansive versions of the classical sub-rules.

The public law of the activist, social democratic state expressed concern for the level and distribution of goods more directly. The activist state placed into question levels and distributions of important goods that seemed inconsistent with social democracy's guiding premises: If market transactions resulted in outcomes where people did not have "enough," according to prevailing social democratic norms, those outcomes certainly could be changed by legislation, and sometimes had to be changed pursuant to constitutional command. The classic U.S. state action case of Shelley v. Kraemer illustrates the shift from the focus on intent in classical legal theory to a focus on outcomes in the activist state. The Supreme Court there held that a state court's injunction against the transfer of property from a white seller to an African American buyer, issued to enforce a covenant restricting such transfers, was unconstitutional state action, even though the state courts were enforcing a rule neutral as to race that called upon them to enforce all restrictive covenants that left open a sufficiently large market for land sales. What made Shelley difficult for commentators was that the state courts there were enforcing a racially neutral rule, not one intentionally designed to disadvantage African Americans. The hard part of Shelley was not that state court enforcement of a common-law rule was state action, but that the rule it was enforcing was not one that classical legal theory would have condemned. Shelley's holding on the merits makes sense only on a theory of equality that condemns some distributions of important goods like housing.

The relation between an expansive state action/horizontal effect doctrine and the activist state can be seen throughout the Canadian cases. Dolphin Delivery, the Canadian Supreme Court's first state action case, distinguished an earlier lower court case in which a young woman brought proceedings in the local human rights commission against a private hockey association for excluding her from a boys' team. The human rights commission refused to act. The applicable statute did ban gender-based discrimination, but it contained an express exception "where membership in an athletic organization or participation in an athletic activity is restricted to persons of the same sex." The provincial supreme court held that the exclusion violated the Charter's equality guarantee. The Court in Dolphin Delivery approved that result. It described the case as "a law suit between private parties," but said that the hockey association had "acted on the authority of a statute," which "removed the case from the private sphere." Analytically this is hardly satisfying: The purported exclusion of the hockey association's discriminatory action could have been described as merely confirming the hockey association's pre-existing common-law rights of property and contract, which it exercised in excluding the complainant from the hockey team. The Supreme Court's intuition, though, is sensible enough in an active state, where – having entered a field – the state displaces the common law and converts all actions by private entities into actions authorized by the state.

The Canadian Supreme Court acknowledged this line of argument in the gay rights and medical care cases. The gay rights decision analyzed the problem as involving a legislative omission, or, equivalently, as involving the underinclusiveness of the human rights act. Characterizing the problem as one of omission is misleading. The enacted human rights act did not "omit" sexual orientation; it simply left in place the pre-existing background rights of property and contract. Finding a statute unconstitutional because it is underinclusive means that the Charter sometimes imposes affirmative obligations on the government: Once the government enters a field, such as restricting the contract and property rights of private entities in the service of the Charter's equality norms, it must occupy the entire field to the extent of those equality norms. The activist state, in turn, is defined by the fact that it has affirmative obligations. An expansive state action/horizontal effect doctrine allows the courts to collaborate with legislatures in defining the scope of those obligations. A central passage in the medical care case makes the same point. According to the Court, hospitals "act as agents for the government" in providing medical services. The Court continued, "The Legislature, upon defining its objective as guaranteeing access to a range of medical services, cannot evade its obligations under [the equality provision] to provide those services without discrimination by appointing hospitals to carry out that objective." The active state, having entered the field of subsidizing medical care, must do so fully; the legislature cannot define however it wants the "range" of services it is willing to provide within that field, but must instead secure judicial agreement on the range of services to be provided. Here too the activist state, through its legislature and courts, takes on affirmative obligations of providing services.

The Judicial Role in Light of the Equivalence of State Action

Social democracy affected private law by encouraging judges to develop the background rules of property, contract, and tort to respond to concerns about the level and distribution of important goods. It affected public law by encouraging judges to give constitutional norms horizontal effect. And, importantly, these two effects are in fact only one: The state action/horizontal effect doctrine is the doctrinal vehicle whereby background rules of property, contract, and tort are made subject to constitutional norms 15 dealing with the level and distribution of important goods.

Another way of putting the point is this: To ask whether the state action/horizontal effect doctrine should be expansive is to ask whether a nation's constitution guarantees social welfare rights – that is, whether the constitution mandates some level and distribution of important goods even if that level and distribution are not achieved through the operation of markets in which people invoke their background property and contract rights. But, the same results can be reached by adjusting the background rights themselves. The equivalence of the state action/horizontal effect doctrine and the development of background rules of property, contract, and tort poses an important question about the judicial role. It is conventionally asserted that courts are ill-suited to implement social welfare rights. For example, Cass Sunstein criticizes a constitutional provision guaranteeing a "right to an income conforming with the quantity and quality of work performed":

> This provision will have one of two consequences: (a) If the provision is to mean something, courts will have to oversee labour markets vary closely, to make sure that every bargain produces the right wage. We know enough to know that government is ill-equipped to undertake this task. Courts are in an even worse position to do so. And if courts are going to oversee the labour market, it will be impossible to have a labour market. (b) The relevant provisions will be ignored – treated as aspirations not subject to legal enforcement. This is a better outcome than (a), and courts in Eastern Europe should be encouraged to reach this conclusion. But it is hardly desirable to have a system in which many constitutional rights are ignored.

Of course, courts "oversee the labour market" through their development of background rules of property and contract. There can be no distinctive incapacity of courts that allows them to develop those background rules in an acceptable manner but makes them unable to develop social welfare rights – or, equivalently, unable to work out the contours of the state action/horizontal effect doctrine – equally acceptably. Put another way, we think we know that courts can develop background rules of property and contract acceptably; we know that courts must develop some doctrine of state action or horizontal effect; we may believe that courts cannot develop social welfare rights acceptably. The difficulty is that those three views are incompatible.

Addressing the Trilemma

The incompatibility among the three propositions I have described can be resolved in several ways. The most obvious is to deny that courts can in fact develop the background rules in ways responsive to concerns about the level and distribution of important goods. This would be to return to classical legal theory, specifically in private law, by constitutionalizing the common law. The U.S. experience with classical legal theory suggests the difficulty of that course. The New York Court of Appeals once held that legislation altering the common law could be unconstitutional. The case involved a workers' compensation statute and what the court took to be the common-law requirement that liability could ordinarily be predicated only on fault. The statute modified the common law either for reasons not encompassed within the government's police power, or by making a larger departure from the common law than the police power, understood as a defence against hard-to-detect occasions of fraud or coercion, could justify. The court's theory implied that judicial modification of the common law would also be unconstitutional, if the courts departed as substantially from the common law as the legislature had.

The New York court's result did not survive. Perhaps it was analytically coherent, although there surely would have been difficulty in working out how much the courts could modify the common law before they crossed the line into constitutional violation. Even if a court might construct an analytically defensible account of limitations on the power to alter the common law, doing so would entail reverting to a world without an active, social democratic state. I think that such a possibility is too remote to be worth serious attention.

The trilemma matters most in nations with thin systems of social provision. As Professor Sunstein also suggests, nations with thicker social welfare systems might accommodate constitutional social welfare rights. But, as social provision becomes increasingly thick, the need for judicial enforcement of social welfare rights, or for the development of background rules to address concerns about the level and distribution of important goods, or for a worked-out state action doctrine diminishes. The trilemma may persist in theory, but the practical consequences of a system's inability to resolve it are small. Sweden and the Netherlands have quite substantial systems of social provision, and guarantee social welfare rights in their constitutions. Yet, both have extraordinarily narrow systems of judicial review. The constitution of the Netherlands provides expressly that "[t]he constitutionality of Acts of Parliament and treaties shall not be reviewed by the courts," although the courts will enforce treaty provisions that are directly applicable in domestic law, even in the face of contrary legislation. Sweden's courts have the power of judicial review, but they are instructed to "set aside" a statute "only if the fault is manifest." According to one overview, the Swedish highest courts had not found a statute unconstitutional at the time of publication in 1990. The need for courts to grapple with the trilemma is substantially reduced in the presence of substantial systems of social provision developed by legislatures.

Putting nations with thick systems of social provision to one side, then, I want to consider several variants of judicial review that accept the proposition that the state action/ horizontal effect doctrine, social welfare rights, and background rules of property and contract are equivalent. They are, in order, passive review, strong-form judicial review, weak-form judicial review, and what might be called superweak-form judicial review. In the end, I suggest skepticism about the possibility that any variant will resolve the trilemma in a satisfactory way.

Courts apply passive review when they employ a standard of irrationality or intentional discrimination to assess claims that the level or distribution of important goods is inconsistent with the constitution, or, equivalently, when they do not develop an expansive state action/horizontal effect doctrine. How, though, does passive review accommodate the judicial role in developing the background rules of property and contract? Here some considerations arising out of judicial structure may be significant. Suppose a constitutional court abjures enforcing social welfare rights and (necessarily, for consistency) construes the state action/horizontal effect doctrine narrowly. In a social democratic state, concern over the level and distribution of important goods does not disappear; it simply shifts to the courts having responsibility for developing the background rules of property and contract. Still, each court may maintain a coherent doctrinal structure if the courts are structurally separate, that is, if there is a constitutional court and what we can call ordinary courts. I believe that the United States is the only advanced system with a structure that is completely effective in separating its constitutional court – the Supreme

Court – from the courts responsible for developing the background rules, that is, from the state courts.

Other constitutional systems do not maintain this insulation nearly as effectively. The Canadian Supreme Court, for example, has the power to develop the common law directly. Suppose that court had adhered rigidly to Dolphin Delivery, refusing to apply the Charter in ordinary private litigation where the parties relied on common-law rights and defences. Still, the court could – and has – developed the common law in light of the norms it finds in the Charter. The German Constitutional Court's influential doctrine of indirect horizontal effect connects that court to Germany's ordinary courts. Under the doctrine of indirect horizontal effect, the specialized constitutional court articulates constitutional norms and supervises the ordinary courts to determine whether those courts have adequately taken constitutional norms into account in their development of the background rules. Absent a strict separation between the constitutional court and the ordinary courts, passive review seems an unstable solution to the trilemma of state action/horizontal effect, social welfare rights, and the background rules: A court constrained by a narrow state action/horizontal effect doctrine will effectively enforce social welfare rights by developing the background rules itself or through its supervision of the ordinary courts.

Strong-Form Judicial Review

Professor Sunstein assumed judicial review would take a strong form. But, strong-form judicial review is probably as unstable as passive review, though for a different reason. Professor Sunstein's concern is not, I think, with judicial regulation of the labour market in the abstract; it is that courts lack the capacity to regulate the labour market, and (generalizing) other markets as well, to the degree of detail required by guarantees of social welfare rights. The problem, I believe, is not that courts cannot at any particular time promulgate what would effectively be a code for the labour and other markets. It is, rather, that private actors and legislators can readily adjust their behaviour and legal relations to avoid the obligations the judicially promulgated code places on them.

The problem is perhaps more apparent with respect to background rights than with respect to social welfare rights, and was expressed most clearly in Robert Nozick's criticism of what he called patterned accounts of justice. Such accounts specify a just level and distribution of important goods. According to Nozick, such accounts failed to appreciate the implications of the fact that markets are dynamic. A court might specify background rights at time-1 in a way that, at that time, produced the constitutionally required level and distribution of important goods, but market transactions, all conforming to the background rules, would inevitably change the level and distribution. In the area of public law, we can think of the full specification of a set of social welfare rights to the appropriate degree of detail as something like the tax code or regulation of campaign finance. We have enough experience to know that legislators and private actors will find ways to disrupt the social provision set out in the specification.

Weak-Form Judicial Review

Neither passive nor strong-form judicial review seem likely to offer stable solutions to the trilemma I have described. But, the conventional wisdom about the inability of courts to enforce social welfare rights (or, again equivalently, to administer an expansive state action/horizontal effect doctrine) arose at a time when the only options for constitutional courts seemed to be passive or strong-form review. A new form of judicial review has arisen in the past few decades, and its invention might alter our judgments about judicial capacity.

The new form of judicial review comes in several variants, but in each a judicial determination of what the constitution requires is explicitly not conclusive on other political actors, who can respond to the court's decision through ordinary politics. The notwithstanding clause in Canada's Charter of Rights is one variant. Under that provision, parliaments can specify that their enactments will take effect for a five-year period, notwithstanding their inconsistency with certain Charter guarantees. The notwithstanding clause makes it possible for legislatures to respond to judicial interpretations of the Charter by enacting legislation predicated on a different view of the judicial review do allow political actors to respond by amending the constitution in response to a judicial decision with which the political actors disagree. Weak-form systems differ in that political actors can respond without invoking any supermajoritarian amendment procedures. It follows that a constitutional system in which constitutional amendment is easy, both in form and in practice, is, in my terms, a system with weak-form judicial review. (2) The Warren Court occasionally hinted that the U.S. Constitution authorized a particular type of weak-form judicial review, in which courts and legislatures could engage in a dialogue about what the Constitution required.

The British Human Rights Act (1998) provides a different model of weak-form judicial review. The Act requires courts to interpret statutes to be consistent with the European Convention on Human Rights, if they can fairly do so. If such an interpretation is impossible, the Act directs courts to issue a statement that the statute is incompatible with the Convention, and authorizes government ministers to respond in a variety of ways, including modifying the statute on their own, introducing fast-track legislation to modify the statute, introducing such legislation in the ordinary course, or doing nothing. The New Zealand Bill of Rights creates an even weaker form of judicial review, simply imposing an obligation on courts to interpret legislation to be consistent with the Bill of Rights' provisions, but providing no remedy if parliament enacts a statute that clearly violates the Bill of Rights. The Grootboom decision of South Africa's Constitutional Court provides yet another model for weak-form judicial review. There a "group of people... lived in appalling conditions, [and] decided to move out and illegally occupied someone else's land. They were evicted and left homeless." The government had designated the land they took over for subsidized low-cost housing. South Africa's Constitutional Court held that the country's constitutional guarantee of "access to adequate housing," and its imposition on the state of a duty to "take reasonable legislative and other measures, within its available resources, to achieve the progressive realization of this right," imposed a "minimum core obligation" to adopt a reasonable legislative program aimed at securing housing for all. In particular, the Constitutional Court evaluated the government's existing housing programs, using a standard of reasonableness, and held that the programs were not a reasonable method of implementing the constitutional guarantee because they did not have "a component catering for those in desperate need." The government could provide this component by developing a program of constructing housing for the desperately needy itself, or by subsidizing the construction of such housing by private entrepreneurs, or by providing those in need with vouchers or other forms of "social assistance."

Michael Dorf and Charles Sabel treat approaches like that taken in Grootboom as exemplifying a distinctive variant of weak-form judicial review, part of a group of legal techniques they call democratic experimentalism. A democratic experimentalist court begins with a constitutional principle stated at a reasonably high level of abstraction, such as the South African provision purporting to guarantee access to adequate housing. It begins the experimentalist project by offering an incomplete specification of the principle's meaning in a particular context, such as the requirement that the government's housing programs specifically address the housing needs of those in desperate need. The Court then asks legislators and executive officials to develop and begin to implement plans that have a reasonable prospect of fulfilling the incompletely specified constitutional requirement. The next step involves examining the results of this experiment. Perhaps legislators and executive officials will be able to demonstrate that their programs are moving in the right direction. A democratic experimentalist court might respond by fleshing out the constitutional requirement a bit more, specifying in somewhat more detail what the government must do to fulfill its broad obligation to ensure access to adequate housing. Or, perhaps legislators and executive officials will be able to show that the task they initially set for themselves in response to the court's first decision could not be accomplished within a reasonable time, or with reasonable resources, and propose some modification in the constitutional standard. For example, they might have proposed to build permanent housing for those in desperate need, but, having discovered that land is unavailable at reasonable cost for such purposes, propose now to develop temporary shelters for those people. A democratic experimentalist court could revise its judgment about the constitution's requirements in light of experience.

Notably, that adjustment might be upward, imposing more requirements on the government, or downward, imposing fewer. The revisability of a court's constitutional judgments makes this a weak-form version of judicial review.

There is some reason to believe that weak-form judicial review is unstable institutionally. Canada's experience with the notwithstanding clause suggests, although not conclusively, that the clause has failed to create a distinctive form of judicial review, and that Canada has a rather robust form of judicial review, the notwithstanding clause notwithstanding. The clause has rarely been invoked. The reasons are complex. The clause was partly discredited by its use in the long-running conflict over Quebec's status within, or potentially outside, Canada. In addition, politicians seem unwilling to present themselves as attempting to "override" the Charter, rather than, as might have occurred, being willing to present themselves as offering reasonable interpretations of Charter rights that simply happen to differ from the interpretations the Supreme Court offers. As some early commentators predicted, the notwithstanding clause may have encouraged judges to act rather aggressively in developing Charter rights, by letting judges think that legislatures had the power to revise whatever the judges did. Then, with the notwithstanding clause falling into desuetude, Canada was left with empowered courts exercising strong-form judicial review.

Experience with the British Human Rights Act is too thin to be instructive yet, although commentators have worried about whether courts will "distort" legislation in interpreting it to be compatible with the European Convention, and about whether ministers will be willing to do nothing in the face of a judicial declaration that a statute is incompatible with the Convention. Even the extremely weak New Zealand Bill of Rights has been criticized as creating, in practice, a strong form of judicial review.

The conceptualization of democratic experimentalist judicial review is even more recent than that of other versions of weak-form review. But, to the extent that the model has been developed out of reflection on institutional reform litigation in the United States, there is reason to be skeptical as well. The difficulty is that democratic experimentalist review requires some degree of collaboration among courts, legislatures, and executive agencies, in a setting where the courts are attempting to change what the other actors have already decided to do. Those other actors made their decisions because of the incentives they had, which remain in place when the court adds another incentive to the mix. The unsurprising result has been a reasonably high degree of resistance or evasion of the initial judicial intervention, even if that intervention seems to an observer relatively mild.

The courts' response in the face of resistance or evasion is likely to be different from its response to collaboration. The courts might move in quite contradictory directions. Faced with resistance or evasion, the courts might insist on a "plan that promises realistically to work, and promises realistically to work now," to quote from the U.S. Supreme Court opinion expressing the Court's displeasure with resistance to desegregation. In that direction lies a kind of micromanagement that seems likely to enhance legislative and executive resentment of judicial intervention. Alternatively, in the face of resistance and evasion, the courts might declare victory and abandon the field without the government's operation having changed in any substantial way.

The reasons for skepticism about the stability of weak-form judicial review are clear enough. The incentives on judges to convert weak-form review into strong-form review are obvious: The latter gives them more power than the former. They may be able to accomplish the conversion successfully because of the ideological valence of the phrase protecting human rights. Here the language used in Canada is significant. The notwithstanding clause is routinely referred to as creating a power to override Charter rights. But, as suggested above, what politician wants to be in a position of overriding rights?

Superweak-Form Review

Professor Sunstein notes the possibility that some constitutional rights "will be... treated as aspirations not subject to legal enforcement," and thinks it "hardly desirable to have a system in which many constitutional rights are ignored." Yet, to say that constitutional provisions are not legally enforceable but express aspirations is not to say that they necessarily will be ignored.

The constitutions of Ireland and India set social welfare rights apart from other constitutional rights in sections that identify social welfare rights as "directive principles of public policy." These principles are not legally enforceable. Rather, they encourage legislatures to enact statutes consistent with the principles, that is, to move in the direction of social democracy to the extent politically and economically feasible. Unlike weak-form judicial review, however, these provisions do not even indirectly authorize the courts to treat the directive principles as legally enforceable.

The directive principles might be taken to provide guidance in interpreting statutes. The interpretive role directive principles can play in court gives them some characteristics of judicial review, but in an even weaker form than under the Human Rights Act. But, once the principles have such a role, the trilemma recurs.

The constitutions state that the courts may not directly enforce the directive principles, and therefore may not directly elaborate constitutionally guaranteed social welfare rights. But, in suggesting that the courts give the directive principles an interpretive role, the constitutions encourage the courts to develop the background rules of law in a way that it analytically equivalent to directing them to elaborate social welfare rights. Even superweak-form judicial review appears to be an unstable solution to the trilemma.

FAMILY WELFARE

Welfare of each citizen is the AIM of family welfare Department. It is tried to achieve mainly through saving the lives of mothers and children and improving their health status as well as checking the population growth.

Programme

Different programmes like family planning (later on renamed as family welfare) and programmes like Maternal and Child Health, Universal Immunisation Programme, Diarrheal Control Programme, Acute Respiratory Tract Infection Control Programme, and other nutritional deficiency control programme (later on included incer one programme 'Child Survival & Safe Motherhood') were implemented with same objectives previously. During Ninth Five year plan period these all programmes were brought under one umbrella with greater service packages and wider coverage i.e. Reproductive & Child Health (RCH) Programme in year 1997 in India.

Implementation

Under the Guidance of Secretary & Commissioner (Family Welfare), Commissioner (Health) and Additional Director (Family Welfare) and through primary health care approach Family welfare department is striving to achieve complete welfare of the citizen by organizing and implementing RCH programme through out the state. The state Family Welfare department is also carrying out special schemes like Integrated Population Development Project, link couples, rapid referral services, moped loans, National Maternity Benefit Schemes etc. The department is actively working for polio eradication and Intensive Pulse Polio Campaign and surveillance for polio cases are being carried out.

Fund Assistance

With the assistance of World Bank 13 Districts, Surat, Valid, Dang. Bharuch, Panchmahal, Kheda, Ahmedabad, Mehasana, Havnagar, Rajkot, Amreli, Junagadh, Jamnagar, special RCH project t and one sub-project in Baroda district is being carried out. In five weaker Districts with poor basic facilities with the assistance from UNFPA additional components of RCH as an Integrated Population Development Programme are being implement. These districts are Sabarkantha, Banaskantha, Kutch, Surendranagar and Dahod. With good coordination and team efforts improvement in quality and coverage of care at various levels are being achieved.

Reproductive and Child Health

Introduction RCH programme was launched in Indian on 15th October 1997 envisages provision of client centred, need based, good quality, integrated RCH services for improving the health of women and children. Paradigm Shift Under the RCH program all aspects of women's reproductive health across their reproductive cycle, from puberty to menopause are covered. RCH program addresses the needs that have emerged over years of implementing Family Welfare Program. As opposed to the Family Welfare program, the RCH program aims to be more in tune with the ground realities concerning...

- Overall health needs of women and children,
- Implementation needs of health workers,
- Local demographic needs and conditions.

Under this Programme the emphasis shifted to decentralized planning at district level based on assessment of community needs and implementation of programme at fulfilment of these need. New interventions such as control of reproductive tract infection, gender issues, male participation and adolescent health in addition to the services offered under the CSSM and the Family Welfare Program are also taken up.

Components

1. Effective Maternal & Child health care;
2. Increased access to contraceptive care;
3. Safe management of unwanted pregnancies;
4. Nutritional services to vulnerable groups;
5. Prevention and Treatment of RTI/STI;
6. Reproductive Health Services for adolescents;
7. Prevention and treatment of Gynecological Problems;
8. Screening and treatment of cancers; specially uterine, cervical and breast.

Life-cycle Approach

Women's health is important during all phases for their lives, frcm childhood to adulthood. The Reproductive and child health program addresses women's health across their life cycle. To ensure good health across the life cycle, all components of the RCH program are implemented fully towards improving the overall health of women and that of society as a whole.

Program Interventions

The RCH program is Implemented based on differential approach. Inputs in all the districts have not kept uniform. Based on the the capability of the health system in the district, all the districts of Gujarat have been categories into A B and C categories.

WELFARE OF THE DISABLED AND THE AGED

The objective for the disabled is to provide comprehensive measures necessary for prevention of disability and development of physical, mental and social capabilities of people with disabilities.

Tamil Nadu leads other States in implementing the various provision of the Persons with Disabilities Act, 1995, this act is being implemented to make as many disabled as possible active self-reliance and productive contributors to the State. The state intends to provide comprehensive, rehabilitation services, which include provision of special education, vocational training, placement in jobs, assistance for self employment and free supply of appliances to improve their mobility with the ultimate objective of making the handicapped selfreliant and economically independent. There are 266 special schools – 25 Government schools, 58 aided schools, 182 unaided schools and 1 municipal school functioning to provide special education to the disabled children. Financial Assistance given to severely disabled persons has been enhanced from Rs.200/-to Rs.500/- per month from 2006 onwards. During 2007-08, an amount of Rs.1 crore is provided for purchase of aids and appliances to benefit 9006 disabled persons. In order to provide a thrust for the rehabilitation and welfare of Mentally Disabled, an amount of Rs.13 crore has been made for providing assistance to reputed NGOs, for maintaining special institutions for mentally retarded during 2007-08. The welfare programmes are to be carried out by the NGOs viz., provision of maintenance allowance, creation of early intervention centres, residential and non-residential schools and adult mentally retarded homes for both boys and girls in every district. During 2008-09, an amount of Rs.15 crore is proposed.

Financial assistance of Rs.10,000/-is also given for the normal persons marrying blind/deaf and dumb and orthopaedically disabled. For 2008-09, an amount of Rs. 1.32 crore is proposed. An amount of Rs. 68.89 lakh is proposed for 2008-09 to NGOs for providing hostel facilities to the blind students.

Establishment of Disabled Welfare Board

The Government have established a separate welfare board for disabled to ensure the continuing government attention and assistance for the disabled in the future. An amount of Rs.1 crore has been provided for the establishment of welfare board and also to implement social security scheme for the disabled during 2007-08. For 2008-09, an amount of Rs.1.15 crore is proposed for this scheme.

Programmes for Rehabilitation of persons with disabilities has been implemented in 6 districts namely, Tiruvannamalai, Theni, Kanchipuram, Ramanathapuram, Thanjavur and Tiruvarur at a cost of Rs.1.90 crore during 2006-07 to benefit 1.17 lakh persons benefit under this scheme. It has been further extended to 5 districts viz., Tirunelveli, Sivagangai, Krishnagiri, Pudukottai and Dharmapuri in the year 2007-08. For 2008-09, an amount of Rs.2.43 crore is proposed for this scheme.

Social Safety net for the Aged

The objective for the aged is to provide a social security net for the aged poor through provision of pension and basic necessities such as noon meal, free sarees, dhoties etc. In order to provide social security to old age population/physically handicapped/destitute widows/deserted wives and destitute agricultural labourers who have no means of subsistence and have no relatives, old age pension schemes are being implemented. As on 30.9.2007, 5.49 lakh persons are benefited under old age pension (normal) scheme. For 2008-09, Rs.314.58 crore is proposed for this scheme. The old age people have also given midday meals plus 2 kgs of rice per head per month or

4 kgs of rice per head per month for those who do not take meals at the NMP centres supplied through fair price shops and 2 dhoties/sarees at the time of Pongal and Deepavali festivals. For 2008-09, Rs. 4605.88 lakh is proposed. In order to give proper institutional care to the elderly, the Govt., provides grant to the Voluntary Institutions for running 30 old age homes. About 1029 old age persons are being benefited. An amount of Rs.2 lakh per old age home is given as grant by the State Govt.

Besides Annapurna scheme is also being implemented in the state. Under this scheme 10 kgs of rice per month supplied free of cost to the destitutes/senior citizens with the target of 71,974 beneficiaries fixed by the Government of India. For 2008-09, Rs.6.35 crore is proposed for this scheme.

Plan Outlay for 2008-09

The outlay approved for Social Welfare for Eleventh Plan (2007-12) is Rs.4349.60 crore. The outlay provided for Social Welfare sector for 2007-08 is Rs.997.53 crore. An amount of Rs. 1002.59 crore is expected to be incurred during the period. The outlay approved for Women's Development and Child Rights and Welfare of the Disabled and the Aged under the Social Welfare sector for 2008-09 is Rs.943.74 crore. Of this, an amount of Rs. 384.39 crore and Rs.0.43 crore is earmarked for Scheduled Caste Sub Plan and Tribal Sub Plan respectively.

WELFARE OF THE AGED- MINISTRY OF SOCIAL JUSTICE & EMPOWERMENT

Ministry of Social Justice & Empowerment Under the ministry, special care is being taken for the welfare of the Aged.

The Government of India announced a National Policy on Older Persons in January, 1999. This policy provides a broad framework for inter sectoral collaboration and cooperation both within the government as well as between government and non-governmental agencies. In particular, the policy has identified a number of areas of intervention; financial security, health care and nutrition, shelter, education, welfare, protection of life and property etc. for the wellbeing of older persons in the country. Amongst others the policy also recognizes the role of the NGO sector in providing user friendly affordable services to complement the endeavours of the State in this direction. While recognizing the need for promoting productive ageing, the policy also emphasizes the importance of family in providing vital non formal social security for older persons. To facilitate implementation of the policy, the participation of Panchayati Raj Institutions, State Governments and different Departments of the Government of India is envisaged with coordinating responsibility resting with the Ministry of Social Justice & Empowerment.

National Council for Older Persons

A National Council for Older Persons (NCOP) has been constituted by the Ministry of Social Justice and Empowerment to operationalise the National Policy on Older Persons. The basic objectives of the NCOP are to :

- advice the Government on policies and programmes for older persons
- provide feedback to the Government on the implementation of the National Policy on Older Persons as well as on specific programme initiatives for older persons
- advocate the best interests of older persons
- provide a nodal point at the national level for redressing the grievances of older persons which are of an individual nature
- provide lobby for concessions, rebates and discounts for older persons both with the Government as well as with the corporate sector
- represent the collective opinion of older persons to the Government
- suggest steps to make old age productive and interesting
- suggest measures to enhance the quality of inter-generational relationships.
- undertake any other work or activity in the best interest of older persons.

There are 39 members in the council. A seven member working group has also been constituted from amongst the members of NCOP. The Working Group has so far held two meetings to discuss ways and means to achieve its objectives.

Old Age and Income Security

The Ministry has also launched a project called "Old Age Social and Income Security (OASIS)". An Expert Committee is constituted under the project. The first report of the Committee and the existing income security instruments available to older persons have been comprehensively examined. The report also contains detailed recommendations for enhancing the coverage, improving the rate of returns and for bringing about a qualitative improvement in the customer service of Public Provident Fund, the Employees Provident Fund, the Annuity Plans of LIC, UTI etc. The recommendations of the Committee are being examined by the Ministry of Finance for further action. Meanwhile, Phase II of the project is looking at the pension and gratuity schemes of the central government and old age pension provided under National Social Assistance Programme (NSAP). At the core of the second phase of project OASIS however, lies the designing of a new, fully funded, contributory pension programme for the balance (uncovered) workers including casual/contract workers, self-employed, farmers etc.

Revision of the Schemes of the Ministry

In order to facilitate implementation of the National Policy, and to bring about a qualitative improvement in the programme intervention of the Ministry, both the on-going schemes were revised during 1998-99.

(i) Scheme of Assistance to Panchayati Raj Institutions/ Voluntary Organizations/Self Help Groups for construction of old age homes/multi service centres for older persons. The scheme has been revised to enhance the one time construction grant for old age homes/multi service centres from Rs. 5.00 lakhs to Rs. 30.00 lakhs to eligible organizations.

(ii) An Integrated Programme for Older Persons has been formulated by revising the earlier scheme of Assistance to Voluntary Organizations for programmes relating to the welfare of the aged. With the aim to empower &

improve the quality of Older Persons, the programmes hopes to :

a. Reinforce and strengthen the ability and commitment of the family to provide care to Older Persons.
b. Foster amiable multi-generational relationships.
c. Generate greater awareness on issues pertaining to older persons and enhanced measures to address these issues.
d. Popularise the concept of Life Long Preparation for Old Age at the individual level as well as at the societal level.
e. Facilitate productive Ageing.
f. Promote Health Care, Housing and Income Security needs of Older persons.
g. Provide care the destitute elderly.
h. Strengthen capabilities on issues pertaining to older persons of local bodies/state governments, NGOs and academic/research and other institutions.

Strategy : Developing awareness and providing support to build the capacity of government, NGOs and the community at large to make productive use of older persons and to provide care to older persons in need; Sensitising children and youth towards older persons; reinforcing the Indian family tradition of providing special care and attention to older persons and organising older persons themselves into coherent self help groups capable of articulating their rights and interests.

WELFARE OF AGED

Old Age Pension : The scheme of Old Age Pension was started during 1974-75 in Mizoram. It was given to 150 Old Age persons @ Rs 30/-p.m. per person who have no supporters or near relatives to support them. The amount of pension was raised to Rs 60/-during 1981-82 and then to Rs.250/-per month per beneficiary for 10525 benficiaries.. Govt.of India sanctioned additional fund for 4991 beneficiaries @ Rs.200/-per month w.e.f 1st Nov.2007.

Old Age Home : Old Age Home had been opened in 1989 under Social Welfare Department at Aizawl for the Homeless aged persons. It is the Home of its only kind in the state of Mizoram. Old Aged persons (60 +) having no supporter/relative and who are resident of the state of Mizoram are admitted in the Home. The Home provides recreational facilities and other programmes, The Home, a capacity for 25 inmates is located at Luangmual Govt. Complex. Application in plain paper for admission into the Home may be submitted to the Director, Social welfare Department.

All Administration of Old Age Home rested with the Care Taker, Old Age Home, however subordinate staff assisted the Care Taker. All necessary decision at various level under the Care Taker are being made with due approval of the Director, Social Welfare Deptt.

WELFARE OF WOMEN AND CHILDREN

The department of Women and Child Development in Bellary district working for the welfare, rehabilitation and development of women and children. The children are covered under integrated child development programme and also provision is made to protect them in correctional institutions. Various schemes are also in operation for the development of women by Women Development Corporation The schemes of the department of disabled welfare are also operated by this department at district level.

The national policy for children, 1974 is founded on the conviction that child development programs are necessary to ensure equality of opportunity to these children. So, integrated child development service was launched on 2nd October 1975, in persuance of the said policy.

It is a powerful out reach programs to help and to achieve major national nutrition and health goals embodied in the national plan of action for children. It provides increased opportunities for providing early development, associated with improved enrolment and retention in the early primary stage and releasing girls from burden of sibling care to reduce the I.M.R.(Infant Mortality Rate).

Programmes of the Department

Correctional Institutions: There are four correctional Institutions working in Bellary city out of them three institutions viz. (1) Juvenile Home (Senior) (2) Juvenile Home (Junior) and (3) Observation Home, are running under the provisions of Juvenile Justice Act 1986 and another institution viz Stree Seva Niketana for women is running under the Act suppression of immoral Traffic in women. One Institution for Deaf and Dumb boys is also running. In all these Institutions Women and Children are provided, security, basic necessaries of food, shelter, clothing and also they are receiving education and training in several crafts.

Integrated Child Development Scheme: In Bellary district, ICDS is covered in 7 taluks with 8 blocks in 7 rural areas and one block in Bellary urban area. The objectives of the schemes are following :

a) To improve the nutritional and health status of children in a age group of 0-6 years.

b) To lay the foundation for proper psychological, physical and social development of child.

c) To reduce the infant mortality, morability, mal nutrition and school dropouts.

d) To enhance the capability of the mother to look after the normal health and nutrition needs through nutrition and health education.

The department provides the following package of services

:

i. Providing supplementary nutrition.

ii. Providing immunisation, vitamin A and folic acid.

iii. Providing health checkup.

iv. Providing referral services

v. Providing nutrition and health education through camps

vi. Pre-school education to children under age group of 0-6 years. 2.3 State Sector Schemes

This department under state sector provide several schemes benefits to rural women and girls like attendance scholarship for rural girls to encourage them for higher education, financial assistance to law graduates women for under going training and job oriented schemes to rural girls and also runs hostel for rural girls and loan schemes like Vikasini,Udyogini, Mane Belaku,etc to women where-in marketing shed and loan is provided to strengthen women economically. Taluka Panchayat schemes implemented through Zilla Panchayat are following

i. Namma Magalu Namma Shakti – This scheme provides Rs.2500/-insurance facility to girl child at the age of 5 years and from 6th year the girl will get annual dividend on the deposit and at the age of 18 years she will receive lumpsum of Rs.4,410 is provided she is un-married. This scheme aims at discouraging early marriages.

ii. Widow and Devadasi Re-marriage scheme in rural areas.

iii. Maintenance of nine destitute cottages wherein food shelter, clothing bedding, is provided for destitute school going children.

iv. Also runs creches for working mothers in Bellary Urban and Rural areas.

v. Maintenance grants to Mahila Mandals etc.

Central Sector Schemes

National Maternity Benefit Scheme-This scheme is sponsored by Central Government and it is implemented by the department at District Level through ICDS projects. Under this scheme Rs.500-00 is paid in one installment to Women under pregnancy to meet her delivery expenses. It may also be paid after delivery. The benefit is admissible for the first two births. 2.Balika Samrudhi Yojana :Under this scheme Rs.500/will be given to the nursing mother of a girl child belonging to BPL families.This is limited to 2 female live births.

Disabled Welfare

Women and Child Development Department is implementing the schemes the disabled welfare, providing tricycle to physically handicapped persons who are above 18 years, scholarships to handicapped students, mobility sticks and Braille watches to blind persons, hearing aids to deaf and dumb, training programs like " Hosa Hejje " to disabled persons through NGO in Bellary district. It also provided loan schemes like Adhara to Physically handicapped to strengthen them economically.This is a scheme of providing identification cards to PH persons.

Women Development Corporation Schemes

Women and Child Development Department also carries out women development corporation schemes like training programmes and financial assistance to women through Mahila Mandals, training cum production schemes, loans schemes like Udyogini, Vikasini, Mane Belaku etc. to strengthen women economically.

WELFARE SCHEMES FOR PHYSICALLY CHALLENGED PERSONS

The following schemes are being implemented by the Government for the welfare of the persons with disabilities:-

(i) Deendayal Disabled Rehabilitation Scheme (DDRS):- Under the scheme, funds for the welfare of persons with disabilities are provided to the non-governmental organizations for projects like special schools for disabled, Vocational Training Centres, Half Way Homes, Community Based Rehabilitation Centres, Early Intervention Centres for Disabled and Rehabilitation of Leprosy Cured Persons etc.

(ii) Assistance to Disabled Persons for Purchase/Fitting of Aids and Appliances (ADIP):-Under the scheme, aids/ appliances are distributed to the needy persons with disabilities which includes mentally challenged children also.

(iii) National Institutions:-The Ministry supports seven autonomous National Institutes which provide rehabilitation services and undertake manpower development with the overall objective of providing rehabilitation services for different types of disabilities.

(iv) The National Handicapped Finance & Development Corporationprovides concessional credit to persons with disabilities for setting up income generating activities for self employment.

(v) Scheme for Implementation of Persons with Disabilities (Equal Opportunities, Protection of Rights and Full Participation) Act, 1995 (SIPDA):-Under this Scheme, assistance is provided for setting up of District Disability Rehabilitation Centres, Regional Rehabilitation Centres, creating barrier free environment in public buildings, awareness generation etc.

(vi) Scheme of Incentives to Employees in the Private Sector for providing employment to persons with disabilities:- Under this Scheme, launched in April, 2008, the Government of India provides the employers' contribution for Employees Provident Fund (EPF) and Employees State Insurance (ESI) for three years, for persons with disabilities employed in the private sector on or after 1.4.2008, with a monthly salary upto Rs.25,000/-.

WELFARE OF WEAKER SECTIONS

The National Scheme for Liberalization and Rehabilitation of Scavengers aims to provide alternate dignified and viable occupation to each scavenger and his/her dependents. The scheme which was modified w.e.f. 1.4.1996, inter-alia, includes TRYSEM norms for training, release of central assistance direct to Scheduled Caste Development Corporation and adoption of cluster approach in the training and rehabilitation programme. The National Safai Karamchari Finance and Development Corporation set up in January 1997 provides loans for higher education to students from safai karamchari community besides providing assistance in selfemployment ventures and technical and entrepreneurial skills.

The National Commission for Minorities, reconstituted w.e.f. 26.11.1996 to focus on effective implementation of 15 point programme for the welfare of minorities, has constituted a High Powered Study Committee for socioeconomic conditions of minorities in India. The Central Government has raised equity share towards National Minorities Development and Finance Corporation from 25 per cent to 60 per cent.

The welfare of STs and SCs is being closely monitored by the state governments through the Special Component Plan

(SCP) and Tribal Sub-Plan (TSP) with the support of special central assistance provided by the Central government. The consolidated achievements during the Eighth Plan (1992-97) had been 51.53 lakh ST families against the target of 49.78 lakh families. The target for 1997-98 was fixed as 10.97 lakh ST families out of which 9.86 lakh ST families were assisted. A target of 11.01 lakh families has been fixed for 1998-99 out of which 4.13 lakh ST families have been assisted up to 30.11.1998. On going schemes like pre-matric and postmatric scholarship and providing hostel facilities to SC boys and girls continued to be operative in 1998-99.

In addition to various schemes for the development and growth of welfare of disabled persons, a national centre for drug abuse prevention has been established. A sum of Rs.1539 crore has been provided in central sector plan during 1998-99 (BE) for various schemes of welfare of weaker sections of the society including minorities, persons with disabilities and others covered under Social defence.

WELFARE OF WEAKER SECTION

Presidential Directives on Scheduled Castes and Scheduled Tribes were continued to be implemented and monitored on regular basis. Out of the total manpower, 14.6 per cent were Scheduled Castes and 11.5 per cent were Scheduled Tribes.

During the year 2001-02, two commemoration meetings followed bty cultural programmes wre organzied at CWC, Ukkunagaram in connection with Dr.BR Ambedkar and Babu Jagjeevan Ram Jayanthi celebrations-2001. Painting and essay writing competitions were also held for the school children. In addition, a new children's park "Eklavya Park' has been developed at Sector-I and was inaugurated on 14.4.2001. In addition to the above, RINL has a scholarship scheme exclusively for the children of SC/ST employees, under which two scholarships of Rs.250/-per month and one scholarship of Rs.150/ -per month are awarded to the meritorious students among SC/ STs each year. Annual merit cash awards for students belonging to SC/ST communities are being given since the year 1991, coinciding with the birth centenary celebrations of Dr.BR Ambedkar. Based on the pass results of the Xth/SSC examination, 6 cash merit awards of Rs.500/-each and 6 awards of Rs.250/-each are given to the first and second ranked students of SC/ST communities respectively, from each of the schools of RINL.

During-April-Sept, 2002, two commemoration meetings followed by cultural programmes were organized at CWC, Ukkunagaram in connection with Dr.BR Ambedkar and Babu Jagjeevan Ram Jayanthi celebratins-2002. Sports competitions for the employees and their family members were organized on such occasions.

During the year 2001-02 and the period from 1.4.2002 to 30.9.2002, a certain percentage of houses (10% for A&B types and 5% for C&D types) have been reserved for and allotted to the SC/ST employees in the steel plant township.

NATIONAL MINERAL DEVELOPMENT CORPORATION

Manpower

The total number of regular employees in NMDC as on 31.12.2002 was 6073 out of which 1061 persons belong to Scheduled Castes (17.47%), 1122 Scheduled Tribes (18.47%), and 370 to OBCs (6.09%). Being one of the very few public sector enterprises having been incorporated within a short period after independence and the mining resources being concentrated in inaccessible forest domains, NMDC has always had a pro-active attitude in community development simultaneously with its own progress. This philosophy was not something thrust upon NMDC by any Governmental agency or other local pressure groups. It was totally voluntary and arose from a commitment to share the fruits of progress with those concerned or associated with the local area in line with its corporate philosophy to be a responsible corporate citizen. As a part of its social responsibility, NMDC has taken a number of socioeconomic development measures for Scheduled Castes and Scheduled Tribes in and around its various projects, which are enumerated briefly as under:

Education and Training

NMDC has provided free educational facilities for children of Tribals in its schools. The local Adivasi children are provided with uniforms, textbooks etc. The Corporation also provided entire infra-structural facilities including quarters for teaching staff and hostel building for students for running an ITI at Bhansi in Dantewada District, Chattisgarh. In addition, another ITI is being run by DAV at Bhansi for which entire expenditure is borne by NMDC.

A skill development programme was introduced in 1996 which provides necessary training to the 8th pass Scheduled Tribe candidates to acquire necessary skill, knowledge and proficiency in operation of the mines/plants to help them seek employment. They are paid an out–of-pocket expenses of Rs.1000/-per month each to meet their sustenance and incidental expenditure, besides being provided subsidized breakfast, lunch and uniforms.

Medicare

NMDC provides free medical treatment (both out patients and in patients) to Scheduled Castes and Scheduled Tribes residing in and around its projects. NMDC organizes regular eye camps, provides counselling in the matter of family planning/ welfare to the local Adivasis besides undertaking free family planning operations in the project hospitals. Regular health check up programme for the benefit of school children is also being organized.

Drinking Water Facility

NMDC constructed a number of hand pumps/water tanks in nearby villages, Similarly, a number of open wells and tube wells have also been provided in the surrounding villages.

Peripheral Development

(i) NMDC has established a number of public health centres in nearby villages where the project Doctors visits them.

(ii) The Corporation has taken up electrification work in nearby villages.

(iii) NMDC has taken up laying of all-weather roads connecting various villages. Similarly improvement of approach roads and black topping of roads connecting the surrounding village has been taken up.

The Bailadila Projects contributed in bringing about a metamorphosis in the attitudes/thinking of the tribals in favour of non-agricultural employment. The tribals and non-tribals employed in the projects generated demand for various forest/ agricultural produce of the tribals thereby allowing their incomes to go up substantially. This has brought prosperity among the tribals in one way.

The improved infra-structural facilities aided the tribals in reaching the markets without much strain. This also provided an opportunity to the local people to mix and inter-act with people from other areas and develop a tendency to join the mainstream of the society. Such interaction had another dimension related to the socio-cultural aspects of the tribals who were accustomed to cherishing their own culture without any alien intervention, howsoever positive. A realization has dawned gradually on them of the need to eke out their own living for the betterment of their family through hard work only. As a result, the percentage of tribal employees in the total work force of the projects is substantially higher than what the Government has prescribed. However, in order to ensure that the fruits of development are evenly distributed, NMDC has initiated a regular consultative process on the one hand with the local village-heads as well as Panchayat leaders and on the other hand with the Unions and Associations functioning in the Project. Periodical meetings are held with the Sarpanches of various tribal villages adjoining the Projects and tentative lists of the developmental works to be undertaken are detailed.

While the process of providing Medicare and drinking water facilities was initiated long back more structured development works in identified thrust areas commenced around 1989 in a big way. Further, the more vigorous campaign in undertaking various community development works were backed-up by the availability of separate budgetary support around this period only. Gradually, construction of approach roads and diversion of nallahs, provision of hume pipe culverts, works relating to footbridges were taken up as per the requirements voiced by the villagers. Further, regular family planning camps and free eye camps were started supplementing the Governmental efforts.

Apart from the aforesaid direct benefits, the investment in Bailadila Sector has also created secondary and tertiary job/ business opportunities to the local population. The development of infrastructure facilities like roads, railway line, public transport, hospitals, schools, installation of a T.V. tower/receiver etc. has also opened opportunities for social and economic growth of this otherwise inaccessible area. This has provided ready market for their "produce", which otherwise was not available.

KUDREMUKH IRON ORE COMPANY LIMITED

The total number of employees in KIOCL as on 31.12.2002 is 2184 out of which 327 persons belong to Scheduled Caste (14.97%), 88 persons to Scheduled Tribe (4.02%) and 300 persons to Other Backward Classes (13.73%). Besides, there are 135 women (6.18%), 37 Physically Handicapped (1.69%) and 79 Ex-servicemen (3.61%).

Welfare Measures

The Company has set up full fledged facilities at Kudremukh and Mangalore by establishing a modern township, hospital, recreation facilities etc. 10% of type "A" and "B" quarters and 5% of "C" & "D" type quarters are reserved for SC/ST employees. During the year 2001-2002, 15 merit scholarships and 40 merit-cummeans scholarships were sanctioned to children of employees. Out of 55 scholarships, 20% of the scholarships i.e. 11 scholarships were sanctioned to the children of SC/ST employees. The qualifying standard of eligibility i.e. First Class or 60% whichever is higher, is relaxable to 50% in the aggregate marks for sanction of scholarship to children of SC/ST employees.

Manganese Ore (India) Ltd.

Manganese Ore (India) Ltd. is a labour intensive organisation having an employment of 7358 employees as on 31.12.2002. MOIL has undertaken several measures for welfare of weaker sections and some of them are as under:

MOIL has adopted a Tribal Village namely Gondi which is close to Ukwa mine in Madhya Pradesh. The company has introduced a wide range of development activities such as repair of road, construction of houses for homeless tribals, construction of school building to impart education to tribal children, etc. as a part of their on going Social Welfare Promotion Scheme. MOIL has been giving financial assistance to social institutions who are working for rehabilitation of the aged and handicapped persons. The company has donated tricycles to handicapped persons and provided sewing machines or development and upliftment of tribal women.

MSTC Limited

The presidential Directives issued from time to time pertaining to policies and procedures of the Government in regard to reservation, relaxation, concession, etc. for the SC/ST/OBC candidates are kept in view while taking action/decision on any matter laid down therein. Best efforts were made to comply with the directives in matters concerning recruitment and promotion. Adequate representation of SC/ST/OBC members was made available in both Departmental Promotion Committees as well as Selection Committees (in case of recruitment)

In order to improve the efficiency of the employees belonging to the reserved categories and to prepare them to take up higher positions in future, special attention was paid to their training and development in their respective fields of function. During the year 2002-2003 (till 31.12.02) 6 SC and 2 ST employees of the company were sponsored for training programmes, both inhouse and institutional. Apart from this, all possible cooperation and assistance was provided to the MSTC SC/ST Employees' Council, which functions primarily to safeguard the interest of the reserved sections of employees of the company.

Bibliography

Ahmed, Mesbahuddin : *The British Labour Party and the Indian Independence Movement, 1917-1939*, Envoy Press, 1987.

Appadurai, A. : *The Social Life of Things; Commodities in Cultural Perspective*, Cambridge: CUP., 1986.

Arthur Berriedale : *The Religion and Philosophy of the Veda and Upanishads*, Cambridge, Harvard University Press, 1925.

Bala Kiran : *Social and Economic Development of Scheduled Tribes*, Deep & Deep, Delhi, 2000.

Banton, M. : *Political Systems and the Distribution of Power*, London: Tavistock, 1965.

Beauchamp, Tom L.: *Philosophical Ethics*, New York: McGraw Hill, 1991.

Berreman, Gerald D., : *Social Inequality: Comparative and Developmental Approaches*, New York: Academic Press, 1981.

Desai, A.R. : *Social Background of Indian Nationalism*, Bombay, Popular Prakashan, 1966.

Ehrenfeld, David W. : *The Arrogance of Humanism.* New York, Oxford University Press, 2003.

Flavia Agnes: *Law and Gender Inequality : The Politics of Women's Rights in India,* Oxford University Press, 1999,

Heinsath, Charles : *Indian Nationalism and Hindu Social Reform*, Princeton, Princeton University Press, 1964.

Hopkins, Thomas J. : *The Hindu Religious Tradition*, Encino, California, Dickenson, 1971.

Humphrey, C. : *Karl Marx Collective; Economy, Society a d Religion on a Siberian Collective Farm,* Cambridge: CUP, 1983.

Jaya Sagade: *Child Marriage in India : Socio-Legal and Human Rights Dimensions*, Oxford University Press, Delhi, 2005.

Johnson, S. B.: *Social Mobility Among Untouchables*, Vikas, New Delhi, 1979.

Jones, Ernest : *The Life and Work of Sigmund Freud*, Basic Books, New York, 1961.

Kurtz, Donald V. : *Political Anthropology: Paradigms and Power*, Boulder, CO: Westview, 2001.

Lamont, Corliss: *The Philosophy of Humanism.* Humanist Press, 1997.

Levinson, D.: *Family Violence in Cross Cultural Perspective*, Newbury Park, Sage, 1989.

Macpherson. C. B.: *The Political Theory of Possessive Individualism: Hobbes to Locke,* Oxford, Oxford University Press, 1962.

May, Rollo : *Psychology and the Human Dilemma*, Norton, New York, 1996.

Mittal, Kewal Krishan: *Materialism in Indian Thought,* New Delhi, Munshiram Manoharlal Publishers, 1974.

Mullaly, R.: *Structural Social Work: Ideology, Theory, and Practice*, Toronto, Canada: McClelland and Stewart, 1993.

Nicholas Terpstra: *Lay Confraternities and Civic Religion in Renaissance Bologna,* Cambridge University Press, 1995.

Petrosyan, M.: *Humanism: Its Philosophical, Ethical, and Sociological Aspects.* Progress Publishers, 1972.

Potter, Karl H.: *Encyclopedia of Indian Philosophies,* Princeton: Princeton University Press, 1983.

Prajnanananda, Swami: *Schools of Indian Philosophical Thought,* Calcutta, Firma K. L. Mukhopadhyay, 1973.

Robertson, A. F. : *The Dynamics of Productive Relationships,* Cambridge: CUP, 1987.

Steve Max: *Organizing for Social Change: A Manual for Activists in the 1990s*, Midwest Academy, Seven Locks Press. 1991.

Wilson, S.J.: *Confidentiality in Social Work:Issues and Principles.* New York: The Free Press, 1978.

Yolton, J. W.: *John Locke: Problems and Perspectives*, Cambridge Uni. Press, 1969.

Index

H

I

J

L

M

N

O

P

R

S

T

U

V

W

Y

□□□